NURTURING INDEPENDENT LEARNERS

Nurturing Independent Learners

Helping Students Take Charge of Their Learning

DONALD MEICHENBAUM
University of Waterloo, Ontario

&

ANDREW BIEMILLER
University of Toronto, Ontario

Brookline Books

ISBN 1-57129-047-8

Library of Congress Cataloging-In-Publication Data
Meichenbaum, Donald.
   Nurturing independent learners : helping students take charge of
their learning / Donald Meichenbaum & Andrew Biemiller.
     p.   cm.
   Includes bibliographical references (p.) and index.
   ISBN 1-57129-047-8
   1. Mastery learning--United States.   2. Academic achievement-
-United States.   3. Knowledge, Theory of.   I. Biemiller, Andrew,
1939-   . II. Title.
LB1031.4.M45   1998
370.15'23--dc21   97-50477
                                              CIP

Cover design, book design and typography by Erica L. Schultz.

Printed in USA by Data Reproductions Corporation, Auburn Hills, MI.
10 9 8 7 6 5 4 3 2

Published by
BROOKLINE BOOKS
P.O. Box 97
Newton, Massachusetts 02464
(617) 558-8010
Order toll-free (within the U.S.): 1-800-666-BOOK

Contents

CHAPTER NINE
Planning and Implementing Consultation Settings 159

CHAPTER TEN
Creating Authentic Settings:
Fostering Task Planning and the Application of Skills 192

CHAPTER ELEVEN
Applying the Three-Dimensional Model of Mastery
to Analyze Selected Educational Programs 227

List of Highlight Boxes

List of Tables

List of Figures

To my daughter Lauren, a dedicated and gifted teacher whose collaboration was the inspiration for my involvement in this project.

— D. Meichenbaum

To my wife, Sandy, from whom I have learned much of what I know about teaching and about living.

— A. Biemiller

We wish to acknowledge the Waterloo County and Toronto School Boards; the Experimental School at the Institute of Child Studies, University of Toronto; the Laidlaw Foundation and Canadian Social Science Research Council; and our many graduate students.

Prologue

Teachers are confronted with a major challenge. By the time students reach high school, they may differ by *as many as six grade levels* in their academic abilities. This book will analyze the nature of these differences, explore how they emerged, and consider what teachers can do to address such varied abilities in their classrooms. We begin in Chapter 1 by examining just how extensive these differences are in specific academic areas. In Chapters 2 and 3 we consider what distinguishes those who thrive in school from those who falter. Some students are budding experts, or at least intelligent novices, as they undertake new and more challenging tasks. They achieve in school, enjoy school, and in turn, are held in high regard. We will use the literature from the area of expertise (Chapter 2) to understand why smart students keep getting smarter, while slower students fall further and further behind. How such marked individual differences emerge is the focus of Chapter 4. Until we better understand how such differences arise, we are unlikely to develop more effective interventions that can be implemented on both a preventive and a remedial basis.

How can we work to reduce or remove the differences between the "haves" and the "have-nots" without penalizing those students who are achieving? The answer to this challenging question led us to develop the three-dimensional theoretical model of instruction described in Chapter 5. In order to develop mastery and move from being a novice to being an expert in an area of curriculum content, students must become able to construct or plan novel and authentic tasks, using more and more complex skills. They must become self-directed or autonomous in applying skills to novel tasks. Students must not only consume knowledge, but also be motivated to construct and apply knowledge.

How can teachers help their students achieve these lofty objectives? Our answer comes in the form of a theory that provides practical pedagogical suggestions as to how teachers can create learning settings (Chapter 6) that help students:

a) acquire skills and strategies, as described in Chapter 7;

b) consolidate skills and strategies, as described in Chapter 8;

c) increase self-direction through consulting about skills and strategies, in which students assume leadership roles and engage in consultative and reflective skills, as described in Chapter 9;

d) apply and transfer learned skills and strategies to increasingly complex, real-life (authentic) tasks, as described in Chapter 10.

In Chapter 11 we examine a number of successful educational programs that have been used to teach reading, writing, and mathematics, and analyze them from the perspective of our three-dimensional model of instruction. Our proposed model provides a useful framework for understanding why these educational programs have resulted in student achievement. These analyses indicate that there is nothing as practical as a good theory to help teachers organize and understand pedagogical practices and to develop the best teaching approaches.

We conclude in Chapter 12 with a consideration of the research literature on "expert" teachers. What do expert teachers know and do that we can all learn and try? We believe that *most students* can learn to acquire and master academic skills if we can teach more effectively. This faith derives from our combined 60 years of research, our understanding of the literature, our experiences in training beginning and experienced teachers, and our extensive dialogues with teachers, students, principals, and parents. This book is designed to translate basic and applied research and evaluation findings into instructional practices that can enhance child outcomes.

We dedicate this book to those teachers who are willing to join us in our personal journey of improving our educational system.

Donald Meichenbaum
Andrew Biemiller
September, 1997

Chapter One

The Nature of the Educational Challenge

This book is about identifying and meeting instructional challenges in the classroom. Each day, teachers are confronted with students who have varied academic abilities. For instance, by grade 9, the most advanced 25% of students are at least three years ahead of the least advanced 25%. If we limit the comparison to the most advanced 10% on a given subject versus the least advanced 10%, the range between them stretches to 6 grade-equivalent years.

In this chapter, we will consider what these differences look like in the areas of reading, writing, and mathematics. We will then consider the broad educational and social consequences of these marked individual differences. This will set an agenda for how educators can address such heterogeneity in the classroom.

Reading

Of the various academic skills taught in school, the most critical in predicting academic success is reading ability. Learning to read early in life is fundamental to school success in all academic areas (Biemiller, 1993). Children who acquire literacy skills in the earliest grades tend to remain the best readers, writers, and spellers throughout the elementary school years. Children who have difficulty at the start often continue to exhibit relatively weak academic skills. Children with low reading achievement in early grades (by grade 3) have a greater likelihood of school retention, dropout, drug abuse, early pregnancy, delinquency and unemployment (Duncan et al., 1994; Knapp et al., 1997).

The Association for the National Assessment of Educational Progress (NAEP, 1992) reported that two thirds of students in U.S. schools in the 4th, 8th, and 12th grades—including one fourth of high school seniors—are *not* proficient readers. In fact, a recent NAEP evaluation described only 37% of a national sample of high school seniors as "proficient" at reading and only 3% as "advanced," with one fourth of the sample falling below the "base" level in reading (King, 1982). Illustrative of this spread in reading ability are the findings reported by Epstein and her colleagues, who tested students from urban schools in Baltimore, Maryland. The middle schools they were using were racially homogeneous (99% African-American students), and 70% of the students qualified for free lunch. The seventh-grade students in these schools ranged in their reading and language skills from below the first grade to above the 11th-grade level (Epstein, 1992). This remarkable disparity in abilities is further illustrated by the following additional findings:

- While 10% of fourth-graders can read and understand passages that an average sixth-grader can read, another 10% of fourth-graders have difficulty with material that average second-graders can read. Moreover, this pattern of difference increases over the course of schooling.
- 25% of beginning high school students will have problems answering factual questions for which the answers are explicitly available in a short text in front of them.
- 50% of beginning high school students will make errors on questions requiring some degree of inference, and 65% will have difficulty with items containing unfamiliar vocabulary or involving inference requiring more than one logical step.
- Among 17-year-olds who stay in school, nearly 40% cannot draw an inference from written materials. Overall, 13% of 17-year-olds are functionally illiterate; this rate jumps to 40% among minority youth (McGill-Franzen & Allington, 1991).

In order to get a feel for the degree of comprehension deficits that many students evidence, consider the following passage taken from a standardized reading comprehension text.

"A plain, as all agree, is a great stretch of level or nearly level land."
Question: "What is true of all plains?"
Correct multiple-choice alternative: "They have no high mountains."

How many entering high school students do you think fail to answer this question correctly? Would you believe *two thirds?* Such illiteracy can have significant social and economic consequences. For example, among youth who get into trouble with the law involving the courts, 85% evidence functional illiteracy.

About 23 million American adults are functionally illiterate, and among the chronically unemployed, the illiteracy rate is 75%. Thus, the social ramifications of such cumulative deficits in reading are substantial.

Writing Skills

Closely aligned with literacy is the need for graduating high school students to be able to express themselves in writing. The marked heterogeneity in students' writing ability is similar to that in their reading ability. Only about one quarter of high school seniors can state their views and ideas clearly enough to write a persuasive essay. Many students also find writing to be "uninteresting and purposeless" (Bruer, 1993). The students who do not write well report doing little planning and revising when writing papers, and they describe school writing as being "routine, mechanical, and dull." Such attitudes toward writing deter students from developing the motivation and initiating the effort required to practice and refine their writing skills.

Mathematics

While critics bemoan students' lack of competence in reading and writing, it is in the area of mathematics that passions become inflamed. Consider the following illustrative findings:

- Only 16% of eighth-graders will master the content of a typical eighth-grade mathematics textbook.
- Of students in the U.S. starting at an average high school, 25% are unable to multiply by two-digit numbers, and 50% are unable to calculate percentages.
- Only 8% of beginning high school students can regularly solve mathematical tasks that require problem-solving skills, and by the time they turn 17, only 33% will be able to solve math problems requiring several steps.
- A large percentage of graduating high school students are markedly deficient in applying numerical concepts in non-routine situations that go beyond basic procedural mathematical skills.
- Close to half of all 17-year-olds cannot read or do math at the level needed to get a job in a modern automobile plant; for example, fewer than half showed the consistent grasp of functions, decimals and percentages expected of competent seventh-graders (Mosle, 1996).

These findings on mathematical incompetence in a sizeable percentage of students in U.S. schools are frequently contrasted with the successful arithmetical performance of students from foreign countries. For example, after reviewing the cross-cultural research on students' mathematical competence, Geary (1994) concluded:

> In the industrialized world, American children are among the most poorly educated children in mathematics. American children have poorly developed mathematical skills before the end of the first grade and the gap widens with each successive grade ... By the fifth grade, children in the best American classrooms had, on average, mathematics test scores that were below the mean of the lowest-scoring students in Japanese classrooms. In fact, *fifth-grade* children in the lowest-scoring American classrooms had, on average, only slightly better mathematical test scores than children in the best *first-grade* Chinese classroom (p. 236; emphases added).

What is most disconcerting about Geary's findings is that when children in the U.S. enter school, they compare quite favorably in cognitive ability to students entering school in other countries. For example, entering students in the U.S. outperformed students in Asian countries, such as Korea, on informal knowledge. But before the end of the first grade, the Korean children outperformed the students from the U.S. The differences that emerged were *not* due to differences in intelligence. Somehow, what happens—or fails to happen—in schools in the U.S. plays a significant role in contributing to these differences.

While these conclusions are alarming, Cai and Silver (1995) caution that cross-cultural comparisons in math proficiency may be more subtle and complex. Differences between Asian students (Chinese and Japanese) and American students on novel problem-solving tasks are smaller than those on tasks measuring procedural knowledge or computational skills.

Whatever the exact nature of the differences between American and Asian students, teachers are confronted by substantial individual differences that need to be addressed.

Poverty and Minority Status

Before we consider the economic and social costs of heterogeneity in our classrooms, we need to consider the influence of economic and racial differences within U.S. society. Nowhere are these differences in academic achievement more exaggerated than when we consider students who live in poverty.

Twenty-five percent of children (some 15 million students) in the U.S. live in poverty (Huston, 1995).[1] With poverty comes a host of risk factors for health problems (e.g., low birth weight, contagious disease, injury), developmental delays, and social, emotional, and behavioral problems. Low socioeconomic status is often accompanied by parental stress, depression, and related problems that contribute to students' slowed intellectual development. Low income is often accompanied by relatively low levels of social and nonsocial supports for early development and by limited academic supports. Also, as we will discuss in Chapter 4, school systems often spend the least amount of time and money on educating children from poverty. The overall proficiency level of an average 17-year-old in a poor urban setting is equivalent to that of a typical 13-year-old affluent youth.

When poverty is accompanied by minority status, these individual differences are further exacerbated. Fifteen percent of American students are African-American and 11% are Hispanic-American.[2] If present growth rates continue, by the year 2020, minority students will constitute 45% of the school-age population in the U.S., up from the current level of 30%. Both African-American and Hispanic-American students score substantially lower than Caucasian and Asian students in reading and mathematics.[3] In addition, students from families with income below the poverty level (often an accompaniment of minority status) are nearly twice as likely to be held back a grade as their socioeconomically advantaged classmates. Numerous studies have indicated that dropout rate is highly correlated with retention. This is especially alarming when we consider that an estimated 5 to 7% of public school children—about 2 children in every classroom of 30—are retained annually in the U.S. (Hess & D'Amato, 1996; Hirano-Nakanishi, 1986; Shephard & Smith, 1990). Among minority groups, dropout rates are epidemic—an estimated 40% among Mexican-Americans and 30% among African-American students. African-American students are three times as likely as Caucasian students to be placed in a class of educable developmentally delayed, and three times as likely to be expelled; both of these factors contribute to their high dropout rate from school. It is not only academic difficulties that contribute to this high dropout rate. Two of the primary reasons offered by students for dropping out of school are their inability to get along with their teachers and a perceived lack of teacher interest (Neumann, 1996).

The lower performance of minority students may also be influenced by both biological and psychosocial factors. For instance, epidemiological studies conducted between 1988 and 1991 indicated that one in four black children younger than age 6 were affected by elevated levels of lead in their bloodstream, which can result from inhaling lead dust or paint chips. This can cause hearing loss, stunted growth, and damage to blood production, kidney development, and vitamin D metabolism (Garcia-Coll et al., in press). On top of this biological vulnerability, a high concentration of poor black children live in dangerous neighborhoods, and as a result are likely to be exposed to violence, drugs, inadequate housing, and other environmental health risks.

The Economic and Social Costs of Heterogeneity in Our Schools

There is an economic and social price to these cumulative academic deficiencies. Many students who perform marginally in school are placed in remedial or special education classes, from which they do *not* emerge; they rarely reenter the mainstream classroom. Taxpayers spend 2.3 times more money (over $12,000 per year) to educate a student with an academic disability than they do for a student without a disability ($5260), contributing to an annual cost of approximately 300 billion dollars to educate children in the U.S. (Shephard & Smith, 1990).

For those students who make it through the public high school systems, remedial programs may await them at colleges and universities. In recent years, colleges and universities have had a 400% increase in the provision of remedial math courses. Nationally, some 29% of students who attend two- or four-year colleges take at least one remedial course.

What could be done on both a preventive and a remedial basis to reverse these trends? How can teachers conduct their classrooms so that all students will be able to apply what they learn, on their own? We believe all students can learn if instruction is thoughtfully orchestrated and instructional material is carefully calibrated.

We do not call for the implementation of a specific teaching method, nor for a particular pedagogical script; rather, we provide information and guidance on how to enhance teachers' repertoires of skills and options. We are calling not for dramatic changes in teachers' instructional techniques, but rather, for a thoughtful review of how we teach. For our students to become more active and responsible, more self-directed or self-regulating learners, it is critical that our teachers become more flexible and strategic, reflective thinkers. We will offer many very practical suggestions that derive from the educational literature and from our many years of research experience in working with teachers to address the differences between high- and low-achieving students. We will also review some recent success stories in education and demonstrate how our theoretical per-

spective clarifies why those projects have succeeded. In offering these suggestions, we concur with Perkins (1992), who observed that any innovative instructional approach should not escalate the teacher's workload; should allow the
teacher a creative role; and should avoid extreme demands on the teacher's
skills and talents.

The urgent need for such instructional procedures is highlighted by the trend
for more and more schools to move toward academically heterogeneous classrooms. The "untracking" of secondary schools and the reduced use of ability
groupings at the elementary levels have underscored the urgency of finding
ways to effectively address individual differences in classrooms.

Surely, there is much to be concerned about in education—but there is also
much to be proud of. There are more educational researchers conducting more
meaningful in-classroom collaborative research with front-line teachers than ever
before. We have been involved in several such classroom projects, which we will
describe later in this book. Educational researchers and teachers have learned a
great deal about how to teach more effectively. This book is designed to bridge
the gap between what we know and what many teachers actually do in their
classrooms. As Brown and Campione (1996) observe:

> Although the rhetoric and vocabulary of educational reform efforts
> have changed noticeably over the century, changes in classroom prac-
> tice appear to lag behind (p. 320).

Our goal is to address this lag. As researchers, we have spent many hours observing in classrooms and working with children who thrive and children who
do not. We begin our analysis with a consideration of what distinguishes those
who succeed academically from those who falter. A consideration of these differences will set the stage for what can be done to close the gap between high-
and low-achieving students.

Endnotes

1   What is most alarming about these statistics is that the National Commission on
    Children indicates that the number of children living in poverty increased by roughly
    two million in the U.S. between 1980 and 1990, and this trend is continuing (Sherman,
    1994).

2   When discussing minority groups, it is important to recognize their marked hetero-
    geneity. For example, consider the Latino population: the largest Latino group in
    the continental U.S. is Mexican-Americans (64%), followed by Central and South
    Americans (13%), Puerto Ricans (11%), and Cubans (5%). There are substantial
    cultural differences and academic achievement differences among these groups.

English as a second language (ESL) plays an important role in contributing to the academic difficulties Hispanic American children experience in school (Neumann, 1996).

3   The National Assessment of Educational Progress has noted that in some academic areas, including math achievement, the scores of blacks and Hispanics have significantly improved, while there has been little change in the scores of whites (Grossamer et al., 1984). In spite of these gains, students raised in poverty are, overall, badly disadvantaged by the educational system.

Chapter Two

Toward an Understanding of Individual Differences in the Classroom: An Expertise Perspective

Why Study Experts?

What exactly distinguishes those students who thrive and succeed in school from those who falter and fall further and further behind? Most attempts at answering this challenging question focus on the students who *don't* achieve academically. A plethora of explanations have been offered that cover a full range of possible factors—including genetic influences, developmental differences, psychosocial variables such as poverty and racism, inadequate parenting, deficient instruction, restrictive learning opportunities, and limited resources. Enumerating the possible factors yields a litany of the social ills that plague society.

An alternative explanatory strategy is to consider the distinctive characteristics of those students who succeed in school and the nature of their supportive learning environment. If educators could better understand what factors contribute to these students' accomplishments, they might be able to figure out how to narrow the gap between the academic "haves" and the "have-nots" in their classrooms. To address the question of individual differences, we undertook a research project designed to identify students who were noted for their academic accomplishments and budding expertise, and then carefully observed them in class. We wanted to know what such competent children do in class, what they say to themselves while performing academic tasks, what they say to others, and what others say to them.

Before we share the results of this research program (see Chapter 4), it is instructive to first pause and consider what we know about the nature of expertise, in general. Our analysis of expertise influenced what we looked for in the budding "experts" whom we studied in classrooms. The relevance of the literature on expertise is underscored by John Bruer, who proposed that "learning is the process by which novices become experts" (Bruer, 1993).

In presenting this material on expertise, we do not expect all students to reach extremely high levels of achievement. No matter how hard we try, most of us are unlikely to be able to become Olympic athletes or world-class chess champions. A combination of talent, skill, commitment, practice, and mentoring would be required for each of us to achieve at the highest level of competence. Yet while we are not proposing that everyone is going to become an expert, we do believe that educators can learn a great deal from studying the characteristics and histories of exceptional achievers.

The Literature on Expertise

We each spend a great deal of time in search of excellence. We attend concerts, dance recitals, and athletic events in the hope of catching a stellar performance. We have a favorite restaurant where the chef has that "perfect touch" and excels at creating desserts or other dishes. We delight in our favorite novelist, singer, or actor. We hire experts to help us with our computers, our taxes, our cars, and our health. We want our children to find their way into the classroom of the expert teacher who can make a difference in their lives. In a similar spirit, teachers also have recollections of their favorite or most expert students.

In short, we spend a great deal of time, effort, and money in search of excellence, and we are in awe when we encounter expertise. But what exactly do experts do that makes them so excellent? What are the talents, knowledge, skills, and drive that contribute to their expertise? What distinguishes the expert from the novice and from the experienced nonexpert? We believe that the extensive literature on expertise can yield important pedagogical guidelines for educators to help all of their students become more expert.

Psychologists have studied many types of experts and compared them to their less accomplished colleagues, usually novices (Ericsson & Charness, 1994). The impressive array of expert populations studied includes:

- expert players of chess, bridge, GO, and Othello;
- expert actors, dancers, artists, and musicians;
- experts in music notation, sight reading, composition, and recalling musical melodies;

- experts in science, writing, reading (prose and maps), solving problems (in algebra, chemistry, physics, and social science research), abacus and mental multiplication calculations;
- athletes expert in such sports as basketball, track, marathon running, field hockey, baseball, tennis, table tennis, golf, miniature golf, cricket, squash, badminton, volleyball, snooker, figure skating, swimming, gymnastics, wrestling, weight lifting, and karate. Researchers have also studied sports fans who are most knowledgeable and expert in the areas of football and soccer, horse racing, and even sports referees;
- experts in computer programming, electronic circuit design, medical diagnoses (e.g., radiologists and dermatologists), auditing (detecting fraud), and control of simulated cargo ships;
- experts in such specialties as typing, juggling, Morse Code, and memorization (e.g., waiters who are exceptional in the recall of their patrons' drink orders); and
- children who are experts in their knowledge of dinosaurs.

Before we consider what the literature has to say about the nature of expertise, reflect for a moment on an area in which you yourself demonstrate a level of expertise (or at least a high level of competence). You may be an expert at carpentry, gardening, skiing, selecting wines, baking brownies, providing social support for others, or teaching. What exactly contributes to your expertise? Consider whether the following attributes apply in your case, in your area of specialization.

1. Do you have a good deal of knowledge—not only about what to do, but also about how and when to do it?
2. Is your knowledge organized in an efficient, readily retrievable manner, so you can identify goals, patterns, and critical features of a task, and then plan task solutions?
3. Does such knowledge elicit deliberate, strategic performance that you can thoughtfully monitor on an ongoing basis, so that you can change what you do according to the changing demands of the situation and the constraints of the task?
4. Are aspects of your performance "second nature," or automatically produced in a routine and effortless fashion, so you can direct your attention to and reinvest your energies in other aspects of a task?
5. Can you describe to others what you do or what they can do to achieve greater expertise?

6. Do others put you in a consulting role—asking you for directions or suggestions, and deferring to your advice—thus providing you with multiple opportunities to exercise and further develop your level of expertise?

7. Do you invent new ways of performing tasks, resulting in the construction of new knowledge and skills?

8. Are you motivated to persist at a task in order to put in the time and effort required to further develop and fine-tune your level of expertise?

9. Do you seek and undertake new tasks that challenge you and create optimal learning situations so you are working at the edge of your knowledge and skills?

10. Do you engage in extensive deliberate and effortful practice, during which you monitor your performance with full concentration?

11. As you developed your expertise, were you supported (mentored) by one or more persons? What did your mentors do to inspire, support and nurture your expertise? What opportunities did you have to apprentice with an expert?

The answers to these questions will reveal that knowledge, strategies, and motivation are the building blocks needed to develop expertise. These answers emerge from the literature on expertise, to which we now turn our attention.

Distinguishing Characteristics of Experts

Psychologists have used a variety of diverse assessment approaches to study how experts differ from both novices and experienced non-experts. Researchers have conducted detailed naturalistic observational studies of experts "doing their thing." In order to tap the "inner world" of experts, psychologists have asked them to think aloud or draw diagrams or procedural flow charts of what they are doing while performing a task. On other occasions, experts have been interviewed before, during, and after demonstrating their abilities.

Psychologists have also studied experts in controlled laboratory settings where the task stimuli presented to both experts and novices could be carefully manipulated and controlled. Some of the most famous studies in this area of expertise were conducted by de Groot (1966) and by Chase and Simon (1973a, 1973b) with chess players. They exposed expert chess masters and novices to a 5-second glimpse of a mid-game chess match. When asked to reproduce what they had just seen, the chess masters could reproduce the positions of 20 or more of the pieces that were displayed on the board. Novices could only manage to recall 4 or 5 pieces. The superiority of the experts was removed, however, if the pieces to be recalled were placed on the board at random. Thus, the difference between the two groups was not that the experts had better memories *per se;* their advantage only emerged when the chess pieces were arranged in a meaningful fashion that simulated a true game. Under these game-like conditions, when the expert chess players looked at the board, they saw functional patterns of pieces and useful configurations or chunks. Novices, in contrast, attended to individual pieces.

To appreciate the level of expertise that chess masters bring to this perceptual-recall laboratory task, consider the estimation that expert players develop some 50,000 units (chunks of knowledge) of chess positions over the course of about 10 years (Simon & Gilmartin, 1973). The presence of such knowledge enables experts to recognize and encode a large number of pieces in higher-order units. These findings indicate that experts have stored long-term knowledge that enables them to encode the perceptual display of chess pieces in a very efficient manner.

Experts excel when a situation is typical or familiar. In these cases, information processing is fairly automatic, leading to more efficient performance. The speed of information processing and the size and organization of their working memories contributes to their expertise. As we will see, *knowledge* and *strategy differences* represent important distinctions between experts and novices.

Another difference between experts and novices is *motivation*. For instance, in order to appreciate the drive and motivation that lead experts to practice long enough to develop such extensive knowledge and strategies, psychologists have analyzed the biographies and autobiographies of experts. These biographical accounts indicated that the "best of the best" require a nurturant resourceful environment in order to blossom. One does not become an expert without extensive practice and experience; in fact, it has been proposed that the highest levels of human performance in different domains can only be attained after about 10 years of extended, deliberate, daily practice (Ericsson & Lehmann, 1996). A supportive setting provides the arena to nurture such persistence and drive.

As we search for common features that distinguish experts from novices—in terms of knowledge, strategy, and motivational differences—it is important to recognize that experts also differ from each other in domain-specific knowledge and skills. Each area of expertise requires a specific constellation of talents and skills. The search for commonalities across different classes of experts should not diminish a sensitivity to the uniqueness of each domain. For example, research on expert runners indicates that their extensive practice routines can cause bodily changes that are unique to this sport area. Similarly, research on expert typists indicates that they develop task-specific perceptual and motor skills. Skilled typists overcome speed limitations by reading further ahead than unskilled typists, while simultaneously preparing their fingers for upcoming keystrokes. They also prepare for difficult combinations of keys and learn to quickly type double letters.

One of the major findings that emerges from the research literature on expertise is the presence of specific knowledge and skills. The chess master is most often not expert in other areas. Expertise is usually limited to specific areas, although there may be common features that contribute to the "Renaissance person," or to what Bruer (1993) calls an "intelligent novice."

With the warning that experts do differ on some dimensions, we can now turn our attention to a consideration of what experts have in common. As mentioned above, experts differ from novices in knowledge, strategy, and motivation. We will consider each feature below; in the next chapter, we will examine the implications of these three factors for understanding the marked individual differences that occur in classrooms.

Knowledge Differences

As highlighted in the research on chess players, experts not only know more than novices, but their knowledge is also organized, structured, stored, recalled, and manipulated in a more efficient manner. Subsumed under the heading of knowledge are a number of subprocesses:

1. *Declarative knowledge* constitutes factual and practical information (facts, rules, definitions, etc.). It is colloquially referred to as "knowing *about* things," or "knowing *that*." For example, a reader may know *that* paraphrasing is a useful comprehension strategy.
2. *Procedural knowledge* refers to knowing the procedures for doing something, or "knowing *how*." For example, a reader may know *how to* paraphrase.
3. *Conditional* or *strategic knowledge* refers to knowing *when*, *where* and *why* to do something. For example, a reader may know *when* and *why* paraphrasing is useful.

We will consider each of these forms of knowledge and examine the relevance for understanding expertise in students.

Declarative Knowledge

Experts have extensive, systematized, and organized information in their area of expertise. This knowledge is reflected in a rich vocabulary and extensive information about the rules, strategies, alternative hypotheses, and varied ways to proceed. They possess developed networks of associations and interconnected representations of tasks. These are evident in pre-existing informational chunks, and in well-developed procedural scripts that are stored in their long-term memory. This is also evident in the experts' abilities to put into words the steps that organize their experience and to articulate the goals, subgoals, rules, and procedures involved in performing a task. Experts have much knowledge about themselves as learners and about the factors that influence their performance.

As a result of their extensive, organized, and structured knowledge, experts are able, in the area of their expertise, to perform the following tasks:

- quickly decide what information is important (acquire anticipatory skills);
- demonstrate fast and accurate pattern recognition;
- retrieve information rapidly and reliably;
- automatically categorize a problem and associate a solution procedure with it;
- construct an integrated representation of a task, easily summarize the key features of the task, and accurately draw refined inferences;
- recall information very efficiently from their area of expertise, and access relevant implicit knowledge (e.g., use base-rate data and rule-of-thumb information in formulating decisions);
- retrieve complete solutions that are stored in memory rather than use a step-by-step solution approach; and
- require relatively little study time.

The knowledge-based advantage of experts over novices is also evident when we consider how they approach solving problems. Whereas novices are likely to approach a problem in a general manner, using surface knowledge, experts use a deeper understanding to solve problems. Novices tend to deal with information as isolated fragments that are only vaguely related to higher principles, and they rarely integrate these fragments with abstract theories. When solution algorithms are offered, novices tend to use them in a rote, unthinking fashion. Experts, on the other hand, tend to organize information about specific tasks and skills into higher-order abstractions. This allows them to move to a deeper level of analysis and to perceive multiple levels of meaning.

Two academic examples of how experts organize information on a deep conceptual level come from research on how students solve physics and math problems. Chi and her colleagues (Chi, Feltovich, & Glaser, 1981) asked experts and novices to sort basic mechanical physics word problems according to the similarities in how they could be solved. The novice physics students tended to sort the word problems in terms of specific surface features, such as which problems contained the same physical objects (e.g., all the problems having to do with springs in one pile, and those dealing with pulleys and inclined planes in other piles). In contrast, the experts grasped the word problems in terms of the deeper abstract principles that were required in the solution to the problem (e.g., Newton's Laws, conservation of energy). The students' representations of the word problems were linked to their abilities to reason about them; how students defined the problems determined how they went about solving them.

These different problem-solving approaches were also nicely illustrated in a study by Hegarty et al. (1995). They compared the comprehension skills of successful and unsuccessful students on arithmetic word problems. The unsuccessful problem solvers used what Hegarty et al. called a *direct-translation strategy*: as soon as they saw critical relational keywords such as *more* or *less* in a math word problem, they immediately employed what they thought was the corresponding mathematical procedure, whether or not it was appropriate to the question. Insensitive to the deeper meaning of the questions, the poor problem solvers were responding to the surface features of the tasks. They used algorithmic procedures (problem-solving strategies), but they had little understanding as to why they were using each strategy and what benefit they gained from it.

In contrast, the successful problem solvers used a *problem-model strategy*. They constructed a mental model or theory of the situation described in each problem, and planned their solution on the basis of this model. Instead of the "compute first, think later," "number grabbing," and "keyword" methods that characterized inefficient problem solvers, the more expert problem solvers formulated a verbal or symbolic understanding of the problem before seeking a solution in quantitative terms.

We will consider the pedagogical implications of these research findings in Chapter 7. For now, it is important to appreciate that the ability to learn and apply new skills and procedures is highly dependent upon previously acquired declarative knowledge about problem types and problem settings. Such knowledge is interdependently connected to procedural knowledge (knowing how), to which we now turn our attention; a knowledge base is required to foster strategies, and strategies are essential in constructing and elaborating on one's knowledge base.

Procedural Knowledge

Procedural knowledge is used to generate action. If learning is to occur, the student must transform declarative factual knowledge into if-then action rules. An individual may employ such procedural knowledge in an automated routine script-like fashion. Such "proceduralized" knowledge eliminates the need to search declarative memory; instead, one can implement efficient production rules in an automatic fashion (Anderson, 1982). For example, consider how the novice student learns to drive a car. At first, with each action, the novice may intentionally talk to herself. But with proficiency and practice, such internal dialogue drops out of the repertoire and the behavioral sequence becomes automated. With proceduralized knowledge, the student can turn her attention to other task features such as defensive driving, or engage in parallel tasks such as listening to the radio or even talking on the telephone while driving. If the driver is placed in a novel or difficult situation—such as driving in England where one drives on the left side of the road—she "deautomatizes" the process of driving; intentional internal dialogue reappears.

In the same way that an individual may have a script for driving a car, students may have procedural scripts for performing academic tasks like note taking, highlighting a text, or writing an essay. As we shall see, experts not only have more procedural scripts, but they are also more likely to sequence procedures effectively, to monitor and assess their progress, and to alter their procedures accordingly.

As expertise is developed, more and more scripted behaviors become automated and routinized. Such automaticity is critical because it frees up mental capacity and cognitive resources and reduces the memory load. As a pianist masters procedural drills, her fingers seem to play the piece by themselves. With these basic skills down pat, the pianist can shift attention to other features of the task, such as the interpretation of the music. As a beginning reader learns basic decoding skills, he can shift attention to the complex demands of comprehension.

Procedural knowledge is often difficult to articulate (not immediately "stateable"); it becomes so highly automatized that experts can lose access to it completely. Experts usually know more than they can tell. However, under the right conditions of intentional self-monitoring and reflection (e.g., when the behavioral act is deautomatized), experts can convey the nature of their routines or procedural knowledge to others, as well as to themselves. But these deliberate, intentional cognitions do not drop out of experts' repertoire. Contrary to the belief that expert performance is highly automatized, most types of expert performance are mediated by reportable thoughts involving planning, anticipation, and reasoning (Ericsson & Lehmann, 1996).

Bereiter and Scardamalia (1993) observe that the cognitive resources that are "saved" through automatization do not simply make problem-solving *easier* for experts. Rather, these resources are freed up for higher-level cognitive efforts that experts reinvest into undertaking progressively more challenging tasks.

Conditional or Strategic Knowledge

Conditional or strategic knowledge involves an individual's ability to know when—and when not—to employ a specific skill. The answers to such questions as *when, where,* and *why* reflect the strategic knowledge that guides the performance of experts. A certain amount of declarative ("knowing that") and procedural ("knowing how") knowledge is necessary before conditional or strategic knowledge ("knowing when and where") can be generated and employed. As one moves from being a novice to an expert, declarative and procedural knowledge need to become represented as a series of conditional statements ("if" statements), that become linked to action selection ("then" statements), and to performance ("do" statements). Conditional knowledge influences which skills will be selected and when they will be executed. A series of "if X occurs, then do Y" statements reflect the presence of conditional knowledge. It is conditional knowledge that allows experts to operate in such a strategic fashion. This knowledge is well integrated for experts. Novices may know many separate procedures, but they are usually not coordinated or integrated.

Sternberg and his colleagues have proposed that such conditional knowledge is often acquired incidentally (on one's own) without direct explicit instruction from others. In the same way that individuals learn how to negotiate a different culture by watching, listening, and inferring, students (especially self-directed students) develop action-oriented knowledge by "soaking-up" what goes on in the classroom. This knowledge is characterized as "action-oriented" because it is often implicit and is accessed and activated when the need arises. As Sternberg and his colleagues observe, students often know more than they can tell. Such tacit knowledge allows individuals to develop and employ complex multidimensional procedural rules designed to pursue particular goals that are of value to them. Experts are known for their "practical intelligence" about how to identify problems, invent solutions, handle situations, and elicit help. Moreover, they are likely to associate with other experts who model and reinforce these skills (Sternberg, Wagner, Williams, & Horvath, 1995).

Strategy Differences

A strategy is a plan for solving problems or for constructing and implementing skills in a domain. We employ strategies when we wish to construct a task, when we are being "mindful" of means-ends issues, and when we encounter problems or get stuck when attempting a task. Superior strategy use goes hand in hand with a broad knowledge base to produce expertise. After an extensive review of the literature on expertise, Ericsson and Smith concluded that experts have more varied, more developed, more efficient, and more flexible strategies than novices. When an automated behavior or script is interrupted or blocked, experts draw on more strategies for addressing problems. Experts also more readily monitor the effectiveness of their strategies and performance and alter their behavior accordingly (Ericsson & Smith, 1989, 1991).

An example of differences in strategy use comes from the literature on students who differ in their levels of writing expertise. Expert writers use five or six times as many words in thinking through a writing task as they actually use in their writing. They engage in what has been called an effortful "knowledge transforming" approach to writing that entails planning, searching, evaluating, revising, and editing. In contrast, less expert writers do little more than think of the words they will put down; they settle on a "knowledge telling" approach, writing their thoughts down quickly (often in less then one minute). These less expert writers rarely engage in strategic monitoring and revision, and they rarely consider task constraints or the nature of the intended audience. In general, novices rush to perform, while experts think about their performance and rehearse strategies (Bryson, Bereiter, Scardamalia, & Joram, 1991; Kellogg, 1994).

In comparison to novices, experts explore more *relevant* alternative strategies for constructing solutions to problems. The word "relevant" is important here because experts usually do not consider *all* options; they usually restrict their problem-solving to a limited set of plausible options. This efficient search strategy is in part due to experts' superior recall of domain-specific declarative knowledge. Experts more readily discriminate relevant from irrelevant cues and use these to infer relationships and identify feasible options, with an enhanced appreciation of the implications of their decisions. As skillfulness develops, experts find planning easier, because they need less detail in their plans; they rely on the retrieval of correct answers, rather than on mindful compilations.

Experts tend to organize their strategies and performance over the course of a task. For example, they tend to pause and reflect after solving a problem. This probably helps them to store and later recall effective problem-solving strategies and to make better predictions of what they know. Compared to novices, they tend to engage in more self-explanations of problems and they monitor these explanations. Experts are more likely to put into words—or into some other form of representation (e.g., diagrams, note-taking)—what they have learned, and to share this information by acting as a consultant with others.

Having mastered content knowledge of a particular domain, experts spontaneously display sophisticated use of effective strategies, including strategies they were never taught. They see a new problem as an opportunity to expand their knowledge and competence. And finally, experts are more likely than novices to be aware of, monitor, control, and evaluate the selection and effectiveness of their strategies. They think several steps ahead, skillfully allocating resources. The awareness and control of one's cognitive processes has been called *meta-cognition* (see Highlight Box 2.1). Studies of the metacognitive skills of experts indicate that they have the ability to take charge of their own cognitive functioning in the form of planning, self-monitoring, and fix-up or repair maneuvers such as re-establishing forgotten goals and altering procedural methods. In general, experts engage in more self-regulatory metacognitive activities.

We will have a lot to say about how educators can teach metacognitive skills to their students, but for now it is important to appreciate the critical role metacognition plays in the development of expertise. In order to become expert, an individual has to have knowledge not only about the specific task domain, but also about how his or her mind works—how person, task, setting, and strategy factors influence his or her performance. For instance, how one studies often depends upon the type of exam that is to be given (e.g., multiple-choice recall versus open-ended essay). There is a need to know how setting factors (e.g., the presence of distractors, time pressure, collaborative versus individual efforts) influence performance. There is a need to have some working understanding of the mental resources needed to perform a task and the effort and resource allocation requirements in deploying different strategies.

In short, an expert must know not only how to do a task, but also how to be his or her own "coach"—the one who calls time-out at critical junctions, who reviews game plans, who selects and adapts specific strategies to meet changing task demands, who monitors progress, and who gives "pep-talks" along the way. In short, experts are active, self-directed learners.

Motivational Differences

The emerging portrait might suggest that experts are efficient computer-like machines who can be measured in terms of the size and organization of their domain-specific knowledge, the speed of their information processing, the size

Highlight Box 2.1
WHAT IS METACOGNITION?

One of the terms that comes up over and over in the area of expertise and in discussions of high achieving students is *metacognition*. Students who achieve have been found to evidence heightened metacognitive awareness and a greater number of self-regulatory behaviors. It is critical for teachers to understand what is meant by the concept of metacognition—particularly since teachers are called upon to explicitly model, discuss, and teach metacognition to their students.

The term *metacognition* refers to the cognitions you have about your cognitions, your thinking about your thinking, your ideas about your ideas. It refers to your thinking about yourself as a problem solver who is able to voluntarily plan, monitor, evaluate, and regulate your own cognitive processes. Metacognition reflects your ability to "read" your own mental state and to assess how that state will affect your present and future performance. In this self-assessment process, you bring to bear a good deal of knowledge about specific strategies, tasks, and cognitive processes, as well as knowledge about yourself as a learner.

The following example, described by the psychologist William James, can be used to illustrate metacognition in action. James observed that people often have a feeling of knowing something that they cannot recall. Consider the common "tip of your tongue" phenomenon where you try to retrieve a name you have forgotten (James, 1890). Suppose we notice that you are struggling to remember; as we watch, you work hard at it, but you fail. At an opportune moment we take you aside and say, "We are data snoops and we wonder if you would kindly indulge us for a moment and tell us what you did to try and retrieve the missing name?" Having nothing better to do with your time, you indulge us and describe several things you did when you experienced this phenomenon:

1. You went through the alphabet to see if this strategy would jar your memory ("A ... Alice, no! B ... Betty, no!", and so forth).

2. You tried to recall where you saw this person last. You closed your eyes and pictured the setting and events. (In some sense, you are conveying that you tried to retrieve the missing name by means of imagery association, trying to access the name from the "mental file" in which it is stored.)

3. You approached someone else who you thought knew this person and tried to help him recall the name by asking, "You know the woman who used to live around the corner from me, who wore those tacky dresses—what is her name?" (The ability to access someone else's memory in the retrieval process is a critical skill. In this example, you knew exactly how to elicit help from another person in order to retrieve the missing name; with surgical precision, you provided a prompt—"a former neighbor who wore tacky dresses.")

4. The last strategy you employed was deciding that it was not really important to retrieve this person's name. You convey that you are not going to

expend any more mental effort to remember her name, since this effort will not pay off. You indicate that you are not sure how the mind (memory) works, but you have learned that when you least expect it, something will trigger the recall of a missing name. Nevertheless, you convey some confidence in your ability to retrieve such names. You note that if it were really important, as on an exam, you would continue to work at retrieving the missing name.

Your answer to our question "What did you do to retrieve the missing name?" is what we mean by *metacognition*. Metacognition involves two main factors— our *knowledge* (awareness) and *control* (self-regulation) of our own cognitive processes. First, it involves having a good deal of knowledge about how our heads work. We know when we don't know something, and when knowing something is important or not. We know our own skills and limitations within a particular domain. We know when to give up on a chosen path and try something else. We know how to allocate our attention and control our working memory. We know how to balance time and effort on the one hand, and speed and accuracy on the other. We know how to keep important information in mind while performing some type of operation. We also know that our cognitive processes are influenced by a number of factors: *person* variables (e.g., how fatigued, preoccupied, anxious, or busy we are), *situation* variables (e.g., casual conversation vs. an exam, making decisions under time pressure or not), *task* variables (e.g., recall vs. recognition, multiple choice vs. essay), and *strategy* variables (e.g., using imagery, seeking help).

Second, metacognition also involves elements of control—our ability to plan, to select which strategy we will use (alphabet retrieval, imagery, someone else's memory), and to monitor the relative effectiveness of each strategy in helping us to achieve our goal. When one strategy doesn't work we may switch to another, and then switch back again. We can even select which strategy to use depending upon the demands of the situation, decisions about effort, and other variables.

The critical concern of this book is where we, as educators, explicitly teach our students how to engage in such metacognitive activity. If we observed you in your classroom, where are the opportunities for you to teach metacognitive skills and the "how-to" processes of learning (e.g., self-interrogation, planning how to allocate resources, managing time and effort, summarizing, note taking, self-checking, studying, and a number of compensatory strategies like revising, rereading, asking for help, and selecting and shifting strategies when students sense they have a problem)? Do you teach your students how various person, task, strategy, and situational factors influence their learning processes? When do you use metacognition to monitor your own teaching efforts? How much do you share your own metacognitive processes with your students? Since evaluation often drives instruction, how do you systematically assess your students' metacognitive abilities? How do you encourage your students to self-evaluate their metacognitive abilities?

It is not only *what* we teach that is critical, but also *how* we teach. How shall we teach novices these executive metacognitive skills so they can become more expert? Chapters 7 through 10 will describe specifically how these challenging instructional tasks can be accomplished.

and structure of their working memory, and the flexibility of their strategies to meet the changing demands of the task. But where is the person in the machine? Where are the interest, determination, commitment, persistence, industry, desire for excellence, and passion that lead to the many, many hours of practice required to become an expert?

A major characteristic that distinguishes experts from others is the sheer amount of deliberate practice in which experts engage. This observation is underscored by various researchers, who reported on the developmental experiences of experts in the areas of chess, music and sports. They found that relative to less competent performers, experts:

1. began their activities at an earlier age;
2. demonstrated a higher level of sustained practice for their age group and worked harder on their selected tasks;
3. evidenced interest in their area of expertise before they began systematic practice;
4. engaged in systematic practice that was most often initiated by their parent(s) who actively supported and rewarded their practice habits;
5. continued to practice throughout adolescence in response to efforts of an advanced teacher or coach;
6. reduced leisure-time activities during adolescence as more time was devoted to their area of expertise; and
7. reached maximal or optimal levels of practice by age 20.

(Ericsson, Krampe, & Tesch-Romer, 1993)

These studies indicate that any analysis of the development of expertise needs to take into consideration the motivation and social support that sustain both the level of commitment and the amount of practice. Affective and motivational factors can energize or thwart people's use of abilities and strategies, their level of commitment, their amount of practice, and the quality of their performance. These motivational processes may take the form of specific beliefs, particularly attributions or causal explanations related to the perceived causes of failure and success.

Students' confidence as learners—as well as the ways they view their abilities and the potential consequences of their efforts—can affect the likelihood that they will acquire knowledge and skills and apply them spontaneously in new settings and on new tasks. For instance, research indicates that the kinds of problems and tasks that experts tackle increase their level of expertise. Experts tend to seek out more and more difficult problems, engaging in problems to which previously learned solutions do not readily apply. They continually challenge themselves with solvable problems, so that they develop their level of expertise in a kind of multiplier effect. Experts tackle problems that increase their expertise, working at the upper edge of their competence. They push the boundaries of their abilities, demonstrating dogged persistence, industry, and a desire for excellence. In contrast, non-experts tend to tackle problems and tasks for which they do *not* have to extend themselves.

Any explanation of expertise needs to consider what motivates individuals to invest their effort in becoming experts, develop the commitment to the autonomous pursuit of learning, cope with failure and success, and create more optimal learning situations.

Summary

Expertise is a complex and dynamic process that involves knowledge (declarative, procedural, and conditional), metacognitive awareness, and strategy control, as well as motivational beliefs, attributions, and nurturing and resourceful supports. How do these characteristics of expertise express themselves in classroom settings? How do those students who thrive differ from those who falter in school in terms of their knowledge, strategies, and motivation? In the next chapter we turn our attention to these important questions.

Chapter Three

Application of the Expertise Model in the Classroom: The Characteristics of Budding Experts

In Chapter 2 we examined the characteristics of experts in terms of knowledge, strategy, and motivation. The purpose of this chapter is to consider how these same processes can be used to understand the major individual differences that emerge in the classroom. How do students who thrive in school (whom we will call "budding experts") differ from those students who falter, or even fall further and further behind in each succeeding grade? As educators, we can all conjure up pictures of students for whom schoolwork comes easily, as well as those who have to struggle. If we could ascertain what distinguishes these two groups, this information could be used to improve our educational efforts.

To set the stage for considering how high- and low-achieving students approach and perform academic tasks, consider three responses offered by seventh- and eighth-grade math students. These responses (shown in Table 3.1) were obtained as part of our teacher training project on adapting instructional procedures to the marked individual differences between high- and low-performing students. The students were interviewed about their approaches to math word problems.[1] Note how the two groups differ in their knowledge and understanding about the nature of word problems, and in their dispositions to seek help and persist on the task. These differences are consistent with the observations offered by Chi et al. (1988), who concluded that what distinguishes experts from novices is that "the experts posses an organized body of conceptual and procedural knowledge that can be readily accessed and used with superior monitoring and self-regulating skills" (p. 36). These differences have been found across a variety of academic domains. In the remainder of this chapter, we will consider these differences in more detail, as they relate to knowledge, strategy, and motivational factors.

TABLE 3.1: Metacognitive Interview With High- and Low-Performing Seventh- and Eighth-Grade Math Students

Interview Question	High-Performing Students	Low-Performing Students
1. What are mathematics word problems?	"Questions written out in words. You need to do something to solve them. Draw a picture to help you solve them." "A word problem is similar to a number problem, but instead of the problem being described in digits and symbols it is described in words. A problem may be easier if it is logical and easy to relate to."	"A word problem that has problems." "Like a story about something that happened; it has a question that you have to answer."
2. What makes someone really good at doing word problems?	"They can understand the problem better and use different strategies." "If they understand the word problems and can retell the problem."	"Someone can be good at word problems if they read it and just get the basic facts. Once you understand the problem you can figure from there." "Know all the times tables and division. Need to know how to get the answer."
3. What is the hardest part about doing word problems?	"When there is extra insignificant information, sometimes I have to ignore these facts to make sense of the problems." "Taking one step at a time. If it's not a one-step problem, then you have to do other things first to get the answer."	"If I don't understand it, finding the solution and using it." "Reading and understanding them."
4. What would help you become a better problem solver?	"Trying different ways to solve the problem. I know there are many ways to solve math problems. I could be more accurate, if I put the problem into simpler words." "Practice solving problems. Making up problems and solving them. Or solve real world math problems that have actually happened."	"Being able to read better; don't understand what I read most of the time." "Extra help makes me understand more."

TABLE 3.1 (continued)

Interview Question	High-Performing Students	Low-Performing Students
5. If you were getting ready to take a word problem test, what would you do that would help you the most to do well on that test?	"I would make each problem easier by eliminating unimportant information." "Review them first. Think of our previous math sheets. Study other word problems."	"Have a blank piece of paper to work things out, have an eraser." "Ask the teacher to read some of them for me."
6. Are some parts of a word problems more important than others? How can you tell which parts are the most important?	"When you read the question you should go back and find the part about what the question is asking. Other parts might not have anything to do with the question." "Watch for key words like how many or total or ratio and underline the numbers."	"The question is the most important information in the problem." "It tells the information. It tells the numbers."
7. What do you do if you don't know what a word means in a problem?	"Try to read the sentence with other words to see if I could get the meaning. If this didn't work I'd take an educated guess. If it wasn't a test, I'd ask the teacher." "I could ask a friend or look it up in a dictionary."	"Put up your hand. Ask the teacher." "Go to the next problem."
8. What do you do if you don't get the whole picture or the whole meaning of a word problem?	"You can look at the question you are asked to answer, when you read it again, look for any important facts." "Keep reading it over and over again and write it down or try and draw a picture of the problem."	"Ask the teacher." "Put up your hand."
9. After you have read and understood a word problem, what else must you still do in order to complete the problem successfully?	"You must also solve the problem in number and words. Also, write a sentence explaining your answer." "Think of a strategy to solve the problem. For example, draw a picture or write down the numbers then I carry on from there. Then I try and retell it."	"Do it and if I think something isn't right, do it again." "Show it to my teacher."
10. What about a word problem makes it easy for you?	"A word problem is easy for me when the operation used to solve the problem is easy to do. Adding is much easier than dividing decimals." "When I am able to retell the problem in my own words."	"Simpler words." "The operation is easy, like adding."

Differences Between Low- and High-Achieving Students

Researchers have used a variety of assessment procedures to analyze individual differences. These techniques include standardized tests, performance measures, direct classroom observations, teacher and parent interviews and questionnaires, and laboratory-based measures. No matter which source of information we examine, a common profile of the *low-achieving student* emerges. The students who falter in school are described as "passive, inactive learners." How does this passivity evidence itself? Relative to high-achieving students, low-achieving students tend to:

- have deficits in component skills (e.g., reading comprehension, computational skills);
- have a smaller and less elaborately organized knowledge base;
- use fewer, simpler, and more passive processing strategies;
- respond to tasks and instructions without fully understanding them;
- employ strategies in a rote, inflexible fashion, employing fewer metacognitive self-regulatory behaviors; and
- be teacher-dependent, asking for answers and help sooner and more frequently than do high-achieving students.

Each of these features was evident in the low-performing students' responses to the metacognitive interview. But as Swanson has noted, low-achieving students are not incapable of using strategies per se; rather, they are "actively inefficient." Low-achieving students tend to employ general methods of problem-solving with little strategic precision. For instance, in one study on memory recall, the low-performing students failed to allocate enough study time to retain the difficult items, and they failed to rehearse and self-test for recall. They had difficulty monitoring and predicting how well they would remember. Overall, they were less strategic in undertaking the recall tasks. When they did employ a deliberate strategy, they rarely assessed its effectiveness and failed to fine-tune their learning approach (Swanson, 1992).

A similar profile is evident in classrooms where low-achieving students fail to take charge of their learning. Our own observations indicate that low-achieving students rarely use language to direct their own and others' performance. They initiate little voluntary control and employ limited executive metacognitive skills (Meichenbaum & Biemiller, 1992).

Bereiter and Scardamalia (1993, p. 20) have highlighted a similar behavioral profile in their description of students who are non-expert learners. These students tend to:

- Give little or no thought to how much more there is to learn as they jump to conclusions on the basis of the little they have already learned.
- Make subjective judgments of importance, ignoring events or statements that do not stand out as important in their own right.
- Quickly construct simplistic interpretations, which are then retained in the face of contradictions.
- Dismiss whole topics as boring without attempting to discover what might be interesting in them, while allowing themselves to be captivated by items of tangential interest.

In school, low-achieving students have lower academic goals, evidence less accuracy in assessing their own abilities, and are more likely to give up easily when confronting setbacks and failures. They tend to attribute their failures to a lack of ability and skills, rather than to a lack of effort. In addition, they tend to attribute their success to luck, ease of the task, or some other external attribute— such as the teacher's mood—rather than to what they did. This passive learning style is often compounded by a pattern of impulsivity and distractibility that can have major social consequences, resulting in poor peer relations and behavioral problems (Dweck, 1986).

In contrast to passive and inefficient learners, those who achieve academi- cally are characterized as being "self-directed," strategic students and independ- ent, autonomous learners. *Self-direction* encompasses all the processes by which students exercise conscious, deliberate control over thinking, affect, and behav- ior as they acquire knowledge and skills. Some psychologists prefer the term *self-regulation* (e.g., Zimmerman & Schunk, 1989). High-achieving students are mentally active during the learning process, as they orchestrate and control their own attempts at using performance-oriented strategies, such as self-interroga- tion and self-checking. In addition to their cognitive and metacognitive skills, these students also hold accompanying beliefs that contribute to their commit- ment, effort, and persistence. When taken as a whole, these skills and attitudes represent a sophisticated and reflective approach toward learning, as evident in the high-performing students' interviews in Table 3.1.

Knowledge Differences

Like the experts we discussed earlier, high-achieving students evidence elevated levels of declarative, procedural, and conditional knowledge about school in general, as well as increased domain-specific knowledge. Howard Gardner and his colleagues report interviews with students who were identified as being high or low in their knowledge about how school works and what was needed to succeed (Gardner, Krechevsky, Sternberg, & Okagaki, 1994). Students who were what John Bruer (1993) called "intelligent novices" offered elaborated answers reflecting an awareness of the existence and utility of a number of specific learning strategies and resources. They also had a clear and differentiated view of themselves as learners. In contrast, those students who were low in "practical intelligence" tended to give brief and vague descriptions of what was needed to succeed in school (e.g., "You have to study harder," with little clarification of what this entails).

These different approaches toward learning are evident in the specific cognitive and metacognitive activities that high-achieving students engage in.

- They know more about the subject being taught and access this knowledge more readily.
- They demonstrate greater depth of understanding and greater awareness of related concepts.
- They use larger units or chunks to process information.
- They use what they know to learn more quickly in new domains, relating new skills and knowledge to what they already know.
- They evidence heightened awareness of themselves as learners (e.g., making more accurate predictions of their performance, even before the teacher has graded their tests).
- They engage in more self-explanations and explanations to others as they take on the role of being their own teachers and being consultants to others.

Strategy Differences

High-achieving students are also highly strategic. The ways they approach and plan tasks, the ways they monitor and alter performance during a task, and the ways they reflect, alter, and revise their strategies, all contribute to their high level of performance. These strategies can be clustered into those employed *before*, *during*, and *after* performing a task. Although these strategies will be discussed in a sequential fashion, it is important to recognize that they occur in a recursive (back-and-forth), interdependent fashion, as students cycle and recycle through them.

Before a task is presented, or at the outset of a task, high-achieving students:

1. access prior knowledge and link it with new information;
2. set goals and subgoals;
3. select strategies for achieving the goal and subgoals;
4. plan what to do and how to do it;
5. use information to the fullest (e.g., recall previous instructions, utilize the most important information, ask questions when they do not understand the instructions);
6. organize and transform information; and
7. organize and structure their place of study.

During the course of performing a task, high-achieving students:

1. engage in self-management activities (e.g., time management and resource allocation);
2. use self-directive strategies such as ongoing monitoring, planning, rehearsing, organizing, elaborating and discovery learning;
3. monitor comprehension—noting any lack of understanding or mismatch between initial goals and current performance—and then adjust their strategies and performance responsively and adaptively (e.g., giving themselves directions);
4. rehearse information to be remembered and undertake self-testing in the form of ongoing self-interrogation and self-exams;
5. keep records and results of self-testing;
6. use memory aids effectively;
7. use debugging strategies and take self-corrective steps;
8. seek help and solicit selective assistance, self-selecting exemplary models to observe, and often seeking hints instead of answers;
9. pose more complex questions of themselves and others, and check their answers;
10. explain to others the ideas and procedures to be learned;
11. paraphrase, summarize, and generate explanations that involve creating analogies, metaphors, and examples, so the information to be learned is processed at a deeper level of understanding.

Following a task, high-achieving students:

1. establish a productive environment in which to work and rework, to learn and relearn what has been taught in class;
2. reorganize and correct notes. During class they are likely to use genera-

tive note-taking (putting into their own words what was said), instead of linear note-taking (recording what was said verbatim). This process may take the form of typing into a computer a transformed version of what was taught that day.

3. revise and rework their performance;
4. monitor their progress and keep records;
5. transfer what they learned to novel problems and situations.

Naturally, this extensive list of the competencies characterizing high-achieving students is not complete. But what is most impressive is that high-achieving students have a greater likelihood of performing all these tasks *on their own* and applying their skills on new tasks in novel situations.

Motivational Differences

Knowledge, strategies, and metacognitive abilities are usually not enough to promote student achievement or nurture expertise. Students must also be motivated to use the talents and skills they possess. They must have the *will*, not just the *skill*. A student's will is tied to his or her level of self-confidence and self-esteem. An individual's feelings of self-assurance in a learning situation will influence his or her degree of dedication, effort, and persistence. Motivational factors are an incentive for deploying strategies, especially on transfer tasks. The research literature indicates that the ways experts view themselves and their abilities—and the explanations that they offer themselves and others about their successes and failures—are critical in influencing the learning process. As William James observed, "When an individual stakes a claim to a particular identity they then behave in ways to demonstrate and elaborate on that identity" (James, 1890).

Research by a number of investigators (such as Albert Bandura, Lynn Corno, Carol Dweck, Carol Licht, Bernard Weiner, and others) on high-achieving students has explored a number of factors relating to motivation. High achievers tend to:

- choose challenging tasks;
- evidence persistence on learning tasks and see tasks through to completion even when frustrated;
- give self-consequences depending upon their performance;
- value academic skills and learning;
- volunteer for special projects and bring into class relevant information

not included in the assigned reading;

- hold high expectations of future success and positive beliefs about their capabilities;
- feel confidence (self-efficacy) in their ability to overcome problems and achieve academic tasks;
- be future-oriented about possible achievements (holding multiple positive "possible selves"[2]);
- have an "incremental" view of abilities and intelligence, perceiving these characteristics as developing gradually and resulting from effort—rather than holding an "entity" view of abilities, in which intelligence is viewed as being fixed or innate, and unlikely to change; and
- view school as a place that provides them with opportunities to increase competence, enhance knowledge, and improve skills. This *learning orientation* leads high-achieving students to take personal satisfaction in performing a task and to use internal standards in judging their competence. In contrast, low-achieving students have a *performance orientation* in which school is seen as a setting for demonstrating competence as determined by external judges. Public praise and external rewards are the main source of motivation for such students.[3]

Motivational differences between high- and low-achieving students are further highlighted in the research on the causal explanations students offer for successes and failures. High-achieving students are more likely to view task success as deriving from their efforts and their use of strategies (viz., employing the "tricks of the trade" in order to do well). Successful students tend to attribute failure to not having put out enough effort, not trying hard enough, not using the right strategy, or not having learned the necessary prerequisite skills. As a result, children who attribute their academic outcomes to their own efforts are more likely to be strategic and persistent.

Low-achieving students have a different story to tell when they encounter success and failure. Those who struggle but occasionally succeed see success as deriving more from luck, ease of the task, teacher mood, or external help than from anything they did to achieve. Low-achieving students rather reluctantly take credit for accomplishments, but are all too willing to accept responsibility when it comes to explaining their failures and setbacks.

When confronted by the challenge of not achieving, the student who struggles highlights a lack of ability as the source of failure. The most poignant example of this response that we have encountered was an eighth-grade student who explained the reason for his poor reading comprehension performance: "When I was born," he said, "I think my mother was standing on the wrong line for the genes needed for reading comprehension." While this boy's humor covered up the pain of academic failure, inherent in his quip was a dose of despair and frustration that led him to give up whenever he encountered failure. "What's the use?" was the repeated refrain accompanying his poor performance. It took much work to persuade him to entertain the possibility that good readers achieve because they know "tricks" and strategies and work hard at practicing them. Such a motivational shift was seen as central in moving him from being a novice to becoming a more competent reader. We recognized that he would not immediately perform at the reading level of his classmates, but we set out with him to find a level at which he could read and, in his own fashion, become more expert.

It should be noted that if a student's competence is defined as reaching the reading level of his classmates while in the same grade, then his pessimism may be justified. If instead, competence is defined as performing *eventually* as well as his classmates do now, then pessimism may *not* be justified. Thus, the validity of a student's beliefs about his reading competence depends in part upon how the external world (peers, parents and teachers) evaluates that student, and upon his own self-evaluation, whether in terms of competitive norms or of individual mastery.

In order to improve students' school performance, it is critical to attend to students' attributional beliefs. The attributional beliefs that our students hold can influence several important factors:

1. the goals they set;
2. the commitment they make to achieve those goals;
3. the effort and skills they employ to reach those goals;
4. their choice of strategies to employ;
5. their level of task persistence; and
6. the degree to which they employ learned skills when performing new tasks in new situations.

Without the proper motivation, students are unlikely to make the commitment, demonstrate the persistence, or expend the effort to engage in the amount of practice that is required to move from being a novice to becoming an expert. Inherent in this journey are setbacks, failures, lapses, criticisms, and frustrations. The comments students make to themselves and to others about such setbacks, the stories they construct, and the stories that are generated and shared by significant others in their lives are all critical in determining the paths students will take and the nature of their journeys toward expertise.

The significance of motivational factors in influencing students' achievement was highlighted in the results of the National Educational Longitudinal Study (NELS). This study examined changes in the achievement of 25,000 eighth-grade students (1988) and followed them through the 12th grade (1992). The researchers were interested in determining what student and familial factors predict achievement. The most important factor to emerge from their analyses was one they called "student ambition and plans for the future." Those students who had hopeful, but realistic, visions for themselves as being successful in the future had a much higher level of academic achievement than those students who had weaker visions of themselves. Other associated, but less significant, factors included parental expectations of their children's achievement, student time spent doing homework, parental monitoring of friends and activities, and school attendance rates. Interestingly, whether or not the student attended a private school or came from a single-parent home did *not* predict achievement. Rather, it was the ways students' visions of themselves were shaped within school and families that was critical in predicting achievement levels. As educators and parents, we can help shape and nurture students' visions of themselves.

The "person in the machine," the "student in the instructional setting," has a metaphorical "soul" that must be attended to, nurtured with support, and challenged in a sensitive and timely fashion. The novice must hold the vision of becoming a potential expert—or at least becoming more competent—if she is to elevate her performance. Specific ways that teachers can accomplish these objectives will be discussed in Chapters 7 through 10.

But before we look for possible solutions, we should ask *how* and *when* these substantial individual differences in school performance emerged. Are such individual differences evident across all subject areas and situations? Are there conditions that may mitigate such marked variability in achievement performance? The answers to these critical questions will provide a framework for understanding what can be done to close the gap between high- and low-achieving students. There is some urgency in answering these questions, since the degree of individual difference increases from kindergarten to high school; the gap becomes larger and larger with each passing year.

Endnotes

1. The interview format was developed by Hutchinson (1987, 1993).
2. For a discussion of the concept of "possible selves," see Markus and Nurius (1986).
3. For a discussion of the influence of motivational factors on academics, see Bandura (1993), Borkowski and Thorpe (1994), Corno (1994), Dweck (1986), and Licht (1993).

Chapter Four

How Did The Gap Between Those Who Thrive And Those Who Falter Get So Large?

Children differ considerably in their readiness to profit from school instruction. And there is much evidence that many of these early differences are maintained through elementary and secondary school. Rather than compensating for initial differences, the educational system often tends to advantage the advantaged and to disadvantage the disadvantaged. We suggest that this process, known as a "Matthew Effect" (see p. 45), occurs because schools provide superior learning experiences to educationally advantaged students, and support a transactional process whereby some children gain academic expertise while others become increasingly dependent on academic assistance. In subsequent chapters, we will argue that both organizational and instructional changes will be needed if schools are to provide more equal opportunities for all students. The fundamental organizational change will be to focus on students' mastery of particular academic domains rather than on their age. The instructional change will involve providing most students with the range of experiences now enjoyed by the most advanced students—learning experiences that include developing and using academic expertise, as well as acquiring new skills and knowledge.

We turn now to an examination of the process that leads to the large gap observable in educational achievement. As noted, by the time students reach the first year of high school, the top 10% and the bottom 10% in the same class often differ by more than *six grade levels* in academic ability. If we are going to bring many more students to real mastery of academic skills and knowledge, it is important to understand how these differences came to be. While a great deal of research has been conducted to address this crucial question, we believe the answer can be summarized under four main points, each of which is elaborated upon in this chapter.

1. *Differences at the Beginning of Schooling: Readiness Factors.* Some children begin school more prepared, more "school-ready," due to experiential and constitutional factors.
2. *Stability of Differences in Achievement.* By the end of the third grade, differences become developmentally stable. In other words, by the third grade, children's relative achievement levels become increasingly predictive of their later relative achievement status, as students are launched into achievement trajectories that will likely follow the rest of their school years. This stability also reflects both experiential and constitutional factors.
3. *School Systemic Factors.* Instructional, curricular, attitudinal, and structural features of the school system often inadvertently contribute to and exacerbate the individual differences that exist in students' abilities.
4. *Instructional Practices: A Transactional Perspective.* Early differences lead to differences in the ways students are treated in school by teachers and by peers. These differences may widen the gap in achievement and accomplishment, and students' responses to such treatment may further exacerbate the problem.

While some of the factors that contribute to the growing gap between students lie within individuals, and some lie within the child's home environment, many of these factors can be influenced by teachers and school administrators. What do we do as educators that unwittingly contributes to the differences between the "haves" and "have-nots" in our classrooms? We begin by examining what schools are confronted with from the outset.

Differences at the Beginning of Schooling: Readiness Factors

Increasing numbers of children begin school at risk for school failure (Hodgkinson, 1992; Pallas, Natriello, & McDill, 1989). This fact could be substantiated by any teacher of kindergarten or grade one who can point to substantial individual differences among children in his or her class at the beginning of the school year. Some children arrive at school with far more home support for reading and experience with print, books, and book language than others. When entering kindergarten, some students have large vocabularies, understand number concepts, can follow directions, get along well with classmates, and generally meet the demands of school. Some learn easily, quickly reaching skill levels that permit them to help their classmates and to use their skills on varied tasks in multiple settings. In contrast, many other students begin elementary school lacking some or all of these abilities and knowledge. In many cases, such children can be identified by kindergarten teachers (Biemiller & Richards, 1986).

Currently, 25% to 35% of students enter school with factors that are considered to place them at risk of failing socially and academically. Such factors include poverty, developmental delays, poor physical and mental health, biological and psychological trauma, family indifference, neighborhood violence, parents drug and alcohol abuse, and parental stress and dysfunction (Huston, 1995). These findings were highlighted by Sameroff and his colleagues, who studied the impact of high-risk factors on the intellectual development of 4-year-olds. The IQs of children who had 8 or 9 out of 10 risk factors averaged 30 points below those of children who had no high-risk factors in their backgrounds. The risk factors Sameroff and his colleagues examined included the presence of mental illness in a parent, the level of maternal anxiety, parent interactional style and attitudes, occupational level in the household, maternal level of education, disadvantaged minority status, level of family support, degree of stressful life events, and family size. In short, psychosocial risk factors can put children at high risk for academic failure (Sameroff, Seifer, Baldwin, & Baldwin, 1993; Sameroff, Seifer, Barocas, Zax, & Greenspan, 1987).

How do these initial readiness differences emerge?

Part of the answer to this question involves differences in children's experience (risk exposure) prior to entering elementary school. Children in different families vary in terms of the language (both spoken and printed) to which they are exposed, the emotional support and security they experience, the value placed by their parents on educational attainment, their physical health and medical care, and other factors which affect their readiness to profit from schooling.

As noted previously, most of these environmental differences are partially associated with social class. We know that children who come from economically advantaged households tend to be more successful in school than their less advantaged classmates. Much of their academic success can be credited to the support they receive. In home observations of early language development in 3-year-olds across socioeconomic classes, Hart and Risley (1997) found that children from poor families lag considerably behind children from working-class and professional-class families. The level of positive parent interactions and the amount that parents initiated children's speech in infancy were critical to the development of early language skills.[1]

While parents from advantaged and disadvantaged families report comparable interest in their children's education, the nature of available child supports tends to differ between socioeconomic groups. Many parents from disadvantaged homes pay relatively little attention to their children's grades, and have little involvement in preparing their children for school (e.g., reading to them, teaching them to count, generally engaging them in dialogue). They are also less likely than middle-class parents to provide appropriate support of achievement objectives that are consistent with the expectations of the school (Pianta et al., 1995).

Early experience also affects emotional development. Research on student-teacher relationship variables has found that some children entering school are relatively emotionally secure, outgoing, gregarious, and nonaggressive. Other children show patterns of *social withdrawal*—being dependent on the teacher and evidencing poor peer relationships. Those children who are competently assertive and socially mature make the most academic gains during the first grade. The children's interpersonal styles and communication skills affect the quality of the student-teacher relationship. While teachers see some children as "draining their energy," they see others as "beaming with pride" and "coping with setbacks." These differential interpersonal patterns have a significant impact on the teaching experience children receive not only in school, but also at home (Alexander & Entwhistle, 1988).

This developmental pattern was nicely illustrated by Borkowski and Dukewich (1996), who noted that such differences can begin at an early age. They observed that preschool teachers tend to treat "securely" and "insecurely" attached children differently. Teachers were warmer with, and expected more age-appropriate behavior from, the "secure" children, encouraging self-directed autonomous learning. With the more "anxious-resistant-insecure" children, teachers were more controlling, thus restricting the students' metacognitive learning opportunities. The children's styles of relating "pulled for" different teacher reactions and helped to create learning environments that reinforced the initial differences. A negative transactional cycle emerges early in the child's schooling experience; as we will see, that cycle is difficult to break.

Initial readiness differences also reflect the fact that whenever developmental growth or maturation occurs, there are individual differences in *rates* of growth. A cursory observation of any kindergarten or first-grade class will confirm this fact with regard to height and weight. What is less obvious is that there are also constitutional influences on the rate of development of cognitive capacity. The term *cognitive capacity* refers to the number of things that can be attended to or thought of simultaneously, and to the complexity of those things (Biemiller, 1993). Similarly, there are individual differences in the rate of acquisition of skills, whether cognitive or motoric. Such differences in aptitude may manifest as differences in the amount of time students need to master a task. Most students can learn, but their learning rates may present difficulties (Carroll, 1963, 1989).

The level and rate of maturation affect a child's cognitive capacity and responsiveness to instruction. Such differences are influential in determining school success. Consider that within any given grade, the range of students' chronological ages spans at least 12 months. While some children are old enough and mature enough to develop certain skills in their kindergarten years, others may just be reaching this point by first grade. This normal variation in age has an impact on children's progress or success in school as evident in grade retention rates related to age. Research findings indicate that between the first and fourth grades, about 12% of January- to June-born children have been retained a grade in schools where January-born children are the oldest. In contrast, nearly 40% of December-born children are retained over the same period (Cantalini, 1987; Langer, Kalk, & Searls, 1984). Thus, maturational status clearly influences children's rate of academic progress.

Differences in maturational growth are nicely illustrated in research on gifted children. As Geary (1994) observes:

> Many mathematically gifted children are not "qualitatively" different from their non-gifted peers but rather they develop the same basic mathematical skills at an accelerated rate (pp. 224-225).

Gifted students process information more quickly than their average-ability peers and use more mature problem-solving skills many years before average-ability peers. They learn more quickly and are able to pull together disparate pieces of information to construct new strategies *at a much younger age*. They have a better conceptual understanding of basic concepts and strategies (Geary, 1994).

In summary, children begin school differing in a variety of ways that can influence their readiness to learn. In the same way that students evidence different growth rates in motor abilities, they also evidence different growth rates in cognitive development. Perhaps classroom teachers can learn from those instructors who teach motor skills (e.g., swimming, canoeing, skiing) about how to tailor instruction to the cognitive "growth curves" of their students. As we shall consider, these differences have long-term implications.

Stability of Differences in Achievement

We have seen that children enter school differing in a variety of ways that result in some being more ready than others to benefit from schooling. Do these differences persist? Unfortunately, the answer is *yes*. Patterns of low achievement begin in the first years of formal schooling, and the established pattern remains relatively stable throughout school. The gap evident by the end of the third and fourth grades typically increases in later grades. (Note that performance in first and second grades is relatively *less* predictive of later performance. Some slow-progressing first-graders catch up with their peers in the second grade. This phenomenon is much less common after third grade.) Those students who are making slow progress by grade 3 typically fall further and further behind their higher-achieving fellow students in middle school and high school. It is very hard for a child who is really behind to ever "catch up," in the sense of coming to perform as well as higher-achieving agemates *at the same age*. (However, as we will argue in subsequent chapters, it may be better to emphasize the need for slower-progressing students to reach similar levels of genuine achievement and mastery of skills, rather than attaining similar performance at exactly the same age.)

These slower-progressing students suffer from what Benjamin Bloom (1964, 1976) calls a "cumulative deficit." Incomplete mastery of one skill contributes to the reduced acquisition and performance of the next skill. When students fail to achieve mastery at one academic level, their subsequent performance will become weaker and weaker, and mastery will never occur. A "vicious circle" develops that eventually leads to the substantial differences we find in high school.

Research indicates that achievement measured in the third grade can be used to predict achievement in the 11th grade with an accuracy of 80% or better (Guskey, 1985). As Bloom (1976) observes,

> There is repeated evidence of very high relationships between the achievement of students at grade 3 and their achievement at grades 10 or 11, seven or eight years later. The correlation of the same students' achievement measures at grade 3 and at grade 11 is over .80, suggesting that the rank order of students within a group of 100 or so students in the same school remains virtually the same for 90% of the students. That is, students' achievement in the early grades has a powerful deterministic effect on their achievement throughout their elementary school experiences (p. 18).

Children who acquire literacy skills (reading, writing, spelling) most readily in the early grades tend to remain the best readers, writers and spellers throughout the elementary school years. Likewise, many children who have difficulty at the start of school continue to exhibit relatively weak skills throughout their educational careers.

This pattern of stability in academic performance is not unique to the U.S. In a 10-year longitudinal study involving American (Minneapolis), Chinese (Taipei) and Japanese (Sendai) adolescents, Chen and his colleagues found that 38% to 51% of the variability in the 11th-graders' achievement scores could be accounted for by measures obtained when the students were in the first grade (Chen, Lee, & Stevenson, 1996). The relative stability in academic achievement both across time and across cultures highlights the importance of addressing individual differences at an early age.

The importance of early intervention is further highlighted by findings on how such differences emerge. For example, differences in literacy skills may stem from the fact that the nature of the instructional environment is quite different for high- and low-achieving readers. Less advanced readers are generally given less classroom time to read text than their high-achieving peers. Moreover, when these children are asked to read, the reading tends to be oral—round-robin or choral style—with the consequence that they read far fewer words, stories, and books. Good readers rapidly master word-identification skills and can soon focus on understanding what they read. Poorer readers take much longer to master word-identification skills. This often leads to the neglect of strategies for comprehending larger units of text such as sentences and stories. As a result, many poor readers come to believe that the primary purpose of reading is decoding words and that its primary purpose is to please someone else. Over time, good readers spend more time studying more advanced stories (because they can read them unassisted), and they simply read more. Less advanced readers spend less time engaging in connected independent reading, and they are less challenged to think about the meaning of what they have read. Better readers engage more often in silent reading and related meaning-oriented comprehension tasks. When poor readers receive increased opportunities for reading practice, they demonstrate improved reading comprehension (Brown, 1995; Shany & Biemiller, 1995).

There is evidence that increased attention to assuring early mastery of word-identification skills leads to improved comprehension and generally better academic outcomes. Research summarized by Chall (1983/1996), Adams (1990), and Becker (1977) demonstrates quite conclusively that beginning reading instruction in word identification skills leads to better long-term reading outcomes.

Gersten and Brengelman (1996) demonstrated marked improvement of DISTAR-trained children through the 6th grade, and report that this effect continues through high school. Examination of the DISTAR program suggests that it includes careful attention to developing student awareness of speech sounds (phonemic awareness), in addition to systematically teaching spelling-sound relationships (phonics), while maintaining a significant focus on text meaning (see Adams, 1990).

While research has demonstrated the promise of such early reading interventions, such programs are rarely implemented in schools. In fact, Stahl and his colleagues (1994) report that schools with high proportions of at-risk students tend to spend not more, but *less* classroom time on reading instruction:

> Indeed, data from the most recent National Evaluation of Chapter 1 Programs indicate that schools with large numbers of students from low-income homes schedule nearly twenty minutes less reading instruction per day than comparison schools (p. 118).

This difference in instructional exposure was highlighted by Nagy and Anderson (1984), who observed:

> The least motivated children in the middle grades might read 100,000 words a year while the average children at this level might read 1,000,000. The figure for the voracious middle grade reader might be 10,000,000 or even as high as 50,000,000. If these guesses are anywhere near the mark, there are staggering individual differences in the volume of language experience and therefore opportunity to learn new words (p. 328).

Differences in exposure and practice can significantly contribute to the academic gap in classroom performance. These differences have grave consequences. It has been repeatedly demonstrated that failure to read adequately by the third grade is associated with significantly higher risks of not graduating from high school, early teenage pregnancy, delinquency, and other problems (Kohlberg et al., 1984; Lloyd, 1978; Ross et al., in press).

Palincsar and Klenk (1993) have addressed the gap between high and low achievers in writing. They observed that primary-grade teachers limited low-achieving students' experience with writing to working (primarily alone) on fairly low-level skills (copying words and filling out worksheets), precluding the opportunity to write extended text for the purposes of communicating. Because their instructional time focuses on the mechanics of writing, low-achieving students have an impoverished understanding of the writing process. Again, the problem is that because less-advanced students take longer to master basic skills, they infrequently receive opportunities to use the skills they are learning.[2]

Other investigators have found that spelling, punctuation, and grammar exercises are emphasized more by bottom-performing schools—which tend to be located in urban areas with primarily African-American students—than in top-performing schools (suburban and primarily white). The instruction in the deprived urban schools was primarily grammar-oriented, while the more affluent, suburban schools emphasized writing instruction and opportunities for extended writing (Applebee, Langer, Mullis, Latham, & Gentile, 1994; Valdes, 1992).

A similar profile emerges in the area of mathematics. Sharon Griffin and her colleagues report that many children enter school with a well-developed initial understanding of numbers and with sophisticated counting strategies (Griffin, Case, & Siegler, 1994). Children who lack such number knowledge will treat school math from the start as a rote activity, evidencing little understanding or appreciation of underlying mathematical concepts. This initial lack of understanding can contribute to the cumulative deficit. Griffin and her colleagues have demonstrated that fostering a better understanding of numbers and counting helps bring groups of disadvantaged children to the level of performance seen in groups of more advanced children. (Note, however, that such interventions do not eliminate individual differences.)

The need for proactive action in mathematics was also highlighted by Robert Siegler, who compared the abilities of low-income and middle-income children on simple addition, subtraction, and word substitution problems. He found that both the high- and low-SES groups used multiple strategies adaptively, but they differed in how quickly they accessed and how efficiently they used alternative mathematical solution strategies. The low-performing students—who were more likely to come from the lower socioeconomic group—demonstrated initial arithmetic competence, but when they encountered difficulties (e.g., when their first solution did not work), they evidenced lower confidence and a weaker disposition to use an alternative or back-up strategy to solve the problem (see Griffin et al., 1994). In Chapter 7, we will discuss the important pedagogical implications of these findings, with regard to how teachers need to anticipate and address these initial differences. For now, it is just important to appreciate how such small early differences can set the stage for later, substantial differences.

Bloom (1976a, 1985) notes that these academic differences shape children's "sense of selves" as academic performers. He observed that children's academic self-concept tends to be relatively positive during the first two years of school.

But each academic year thereafter, the top third or fourth of the students become more "positive" about school and about themselves as learners, while the bottom third to fourth of the students become more "negative" about school and about themselves. Bloom goes on to observe that by the end of the eighth grade, the top students feel "very adequate" about themselves in school and desire more education, while the bottom students have feelings of great inadequacy in school and desire to quit school at the first opportunity. These attitudinal and motivational reactions can significantly affect students' performance and further exacerbate initial differences. These differences in self-esteem derive, in part, from the fact that early achievers gain entrance into elite groups that facilitate further successes. As is well known, success breeds success (Day et al., 1992).

While emphasizing that effective early education can reduce some of the differences between children associated with social class, we must be clear that such educational improvements do not eliminate individual differences. For example, Wesley Becker's DISTAR program brought a large *group* of disadvantaged children up to the *group* performance of children in more advantaged schools. It did not eliminate the wide range of performance that occurs within any school. Griffin et al.'s (1994) early math program had a similar effect.

Just as initial readiness differences reflect both constitutional factors and experiences before school, the stability of differences in educational achievement in school reflects a combination of constitutional factors and experiences *during* the school years. As children progress through school, their out-of-school environments continue to range from highly supportive of educational attainment to highly detrimental. In addition, there has been much documentation of differences in how schools treat children, as a function of both social class and individual achievement. We will examine these within-school conditions in the next section. For now, the basic point is that there is a learning gap between children when they start school in their readiness to profit from instruction, and that these initial differences are stable, and tend to become greater over time.

School Systemic Factors: Matthew Effects

In this section, we consider what the school system does, or fails to do, that contributes to the marked individual differences we find in classrooms. We frame this discussion with a Biblical expression offered by the apostle Matthew:

> For unto everyone that has, shall be given and he shall have abundance; but for him that has not shall be taken away even that which he has (Matthew 13:12).

The sociologist Robert Merton took this adage and labeled its basic concept the "Matthew Effect." Keith Stanovich and others have applied the idea of the Matthew Effect to describe the process by which students who possess knowledge or skills "are given," or take, even more; in the classroom, those students who know more learn more. But, as we shall see, the acquisition of expertise by those who "have" often depends on their interactions with those who "have not." Unfortunately, the "have-nots" are much less likely to receive expertise-fostering experience (Stanovich, 1986, 1994).

What is it about instructional practice that results in the "rich getting richer," while the "poor" fall further and further behind? The educational system was not designed to exacerbate such individual differences; rather, education was intended to be an equalizer—resulting in democracy, not meritocracy. How did things go so wrong? In answering this question, we can point to several factors:

- instructional practices;
- curriculum features;
- teachers' attitudes toward lower-achieving students; and
- structural features including ability grouping.

We will consider each of these factors in turn.

Instructional Practices

A consideration of how classroom programs are typically conducted helps to explain why initial differences in ability become exaggerated over time. In most classes, only a small proportion of students have much opportunity to reach high levels of mastery. Consider the impact of what Tharp and Gallimore (1991) have described as a "recitation script." One can find the following features of the script in many classrooms, especially in high schools:

- The teacher lectures in front of the whole class.
- Students are passive participants in the process.
- The teacher asks questions in order to assess the students' comprehension.
- The teacher's questions generally call for low levels of factual recall, with over 20% of the questions that are posed requiring only "Yes" or "No" answers.
- There is little peer-to-peer interaction.

This script neither allows students to develop and master their conceptual understanding nor encourages them to move towards directing their own tasks, using the new skills, strategies, and concepts they have learned in school. Those who are low-achieving to begin with are particularly penalized by this instructional format. Pressley and Woloshyn (1995) have described this traditional teaching approach as consisting of the teacher asking questions, the students responding, and then the teacher evaluating the students' response; thus, they call it the IRE (Initiate, Respond, and Evaluate) approach.

What type of questions do teachers ask? In his influential book *A Place Called School*, John Goodlad (1984) reports that while 50% of class time is spent in group discussion, only 1% of teacher questions invite responses that are neither factual nor routine. The major emphasis of classroom instruction is on memorization and on rote levels of learning, even at the upper grades.

Another important feature of classrooms is teachers' relative insensitivity to individual differences in student abilities. In most traditional classrooms, all students are provided with the same material. McIntosh and his colleagues have reviewed literature on classroom routines and concluded that they are marked by "conformity and overwhelmingly undifferentiated large group teacher-directed instruction. There is very little adaptation of teaching methods to meet the needs of students who are having difficulties" (McIntosh et al., 1985, p. 250). Goodlad (1984), too, reports little "differentiation" of instruction from grade 4 on. Moreover, there is even less accommodation in *content* or content levels.

McIntosh and his associates note that those students who are struggling in class (i.e., the bottom 25%):

- infrequently ask teachers for help;
- do not volunteer to answer questions;
- have low participation rates;
- engage in little self-monitoring of what is being taught or what parts of information are being missed; and
- are passive learners, conveying an attitude of just wanting to get through the school day with minimum difficulty.

These classroom observations led McIntosh to conclude that an implicit "You don't bother me, and I won't bother you" agreement emerges between low-achieving students and their teachers. This leads to low levels of participation, not to mention low levels of learning and mastery. Low-achieving students are likely to use strategies that allow them to just "get by" without meaningful learning (McIntosh et al., 1993).

Research indicates that low rates of classroom participation predict lowered achievement as early as the first three grades. Those who talk more learn more. Nonparticipants have little opportunity to discuss what they already know about a topic and miss the opportunity to relate what they know to new concepts (Good & Brophy, 1994). Further evidence that participation predicts success comes from an unpublished study that found a strong correlation between students' levels of verbal participation on the first day of first grade and their reading achievement at the end of the school year. This pattern persists, as the level of language ability in elementary grades is significantly related to achievement in a majority of subjects (.5 to .6) at the high school and college levels (Biemiller, 1993).

When lecturing, teachers often call disproportionately on the brighter students. This saves time and saves the less able students from embarrassment in front of their peers. The drawback is that only the more able students are able to exercise their verbal grasp of the subject at hand and receive corrective feedback. Moreover, able students often give answers or offer explanations before the slower students can completely solve a problem. There is inadequate time for slower students to be reflective problem solvers. The slower students have few opportunities to verbalize what they are doing and why. Moreover, they are rarely given an opportunity to be peer tutors or helpers, and thus are rarely put into a consultative role (Good & Brophy, 1994).

This problem is evident even when classroom activities are done in smaller groups. If not properly monitored by the teacher, the slower-progressing students may become "gofers" for the more competent students. The advanced students actively "take charge" of the group, resulting in the less competent students becoming "social loafers." Thus, only a small proportion of children actually have much opportunity to engage their competencies. (In Chapter 8, we will consider ways in which lower-achieving students can be taught how to become more effective peer helpers.)

Research also indicates that low-achieving students are on-task for only 40% to 50% of their seatwork time—resulting in limited practice of academic instruction—compared to 85% on-task engaged time for high-achieving students (Englert et al., 1992; Fisher & Berliner, 1995). As a result of this behavioral pattern, low-achieving students can expect to learn approximately one year's worth of content for every two years of schooling in such topics as mathematics. Mercier and his colleagues note that those with learning disabilities are likely to reach an academic plateau after the 7th grade; for example, they are likely to achieve only one more year of growth in math performance from the 7th to the 12th grade (Mercier, Jordan, & Miller, 1994). Differentiated instruction is needed to reverse this pattern. Unfortunately, the current increased emphasis on mixing ability groups ("destreaming"), which results in less instruction being geared to student achievement levels, is unlikely to reverse this pattern.

Similar curriculum differences exist in the ways students from high-poverty vs. low-poverty schools are treated. Jonathan Kozol has documented the "savage inequalities" that exist between poor community schools and more affluent schools (Kozol, 1991). The poor children receive less engaging kinds of education, and their school environment is less stimulating and less positive. These observations are supported by a report published by the U.S. Department of Education (1993) which indicated that students in high-poverty schools—compared to those in low-poverty schools—are exposed to a watered-down and non-challenging curriculum. For example, compared to other students, students from poverty areas:

- receive language arts instruction that relies more on basal readers and textbooks and less on literature and trade books;
- do less creative writing;
- do less silent reading and more reading aloud in turn;
- receive less emphasis on analytic concepts in math instruction through problem-solving, word-problems, or work on mathematical reasoning;
- are given less diverse assignments to do; and
- experience less frequent use of cooperative learning for both reading and math.

Moreover, the research also indicates that teachers in high-poverty schools are more dispirited, frustrated, and dissatisfied with their schools, administration, and colleagues, and they feel that they have little influence on school policy. They are likely to keep much tighter controls on students, thus affording them less autonomy and providing them with fewer opportunities to interact with one another (Solomon, Battistich, & Ham, 1996; Tirozzi & Uro, 1997). As we will consider below, teachers also have lower expectations for economically disadvantaged students.

Curriculum Features

A consideration of curriculum issues further illustrates the ways the school system exacerbates individual differences. Children are taught using the curricula that the "average child" can acquire. Children with more advanced cognitive capacity learn this material more quickly and more thoroughly than others in the class. They are also the first to apply newly acquired skills when application problems or tasks are provided—often reducing opportunities for others to do so. And they are the ones who are asked to provide assistance to their classmates, thus putting into words (thinking aloud) the procedural components of their academic tasks.

Teachers' perceived need to cover all of the material in a given curriculum for children in a given grade imposes significant constraints on teaching opportunities. If teachers are racing to cover all the material, they cannot individualize their instruction or even modify it for different groups. They can't manipulate task difficulty, or pace their instruction.

A good example of this dilemma was offered by Minstrell, who evaluated how physics is taught in U.S. high schools. He began by observing that high-school classes in Europe allow two or three years to teach content that physics teachers in North America cram into one year. Teaching takes time, especially when understanding is a goal. Minstrell (1989) observed,

> We must provide the time students need for mental restructuring.
> Hurrying on to the next lesson or to the next topic does not allow for
> sufficient reflection on the implications of the present lesson (p. 147).

When rushing through subject material, students barely master one set of concepts and procedures before they are required to move on to the next set. When the curriculum is rushed, students (especially those who are struggling) acquire "inert knowledge." They may be able to perform task procedures or recite facts on request, but they cannot explain to others what they have learned, nor apply what they have learned to novel problems or different situations. Teachers try to cover too many topics in inadequate depth, doing what has been called "teaching by exposure" (Carnine et al., 1988). There is an excessive amount of time spent on low-level skills, and little emphasis on conceptual understanding and application.

As John Bruer has observed, current teaching methods and curricula can successfully impart facts and rote skills to most students, but they fail to teach higher-order thinking and learning skills. This is especially critical for low-achieving students. Thus, doing more and more in less and less time is *not* always better (Bruer, 1993). If this observation applies to high-school physics students who are competent, it is doubly true for those students who are struggling to keep up. Teachers need to ask whether they could do *less, better*. An example of how this can be accomplished comes from cross-cultural studies of instruction (see Highlight Box 4.1 at the end of this chapter).

Unless educators learn to adapt instruction to their students' needs, a *mismatch* between academic tasks and student abilities will repeatedly occur. This continuous "mismatching" widens the distance between the "brightest" and the "slowest" students in a class each year.

Attitudes Toward Lower-Achieving Students

Besides the instructional and curriculum factors that contribute to the widening gap between students' achievements, a number of attitudinal and structural factors must also be considered. This was illustrated in a comprehensive study of four senior high schools in California (Oakes & Guiton, 1995), using interviews, observations, and self-reports. The interviews with the school administrators, counselors, and teachers were quite revealing. The school personnel stated:

- "You can tell by the time students finish kindergarten which students will be successful in high school."
- "By the time students get to high school it is all over as to who will achieve."
- "Once students get to high school, they are either intrinsically motivated or not, and this cannot change."
- "Average students will not be able to move to the college track."
- "Below-average students will raise kids just like themselves."
- "Below-average and average students lack the ability to improve their performance."
- "Below-average and average students lack the discipline and motivation to succeed."
- "Below-average and average students are satisfied with just getting through high school and then getting a 'blue collar' job."
- "Because of the way below-average students were brought up, they do not want to learn. They view school as something to get away from."

Imagine the impact of such beliefs on student-teacher interactions and on the expectations that are conveyed to students and their parents. In one of our observational studies we witnessed a high school teacher saying to low-performing students, "You don't have to learn this math material because you will never be able to qualify for college." The low-achieving students were given only the easy assignments, graded mainly on the basis of effort rather than on accomplishments, and treated by school personnel as less capable. It was conveyed to these students that certain types of learning opportunities and jobs were out of their reach. We have come to suspect that some high school teachers see their job as one of sorting able students from others, rather than teaching all students.

While some of the school influences that contribute to the widening gap between the "haves" and the "have-nots" in classrooms are explicit and intentional, others are subtle and inadvertent. What is interesting about the teachers' explanations and attitudes is that they almost always attribute the students' failure, or lack of success, *to the students* and to their circumstances. In no example given by Oakes and Guiton (1995) did school personnel entertain the possibility that they shared some responsibility for the widening gap that occurs in school.

Structural Features

Oakes and Guiton (1995) note that a number of *structural features* also serve to widen the gap between high- and low-achieving students. These features include the number of sections of specific classes that are offered at one time, the nature of the prerequisites to enrolling in certain classes, other policies regulating course offerings, the absence of tutoring, and the promotion of "streaming" or segregation by ability. As one counselor observed:

> Problem kids are neglected or hidden in other classrooms. Good kids get taken care of ... Advantaged students (and their parents) are able to manipulate the system in their favor (Oakes & Guiton, 1995, p. 28).

An example of the tendency for the "smart" students to become smarter comes from research by Ted Schuder and his colleagues on the SAIL program (Students Achieving Independent Learning), in which students in kindergarten through grade 8 were taught strategic thinking skills. When they examined the impact of their program, they found that the teachers used the language arts program with average and high-achieving students, but that the low-achieving students were "systematically excluded from instruction—a common but devastating phenomenon. Many teachers believed that the new curriculum was appropriate for gifted and talented students, but that the low achievers did not have the required skills to participate" (Schuder, 1993, p. 185). This is all too often the refrain when innovative programs are introduced in school. Thus, the Matthew Effect lives on, if it is not anticipated and checked.

Schuder and his colleagues intentionally changed the SAIL program to focus on at-risk children. When these low-achieving students were explicitly taught metacognitive skills such as comprehension monitoring—by means of modeling, coaching, and practice—they, too, were able to achieve.

Educators have recognized the wide gap between high- and low-achieving students and have attempted to accommodate these differences. One solution that has been tried is *ability grouping*, which allows teachers to tailor instructional approaches to students' abilities. However, critics of ability grouping contend that such grouping practices can have "harmful, unintended consequences" (Gamoran et al., 1995; Oakes, 1985, 1990, 1992; Oakes et al., 1992; Page, 1991; Rosenbaum, 1976, 1980; Slavin, 1993).[3] As Jeannie Oakes and her colleagues observe:

> Students in low ability groups tend to receive inferior instruction compared to their high ability peers. Unequal allocation of instruction results in the widening achievement gap between high and low level classes over time (Oakes et al., 1992, p. 575).

Ability grouping creates a resource-rich environment for the high-achieving students, with experienced, well-prepared, and enthusiastic teachers who set high standards. There is a high level of discussion, as students engage in critical thinking and problem-solving activities. In contrast, the ambiance of classrooms of low-achieving students tends to be more fragmented, focusing on isolated bits of information. The high incidence of task-disruptive student behavior further mitigates progress for low-achieving students. Tracking also leads to lower student self-esteem and aspirations, increased student misbehavior, and higher drop-out rates.

At the same time, there is evidence that students make better progress when they are *temporarily grouped* for instruction in specific areas (e.g., math, reading) based on their actual achievement, than when instruction is not adjusted for achievement. If students are heterogeneously grouped for the rest of the day, within-class grouping by performance level for one or two subjects does aid achievement in these subjects (Gutierrez & Slavin, 1992; Slavin, 1987a). The problem appears to be how to differentiate instruction in ways that are both educationally and psychologically beneficial. We will consider the controversy surrounding ability grouping in Chapter 6. At this point, it is important to recognize that in our efforts to help, we can inadvertently, and even unknowingly, exacerbate the very problems we are trying to eliminate.

Instructional Practices: A Transactional Perspective

In the preceding sections, we have examined factors related to the growing gap in educational achievement that we described in Chapters 1 and 2. These include:

(1) Initial differences between children when they start school—what is commonly referred to as "readiness."
(2) The stability of these early differences, leading to successful educational outcomes for some and failure or "cumulative deficits" for others.
(3) School "systemic" factors or practices, including the provision of greater resources for more advanced children, and the use of different instructional approaches and teacher attitudes with children at different achievement levels.

In this final section, we present a transactional perspective that is designed to examine how the interactions between student differences in achievement, external task demands, and support from teachers and fellow students widen the gap between effective, self-directed students and less effective, other-directed students. (We use the term *transactional* to emphasize the interactive causality between students and motivational situations.) We also examine some evidence suggesting that many or most of these less effective students *are* capable of assuming greater responsibility for their own learning and academic task performance when we change some aspects of the learning transaction. Specifically, we argue that *high self-direction and student expertise should not be viewed as an attribute of a child; rather, the process of self-direction depends on the "fit" between the demands of the situation and the ability and interests of the student.*

During the past several years, we have been developing and testing ways of observing self-direction and expertise, both as they occur naturally in school classrooms and in experimental situations. We have focused our attention on children who were nominated by their teachers or peers as being "self-directed" or as "knowing what to do and doing it without having to be told." We have observed over 70 of these teacher-nominated children and 70 of their low-self-directed counterparts from grades 1 to 6 (Meichenbaum & Biemiller, 1992). Our observations were primarily conducted during independent work periods, when children were working on their own assignments. Usually, however, some discussion among children about their assignments was permitted.

We discovered that what children say about their work provides unique opportunities to infer the nature of their cognitive and metacognitive self-regulatory activities. This task-directive speech—whether directed to others (peers, teachers) or to themselves—provides a window into their cognitive processes. As Jean Piaget observed, in the process of relaying thoughts to others, we also relay them to ourselves (Piaget, 1964). For instance, in the midst of seeking assistance from teachers, self-directed children sometimes answer their own questions (e.g., "It's okay, I know what to do now.") It is in the process of formulating thoughts into communicative acts that such thoughts become the object of self-reflection.

Our approach involves coding each sentence produced by each observed child in terms of whether the sentence constituted (a) *spontaneous task-directive speech* (specifying, planning, monitoring, or evaluating performance of their own or another's task), (b) *task-related speech* (a response to another's comment about the task), or (c) *other speech*. We summarize here conclusions from the three observational studies.[4]

- Highly self-directed children initiated more talk about tasks. They spontaneously initiated twice as many task-directive statements per hour (22 or more) as the less self-directed children (11 or fewer). Children who were peer-rated as average in self-direction engaged in no more spontaneous task-directive statements than children low in self-direction.

- The highly self-directed children's higher rate of spontaneous statements about tasks was primarily attributable to their planning ("what next") and monitoring (checking their own or others' progress) statements. Both groups had similar rates of specifying and evaluating statements.

- When expressing emotions about their own work on a task, the highly self-directed children were mostly positive, while the less self-directed children's emotions were about half negative.

- While the two groups of children asked similar numbers of questions, highly self-directed children questioned peers about half of the time, while less self-directed children turned mostly to teachers.

- Less self-directed children tended to be mainly "followers," while highly self-directed children tended to be leaders, leading both others and themselves (i.e., they tended to initiate, direct, and guide other students when performing school activities).

- Differences in teacher language to children in the two groups were also examined. The less self-directed children were more effective at "pulling for" task-directive support from their teacher than at supporting themselves. In contrast, highly self-directed children received many opportunities to practice their metacognitive skills. They were often asked by teachers to help other children and to share procedural information with the class (e.g., "Who can tell the class what we did last time?").

Such differences suggest that teachers and highly self-directed children some-times act as *metacognitive prosthetic devices,* or what we have colloquially called "surrogate frontal lobes," for the less self-directed children, often doing their thinking for them in the form of planning, monitoring, guiding, etc. Table 4.1 provides illustrative samples of verbal exchanges of the two groups.

Our results comparing highly self-directed and less self-directed children are consistent with the findings summarized in Chapter 3 that those who do not succeed in school tend to:

- be passive, inactive learners;
- be more distractible and disruptive, and thus spend less time on task;
- respond to instructions without fully understanding them, and thus be less able to benefit from instruction;
- be eager to finish school assignments without considering the learning involved;

Table 4.1: Examples of Children's Verbal Exchanges

Less Self-Directed (LSD) Children	Highly Self-Directed (HSD) Children
Teacher to LSD Child	*Teacher to HSD Child*
What are you doing?	You did research about Terry Fox. This is just like that.
What do you have to do first?	
Did you check your assignment?	Tell me how you solved that.
You will have to clean up your desk after you are finished.	Look it up in your book. You can find the answer.
LSD Child to HSD Peer	*HSD Child to LSD Peer*
Can you help me?	You don't cut each one individually. You cut the whole thing.
What do they mean by ... ?	
Do you know what I'm supposed to do here?	That glue goes this way.
My card is missing. Where can I find it?	You've done that already, haven't you?
What are we supposed to do?	You forgot to loop again.
Should I ... ?	You can't have two the same.
How did you do that?	Did you ask the other people yet?
	You have already done that.
	If you do X, then Y will happen.

- be teacher-dependent; and
- be the frequent recipients of task-directive speech from both peers and teachers.

In contrast to the less self-directed students, the highly self-directed students can accomplish academic tasks more successfully, and can explain their performance to others. They assume a higher level of responsibility for task accomplishment and achieve a higher level of mastery. These differences are evident in our follow-up findings that revealed that self-directed students are more likely to be nominated by classmates as "someone I would like to do my project with" or "someone I would turn to for help."

This relationship between self-directive behavior and academic advancement is evident in elementary school and becomes more apparent in middle school. For example, elementary children rated high in self-direction by teachers show substantially greater gains in academic achievement over the school year than those students rated low in self-direction (Biemiller & Richards, 1986). In addition, students who use more private speech show larger gains in math achievement from first to third grade. By grades 4 and above, those who succeed academically spontaneously generate and employ more complex strategies and become self-regulated learners. They plan and monitor ongoing schoolwork, know when and how to seek appropriate help, relate new skills and knowledge to what they already know, and demonstrate flexibility when responding to task demands. They assume task responsibility, appropriate ownership, and become autonomous learners (Bivens & Berk, 1990).

Situational Influences:
Evidence that Most Students Can Be Self-Directed

We need to consider two other important findings from our research on self-direction in school children. First, as we followed students across subject areas (e.g., math, English, art, music), we found that children who are self-directed in one academic area are not necessarily self-directed in other areas. The variability in observed self-directive speech and activity across academic domains depends in part on students' skills and interests *within those specific areas.* "Advanced" students are not budding experts in all areas. Conversely, those students who are distinctly low in self-direction in one academic area might demonstrate high or average self-direction in another subject area, in the art room, or on a sports field. This observation led us to the conclusion that self-direction is not a simple trait associated with only some children, but rather a characteristic which emerges in *most* children (and, presumably, adults) *under the right circumstances.*

Our second set of findings has even more relevance to the arguments we will make about the potential of most students to become more expert. We found that when we provided students with tasks that were at their skill level or slightly harder (i.e., challenging), or gave them choice over the difficulty of tasks they worked on, or put them in a consultative role with less able students where they could engage in cross-age tutoring, *the less self-directed children evidenced highly self-directed behavior.* For example, in a cross-age tutoring setting where tasks were not too difficult and low self-directed students were put into a leadership role, the slower-progressing students evidenced the same type of active self-regulated classroom behavior that characterized the self-directed children. In this tutoring situation, we observed a *sevenfold increase* in the spontaneous task-directive speech of low self-directed students, compared to what we observed in their classroom behavior (Biemiller, Shany, Inglis, & Meichenbaum, in press).

The finding that less self-directed students can behave like highly self-directed students underscores the need for teachers to create consulting opportunities for all students. In this research, the consulting opportunity included low-performing fourth-, third-, and second-grade students tutoring students who were one grade level lower, on material that the tutors were competent to teach. (In Chapter 9, we will describe another study in which lower-performing fourth-graders benefited from tutoring second-graders in math.) At present, low-achieving students are rarely placed in a position to provide verbal direction on tasks, and they have limited opportunities to use task-regulatory speech; also, they rarely find themselves in a dominant or leadership role in relation to academic tasks. Being called upon by the teacher to give explanations of tasks is not the same thing as spontaneously doing so, or being asked to help someone else. Low-achieving students typically come to see academic work as an area in which they are normally subordinate—requiring the assistance of others to successfully accomplish assignments. Less advanced students receive little practice in verbally regulating academic tasks, and they have little opportunity to experience themselves as academic leaders rather than followers.

Most children have the potential to be self-directive when working on a task involving well-consolidated skills. It appears that mastery can be fostered if the circumstances are right. Thus, as we said at the beginning of this section, self-direction should be viewed not as an attribute of a child, but as a reflection of the "fit" between the demands of the situation and the ability and interests of the student. Active self-directive learning and "expertise" are not accessible only to a few high achievers or only to very competent children. *Most students have the potential to become more expert.* As we will discuss in subsequent chapters, these findings have very important pedagogical implications for moving students from being novices to becoming more expert independent learners.

Where Do We Go From Here?

The challenge for educators is to arrange for all students to benefit from the educational system, and to help most students become more expert with the skills and knowledge that they have acquired. What can educators do to close the learning gap between the "haves" and the "have-nots"? How can we reverse the "Matthew Effect," so that the large majority of students can effectively use academic knowledge for their own and others' benefit?[5]

Although library shelves are filled with advice about educational practice, often nothing really changes in classrooms. Demonstration projects using the latest findings from research on cognitive science may appear, but few changes will occur throughout the school system or when the demonstration project is discontinued. Report after report from national educational organizations bemoan the state of education, but they make little difference in how teachers teach. When we visit schools, their practices are still all too similar to our own experiences as students some 40 years ago.

We have stressed the reality of individual differences because assuming that *all* children of a given age are—or should be—at the same level of skill and competence at the same time only exacerbates differences. We believe that each child should be treated "the same," in the sense of having opportunities to learn new skills, strategies, and concepts that build on existing knowledge and skills, and of having opportunities to build expertise and self-direction on tasks at which they are competent and can exercise their expertise with others. These are opportunities now enjoyed by those who make rapid progress in academic achievement, but not by the remaining 60 or 70 percent of children. Providing these opportunities to a wider range of students will involve major changes from current educational practice and even academic policy.

What will it take to change the way students are taught? What will it take to close the learning gap? We don't need to overwhelm teachers with a long list of new methods to try. Rather, we believe what is needed is a *theoretical model that explicates the teaching-learning process;* a model that will allow the integration of multiple teaching methods, and that will challenge educators to rethink their efforts.

We believe that most students are capable of mastering academic skills and knowledge in school. The next chapter provides a three-dimensional theoretical model of mastery, and gives suggestions on how such mastery can be increased. We believe that the most valuable tool a teacher can possess is a good theory. In the subsequent chapters, we explore the practical implications of our theory for the understanding and implementation of successful educational interventions. We also examine programs that have begun to provide expertise-fostering learning settings to a wider range of students.

Endnotes

1. Hart and Risley (1997) conducted observations in families' homes and recorded the mothers' verbal interactions with their infant children (7 to 12 months) as they cooked dinner, folded laundry, and watched television. They found that children whose mothers were on welfare heard 600 words per hour, the working-class children heard 1200 words an hour, and the children of professional mothers heard 2100 words per hour. Not only did children from highly verbal families hear more words, but parents also asked them more questions and repeated and expanded on comments the children made. These initial differences showed up on IQ and vocabulary testing at 3 years of age.

2. These reviews refer specifically to elementary school children and include studies in which children of different ages were grouped together for specific subject areas. Slavin emphasizes that such positive effects are only seen in the skills being taught, not in any general aptitude. Reviews of ability grouping in high school do not conclude that ability grouping is beneficial. However, we strongly suspect that the conditions employed in high school studies of ability grouping are rarely, if ever, the same as those used in elementary grades.

3. The first two studies were reported in Meichenbaum and Biemiller (1992). They included observations of 14 highly self-directed and 14 less self-directed children (as nominated by their teachers) in several different schools (grade 1 to grade 6); and repeated observations of two highly self-directed and two less self-directed children in a third-grade class. The third study (reported in Biemiller, Shany, Inglis, & Meichenbaum, in press; Biemiller & Meichenbaum, 1992) involved observational study of 18 children, of whom 6 were peer-rated "high," 6 "average," and 6 "low" in self-direction.

4. We say "the large majority" of children, recognizing that there are students who have special disabilities for particular learning. In the same way that a tone-deaf individual has great difficulty in learning music, or a color-blind individual has special problems in art class, students who have limited cognitive capacities for whatever reason have difficulties performing abstract academic tasks. We suspect that this group of students constitutes less than 10% of the student body, but this percentage may vary depending upon the specific subject matter and aptitude required. While it may take the remaining 90% of students varying time, effort, and guidance to perform the academic task, it is our assumption that they can learn the material if appropriately taught. The challenge for educators is to teach slower students so that instruction is not prohibitively expensive in terms of manpower and time. But this is a trade-off problem and *not* a reflection that some students cannot learn.

Highlight Box 4.1
CROSS-CULTURAL STUDIES OF INSTRUCTION

One way to better understand the strengths and weaknesses of the North American educational system is to examine it through the prism of cross-cultural studies. A number of investigators have compared the performance of North American students to that of students in other countries. These researchers have not only documented achievement differences, but also identified specific factors that contribute to such differences.

As noted in Chapter 1, American children are behind their Asian peers (in Japan, China, and Taiwan) in nearly every dimension of mathematics competence, and this gap increases between the first and the 11th grades. While these findings have been widely cited, less attention has been given to studies of instructional practices that contribute to the poor performance of students in North American schools. A consideration of these factors can provide useful pedagogical guidelines for implementing any needed educational reforms. A number of researchers, led by Stevenson, Stigler, Geary, and Gill, have implicated four major factors:

1. **The amount of instruction**

a) American children receive considerably less mathematics instruction, considering both the average number of instructional days per year (178 in the U.S. vs. 257 in mainland China) and the average amount of time spent per week on mathematics instruction (4½ to 8 hours less in the U.S. than in Asian countries).

b) Greater priority is given to math achievement by Asian teachers and parents than by their American counterparts. This is reflected in the total amount of time spent on math, and in *when* math is taught. Mathematics instruction receives "prime time" in Asia; in many countries, it is the first course taught in the morning.

c) Students in Japan are more likely to attend after-school classes where supplementary instruction is provided.

2. **The content that is taught**

a) In the U.S., the mathematics curricula and the material presented in textbooks are too easy and poorly organized. The easiest types of problems are over-represented in American textbooks.

b) Mathematical topics that are introduced in grades 5 and 6 in the U.S. are introduced in grade 3 or sooner in Japan, mainland China, and Taiwan. U.S. teachers do not challenge students to the same extent as teachers in Asian countries.

c) The U.S. curriculum is often redundant; subject material introduced in early elementary grades is repeatedly taught in subsequent grades. Japanese teachers follow a curriculum sequence that provides in-depth study of topics. For example, they focus on length in grade 1 and volume in grade 2, and they wait until grade 3 to take up the concept of weight—to which they devote a full eight hours. In contrast, U.S. teachers follow a "spiral" curriculum, presenting many topics each year and repeating them with more elaboration throughout subsequent grades. Thus, reteaching is more pervasive in U.S. schools and texts.

d) The representation of numbers is more intuitively related to place-values in Asian language systems than in English. For example, in Asian language systems the number 17 is represented as "one-ten seven," and the number 33 as "three-ten three." This linguistic feature makes place values clearer from the outset of learning to count.

3. Teacher training and teaching style

a) Teachers in Japan receive a clearly defined national curriculum and training guidelines that outline detailed hour-by-hour instructional plans and a suggested review test for each unit. Also, the teacher manuals show how the various topics covered in a semester fit into the overall math curriculum for grades 1 through 6, what students have learned in earlier grades about the topics, and what they can be expected to learn in future grades.

b) The teacher manuals present each unit's goals, key concepts, and mathematical foundations, while pointing out areas that might cause students special difficulties, and describing how teachers can use manipulatives and activities to help students grasp difficult concepts. Teachers are encouraged to tailor these guidelines to the individual needs of their students.

c) There is a better balance between skill instruction and problem-solving instruction in Asian countries. For example, teachers in Japan and Taiwan ask their students questions that "pull for" problem-solving strategies (e.g., "What is the best way to solve this problem?") twice as often as U.S. teachers. Asian teachers are more likely to ask questions that access their students' knowledge of familiar concepts ("context" questions), as well as questions that tap their students' conceptual understanding (e.g., "How is this like what we learned before?").

d) Teachers in Japan may spend an entire lesson solving a very small number of problems, discussing and demonstrating procedural and conceptual failures. Japanese teachers take students through each problem, thoroughly analyzing and reanalyzing the various ways to solve it.

e) Japanese teachers discuss errors extensively to ensure that students understand problems conceptually.

f) Teachers in Asian countries use more manipulatives when illustrating math concepts and use more pedagogically authentic (real-life) problems.

g) A higher level of behavioral discipline is expected by Asian teachers and parents. Classrooms in the U.S. are loosely organized, with a higher frequency of task-irrelevant activities and interruptions of classroom routines (e.g., 20% out-of-seat behavior in U.S. classrooms vs. 4% in Japan). As a result, less instructional time is spent on substantive material in the U.S.

4. **Parent expectations**

a) Asian parents have much higher expectations for their children's achievement than U.S. parents.

b) American mothers have excessively positive attitudes toward their children's academic achievements and toward the efficiency of the schooling their children receive. In contrast, Asian mothers' evaluations of their children's achievement are modest, at best.

c) When math becomes difficult, Asian parents expect and encourage increased effort on the part of their children.

d) Asian parents provide 2 to 4 times as much assistance to their children as U.S. parents.

The cross-cultural findings on mathematics instruction indicate that if teachers and parents value a performance highly and spend a lot of time teaching it, better results will be achieved. It is important to keep in mind, however, that Japanese and Taiwanese instructional approaches that were studied *did not reduce the overall variation in student performance.* On average, Asian students did better than did their counterparts in the U.S., but the range (standard deviation) between more able and less able students was the same as that found in a North American sample (Stevenson & Lee, 1990).

The lesson to be underscored is that even in countries where overall academic achievement has been elevated, marked individual differences still exist. Thus, the pedagogical guidelines to be described in the next section may also apply to Asian countries, where the median performance is higher, but gaps between the highs and lows still exist. The "Matthew Effect" appears to be universal!

In summary, cross-cultural studies indicate that Asian students are more likely than U.S. students to be challenged, to be exposed to well-calibrated, hierarchically arranged mathematical tasks, and to be provided with extensive instruction and practice. Asian students are also more likely to receive useful feedback in a nurturant and supportive environment. They receive extensive instruction and practice on a few problems, leading to conceptual understanding. They are also encouraged to put into words their procedural and conditional knowledge about mathematics problems. The challenge for North American educators is how to incorporate these teaching practices into their classrooms.

(For more details, see Geary, 1994; Gill & McPike, 1995; Stevenson & Lee, 1990, 1995; Stevenson et al., 1986, 1990, 1992; Stigler, Stevenson, & Lee, 1987, 1990.)

Chapter Five

Toward A Three-Dimensional Theory of Mastery: A Tool For Nurturing Independent Learners

This chapter is designed to meet the challenge put forth by the educational psychologist John Carroll (1963):

> What is needed is a schematic design or conceptual model of factors affecting success in school learning and of the way they interact. Such a model should use a very small number of simplifying concepts ... It should suggest new and interesting research questions and aid in the solution of practical educational problems. With the aid of such a framework, the often conflicting results of different research studies might be seen to fall into a unified pattern (p. 723).

In response to Carroll's call for a simplified theoretical framework of factors affecting school success, we offer a straightforward three-dimensional model of mastery. The model explains how novices become experts and what instructors can do to encourage and nurture this process. As noted, there is some urgency for classroom teachers to change the ways they now operate. We believe that the 3-D model will facilitate an evolution of better teaching approaches.

We have reviewed evidence showing that our educational system is proving ineffective in preparing a significant proportion of students for academic success and for effective functioning in society. We also examined the factors that con-

We wish to thank Jennifer Hardacre, Alison Inglis, Rose Marie Nauta, and Lauren Meichenbaum for their constructive editing of this chapter.

tribute to academic success and the ways in which the educational system nurtures mastery in competent self-directed learners, often at the expense of their less competent fellow students. We highlighted educational practices that inadvertently contribute to the ever-increasing learning gap between those who thrive and those who falter in our schools. These practices include the use of instruction that (a) fails to address skill deficiencies effectively, (b) limits the opportunities for low-achieving students to develop and use their expertise and learning skills, and (c) places an unproductive emphasis on competitive performance. We propose that this "instructional deficit" (namely, how we teach or fail to teach) contributes to the six-grade spread in student skills that exists at the beginning of high school.

How can we begin to narrow this gap without penalizing the more competent students? What practical steps can educators take to address the marked individual differences they face? Obviously, we are not the first authors to ask such questions. What is different about our approach is that we propose a *theoretical model of mastery* that guides our pedagogical suggestions. Based on our examination of the expertise literature and our research on self-direction, we have formulated a theoretical model of what is involved in moving from being a novice to being an expert in specific academic areas. We suggest that this model has major implications for understanding the gap between the "haves" and the "have-nots" in our classrooms, and for helping a much larger proportion of students become more expert and achieve in a more masterful fashion.

We begin this chapter with a brief comment about assumptions underlying current educational practices. We then introduce a three-dimensional model of student mastery—providing an initial overview of the model and some of its implications—and consider why language and other forms of mental representation are critical to the development of student mastery. In the five ensuing chapters (6 through 10), we consider very practical techniques that teachers can use to move their students along the three dimensions of mastery. Without a theory, we would have only a hodgepodge of techniques, gimmicks, and passing fads. Our theoretical model will permit teachers to organize their classroom settings and instructional practices and, most importantly, to evaluate the success of their educational interventions.

Underlying False Assumptions

How did our educational system get into the unfortunate position of reinforcing individual differences in students' achievement instead of nurturing success for *all* students? We believe that the answer rests in part on the adoption of two questionable assumptions. The first of these is evident whenever you visit a classroom: the immediate impression conveyed is that *education means "pouring" knowledge into a passive learner.* The second assumption has been captured by two educational psychologists, Ann Brown and Joseph Campione, who observed that traditional school practices are based on the premise *"that there exist proto-typical, normal students who, at a certain age, can do a certain amount of material, in the same amount of time"* (Brown & Campione, 1994).

The view of education based on these false assumptions fails to recognize two key facts: that students are *constructive learners* who are active in determining both what they learn and the degree to which they become independent, autonomous learners; and that children of a given age differ significantly in underlying capacities and learned abilities, as well as in their experience of successfully using academic skills.

We present a more complex model of education. Our conception represents a greater challenge for teachers, but it also represents a realistic hope that a much larger portion of the school population will become fully able to use academic knowledge and skills for purposes valued by themselves and society.

A Model of Mastery

In contrast to the "passive" model of education, we have adopted an active, constructivist model. We believe that the fundamental goal of education is to enable individuals to assume responsibility for accomplishing real tasks in increasingly complex and authentic contexts. In order to reach this goal, students must:

- learn new skills and concepts;
- apply acquired skills effectively by planning and accomplishing a variety of complex, authentic tasks in which the skills are needed; and
- accomplish these authentic tasks independently, without help.

Mastering skills and tasks is a far more complex business than many learning models suggest. Let us begin with an example. Sixth-grader Sheila Smith is learning to use a word-processing program on a computer. She is learning how to perform a number of actions she couldn't perform before, including typing, formatting, moving, saving, and retrieving text. (She is also bringing already-learned skills and strategies into this new context, including knowledge of the meanings and spellings of many words, some phonetic spelling skills, some punctuation skills, etc., as well as strategies for constructing stories, reports, and letters.) If Sheila is expected to learn too many new word-processing skills simultaneously—without sufficient opportunity to practice and get the feel of word processing—she will experience difficulty with tasks which call for these new skills. Furthermore, the level of performance she had previously reached in creating text, spelling, and punctuating may decline.

Sheila is learning word processing as a new way of communicating with others and accessing information. She will use word-processing skills in many tasks, such as writing reports (and later, projects and essays), writing school letters and e-mail to friends, searching computer databases, and eventually performing a variety of tasks in work-related situations. Consequently, she not only practices newly learned skills such as typing and moving text, but early in her word-processing experience, she begins to plan and carry out simple *applications* (e.g., using the word processor to write letters or publish a story). Indeed, her word-processing instruction may have *begun* with the need to produce a clear written document on some subject.

However, just as Sheila can experience difficulty if too many skills are introduced too quickly, she can experience difficulty in *applying* her new word-processing skills if the application task is too complex. For example, if she is expected to construct a story that is more complex, with more words than those she has previously written, she may either forget some of her new word processing skills or fail to produce as complex a story as is expected. Thus, her first assigned word-processed communications should not be too complex. They should be set at—or even below—her present level of writing competence. As her word-processing skills become more fluent or automatic, she can turn her attention to new applied composition challenges.

In teaching word processing to Sheila, our goal (and, we hope, Sheila's goal) is for her to become able to successfully produce clearly written stories, reports, letters, essays, and other communications on her own, using a word processor. Over time, she must become able to *independently* incorporate her word-processing skills into the task of creating or constructing such communications. However, when she first begins to use word-processing skills, she is not independent at all. She is directed by others—her teacher, her peers, and sometimes an instructional computer program. With practice, she will become able to correctly carry out simple tasks involving each skill, without any external direction. With more experience and confidence, Sheila will begin to exercise overt self-direction, telling herself how to carry out procedures, monitoring her typing, and often helping others or commenting on their progress or problems.

This shift from other-direction to self-direction (and to directing others) appears to be necessary if Sheila is to become an independent user of her word-processing skills. In the process of mastering word-processing skills, Sheila acquires new skills and becomes increasingly self-directed both at performing newly-acquired word-processing skills, and at applying those skills to written communication tasks, and later to other computer-related activities. The same shift from other-direction to self-direction must occur with other newly acquired skills.

The Distinction Between Skills, Strategies, and Tasks

Sheila learns *skills* (e.g., typing, saving files, blocking) which she applies in the course of planning and accomplishing new *tasks* (e.g., writing letters, writing reports, etc.). The skills are learned from others. (Most of us don't create or invent the skill of blocking text, nor do we frequently invent new alphabets or words.) In most instances, the teacher decides what skills the learner needs.

Skills are directly taught, but it is critically important not to teach them in isolation. Sheila must see the relevance of the skills she has learned for tasks she wants to accomplish. Thus in addition to skills, Sheila must also learn or discover ways of using her skills on different tasks and in varied contexts. These ways of applying skills or planning tasks are called *strategies*. They are essentially guides (usually verbal) for planning specific kinds of tasks. In the word-processing unit, she will use these strategies to plan and write letters, reports, and even book chapters. (In other domains, there are strategies for understanding texts we read, for finding our way to specific points in a city, for solving mathematics word problems, etc.) Some strategies are taught. Others are discovered or developed by individuals as they go about their tasks.

Word-processing and writing skills and strategies are repeatedly recalled and used in each writing *task*. To successfully plan and accomplish writing tasks, Sheila needs a repertoire of relevant basic skills, special task-planning strategies, and some guided experience actually writing letters, stories, and reports. Each of these tasks will require specific word-processing knowledge, more general knowledge, and strategies for writing (not to mention knowledge of the content to be written about).

Describing Tasks in the Three Mastery Dimensions

Tasks involve (a) *specification* of the goal and relevant conditions; (b) a *plan* of actions or procedures to achieve that goal; (c) actual *implementation* of the task, including performing the actions and monitoring progress; and (d) *evaluation* of the outcome in terms of success in achieving the specified goal, and noting information about one's performance abilities and enjoyment of the task.

Any task to be performed—that is, any situation in which a sequence of actions must be carried out to achieve an intended goal—can be characterized in terms of the level of procedures or skills required, the degree of task planning or application complexity, and the level of self-direction required to carry out the task.

A learner has mastered a *skill* when she can (independently or while leading others):

- perform the skill;
- incorporate the skill as needed when planning and implementing a new task (e.g., when writing a paper); and
- solve problems on her own that may arise in the course of using the skill in various tasks.

She has mastered a *unit* (e.g., a word processing unit) when she:

- has learned the skills and vocabulary in the unit;
- can guide herself in fluently applying those skills in a reasonably wide range of relevant or authentic tasks; and
- can explain the planning of the new applied tasks to others and can help others to succeed in such applications.

As teachers, we work with students so that they can increasingly perform newly learned skills on their own, and can assume responsibility for planning and accomplishing new tasks that require the use of those skills. Over time, we want to see students applying their skills on more and more difficult or complex tasks, and in authentic situations that are often dissimilar to the settings in which the skills were originally taught. We want our students to become independent learners and self-directed experts, being able not only to use, but also to share and to teach what they have learned.

Reaching these goals requires students to progress along three dimensions of mastery. The three dimensions involve various levels of *skill demand*, *planning* or *application complexity*, and *self-direction*. In Sheila's case, she must learn to accomplish progressively more difficult tasks that require increasing levels of skills. She must also learn to perform these tasks on her own as she takes on more and more responsibility for task accomplishment. She should reach a point where she can teach others. If Sheila is to master word processing, she must also be able to apply her skills on writing tasks that are different from the tasks in which she initially learned them. Moreover, with mastery, Sheila can construct new applications for her skills and strategies. These varied features of mastery can be represented on a three dimensional model, as depicted in Figure 5.1.

Explicating The Three Dimensions of Mastery

We begin with a brief overview of how tasks and student performance can be understood and organized in terms of the three dimensions of mastery. We then continue with an examination of how these dimensions interact, and highlight why the self-direction dimension is so important to developing mastery of academic domains.

The Skill (and Vocabulary) Dimension

Skills are routine procedures which we use frequently in the course of carrying out tasks. Examples of skills are adding two numbers, starting a car, and decoding (reading) or encoding (writing) words. This dimension also includes knowledge of vocabulary items (e.g., *add, brake, predict, revise*) needed to talk about both skills and knowledge domains. For example, it is not enough for students to learn how to do mathematics; they must learn how to speak mathematically with others, as well as with themselves.

For the most part, skill domains are organized into hierarchies, with simpler skills and concepts learned first, and more complex and cognitively demanding skills learned later. Thus, we usually learn about small numbers and about addition and subtraction before learning about large numbers and about multiplication, division, and fractions. We learn about simple sound-letter relationships before learning about digraphs, silent *e*, and exceptions. Reading tasks can range from reading single sentences or books with controlled vocabularies to reading novels with complex plots or textbooks about science or history. The skill demands of any task can be analyzed in terms of the number and difficulty of component skills required to perform the task.

The skill demand dimension refers to the level of difficulty or complexity of the skills and concepts required for successful accomplishment of a task.[1] This dimension has been characterized as the OVER dimension—the X axis in Figure 5.1. One goal of instruction is to teach students how to perform more and more difficult tasks, and thus to help them move along the X axis.

Individual student progress with respect to skills in a domain can be directly assessed in terms of the level of difficulty of skills the student can perform. However, the meaning of *perform* depends on the other two dimensions: the planning complexity of the task in which the skill is incorporated, and the level

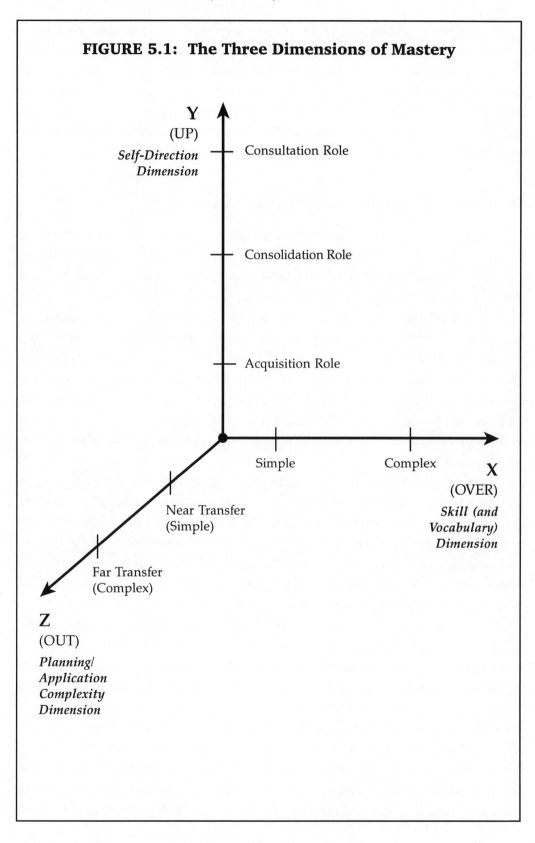

FIGURE 5.1: The Three Dimensions of Mastery

of self-direction accepted as evidence of performing. For example, passing a multiple-choice test item involving a skill represents a different level of performance from spontaneously using the skill when it is needed. In the latter instance, the student who acts on her own initiative must *select* the skill from her repertoire and incorporate it in a task to meet a new specific goal, rather than simply respond to a teacher's request that she perform the skill. Such constructive activity is at the heart of the second dimension of mastery.

The Planning/Application Complexity Dimension

A second goal of instruction is to teach students to transfer skills and strategies they have learned to analogous tasks in new situations. The problem is recognizing which learned skills will be relevant to a new problem or task. The essence of skills or concepts is their automatic character: once well learned, skills can be used without much thought or conscious attention. However, when confronted with a new task—a situation in which one wishes to (or is required to) achieve a particular goal but has no prior plan for doing so—active problem solving must go on. In short, one must create a new plan. With experience, we get better at planning in specific domains. For instance, the first time someone writes a paper (or a paper in a particular discipline), planning takes a lot of time, or the paper is not very well done. With increasing experience of creating similar plans (writing other papers), one becomes more effective. Typically, one develops a strategy for writing papers in a certain discipline. Similarly, the first time a teacher plans a lesson on a particular topic, considerable time must be taken to determine what teacher and student activities will lead to improved student skill or understanding. With experience, an "outline" of an effective lesson emerges, and one is able to plan new lessons more effectively in less time. While all lessons differ from another, and thus each will require some new planning, improvement in the planning process nonetheless takes place.

This "outline" of a lesson is an example of what we mean by a *strategy*. It is essentially a guide for planning lessons, or particular kinds of lessons. (One's strategy for planning phonics lessons may differ considerably from one's strategy for planning math problem solving lessons.) Many people develop effective strategies for various types of tasks on their own. However, in the past two decades, much educational research has indicated that many planning strategies can be effectively taught, and that doing so often brings a wide range of students to higher levels of achievement. An intermediate approach may emphasize both some taught strategies and the examination and use of students' self-invented strategies (see, for example, Pressley et al.'s Transactional Strategies

Instruction, described in Chapter 10).

As with skills and concepts, the planning or application demands of a task can vary greatly. Many routine tasks require little or no planning on the part of the doer—either the plan has already been learned or planning assistance is available. Other tasks require substantial planning. Essentially, the more decisions required to construct a plan, the more complex the plan will be, and the more difficult planning and accomplishing that task will be.

A related instructional objective is to teach students to apply what they know to new tasks that are of value *beyond* the classroom. Such tasks are sometimes called *authentic tasks*. As we will consider in Chapter 10, calls for authentic pedagogy emphasize the need for students to go beyond simply demonstrating that they can perform a given skill. Newly learned skills, concepts, and planning strategies should have "real-world" value (i.e., aesthetic, utilitarian, or personal value).

In the same way that the X-axis ranges from easy to hard skills, the planning application continuum (Z-axis) ranges from near to far transfer, from simple to complex, depending on how many skills or operations must be coordinated and performed in order to construct and accomplish the transfer task.

The key factor in the application complexity dimension is the *number of decisions* that the student must make. Simple tasks and near-transfer tasks involve few decisions. For example, doing a math drill worksheet on addition may require repeated use of adding skills, but no decision needs to be made about whether to use adding or other math operations if this information is specified on the worksheet.

Instruction needs to move students along a dimension where they are called upon to apply what they have learned to more complex and authentic tasks. In almost all cases, reasonably authentic applied tasks involve higher levels of task planning complexity (more variables, more steps, more "if ... then" decisions) than the simplified tasks often used for initial instruction of new skills. Typically, application of skills involves incorporating those skills into new tasks planned by the learner for specific purposes. For example, consider a carpenter building a house, a doctor practicing medicine in an emergency room, or a reporter working on a developing news story. In each case, experienced professionals have some stored general strategies for planning and accomplishing the task at hand. But in each case, the individual must construct a specific plan for a specific task situation. Examples of applying skills in school contexts include tasks in which children read books to enjoy stories, calculate profits when playing Monopoly games, write letters to an editor, plan a school trip, budget their allowances, or complete projects that can be communicated on the Internet or displayed at a museum.

Individual student progress with respect to the planning complexity dimension can be assessed in terms of the complexity of domain-relevant tasks that the student can construct and perform. Again, the meaning of *perform* depends on the other two dimensions: the level of self-direction and the level of skill demand. Children can plan more complex tasks if they are not required to use unfamiliar skills, and/or if they are provided with some assistance.

The impetus toward incorporating new skills while planning increasingly complex tasks may begin from the initial skill-learning context and move OUT (transfer/generalize) to more complex tasks. As noted, the transfer task may sometimes be quite similar to the task and situation in which the skill or strategy was initially taught (*near transfer*). In other instances, the task to be constructed may be quite dissimilar from the task and situation in which the original skill or strategy was taught (*far transfer*, usually involving complex decisions). Over time, teachers attempt to increase the complexity of tasks in which newly learned skills are transferred and incorporated.

Instruction can also move in the opposite direction. The impetus for learning a new skill may begin in an applied context and move BACK from authentic tasks to acquiring the needed skills. For example, teachers of beginning reading may use the class reading of Big Books as an occasion to teach basic phonemic skills. At a higher grade level, we encountered one teacher who wanted to teach his high school students math, geography, writing, and reading skills. These students had a history of academic failure and were at risk of dropping out of school. The teacher was able to convince the school board to take a chance with these students. Since his avocation was flying, he was able to invite these students to learn how to fly. They now had some reason to learn trigonometry (to study angles of descent), geography (to read landing maps), and English (to write letters needed to raise money to support their training). By finding an authentic, highly motivating task, the teacher was able to move BACK from the pilot training to the learning of core academic skills. In turn, the learning of new basic skills (spelling, math, reading, interpersonal planning skills) could be applied in new real-life settings. The apprenticeship model (in this case, learning to be a pilot) provided the impetus for learning component skills.

Just as "necessity is the mother of invention," apprenticeship is the "mother" of skill performance and application strategies. Whether it is learning new statistical techniques to solve dissertation problems or learning vocabulary to master a foreign language, authentic "necessities" are the breeding grounds for mastery.

The planning/application complexity dimension appears as the OUT dimension, or the Z axis in Figure 5.1. In most instances, teachers have their students move both OUT and BACK in a dynamically interactive fashion.

Self-Direction Dimension

In some instances, learners are provided with much support to assist them with task accomplishment and skill performance. At other times, they are expected to perform a task independently or to lead or assist others in accomplishing the task. Thus, a task can range from being *other-directed* (others guide the learner through the performance of the task on a step-by-step basis), to being *self-directed* (the learner is responsible for all aspects of accomplishing the task). The aspects of a task that must be performed include *specifying* what problem should be solved, what task should be undertaken, and what outcome needs to be accomplished; *planning* the task; *implementing* and *monitoring* performance; and *evaluating* and *storing* the results of the task. Depending on the extent to which decisions by others (e.g., a teacher, peer, work supervisor, computer application developer, parent) provide help when needed—or even when not needed—the same task could be characterized as (a) demanding no direction from a learner, (b) requiring some direction from a learner, or (c) requiring complete self-direction. Student progress with respect to self-direction for a given skill or task-planning strategy involves reducing the amount of support necessary for the student to perform a task.

We have identified three phases of self-direction: acquisition, consolidation, and consultation. Each of these phases can also be viewed as representing different roles in the learner's movement toward self-direction. These roles are defined both by specific relationships between a person and a task and by specific relationships between a person and other persons. In school settings, there are usually one or more learners and one or more teachers or peer consultants interacting around a task to be accomplished. We are going to describe three different learner roles that occur with increasing student self-direction, and corresponding teacher roles. The students' roles are *acquiring, consolidating,* and *consulting.* The corresponding teacher roles are *instructing, scaffolding,* and *mentoring.*

Acquiring Roles. When a learner is first introduced to a new task or a task incorporating a new skill, the learner's role is to learn how to perform the skill or use the concept. Similarly, when introduced to a class of problems (task specifications) that can be addressed by a strategy, the learner's role is to learn how to apply the strategy. We describe this initial "learning how" role as an *acquiring* role. When acquiring new skills and strategies, the learner observes, imitates, and acts under the guidance of the instructor—moving toward being able to perform the skill or apply the strategy being modeled.

In learning settings in which students have acquiring roles, teachers usually have *direct instructing* roles. They model, demonstrate, explain, guide, and otherwise provide learners with the plan of new skills or procedures; they "walk" students through performance of a procedure, noting points that should be monitored. In addition, instructors should (but often don't) show how the outcome of the procedure should be evaluated. Teachers also model the use of strategies to plan new tasks (often using think-aloud techniques). For example, a teacher might work through a math word problem, posing strategic questions to herself and answering them. Through this process, she creates a plan for the task.

In summary, the first goal of teaching is *helping students acquire new skills and new strategies for constructing novel tasks in a domain.*

Consolidating Role. As student competence at a given task improves, the student assumes a *consolidating* role. At this stage, students can perform taught skills as demonstrated. Task control shifts from overt direction by the teacher to control by the teacher's plan. When this stored plan is inadequate, the learner may turn to the teacher or a more skilled peer for assistance.

As a student practices a skill in the consolidation role, the skill becomes more automatic—what has been called "scripted" or "proceduralized" (Anderson, 1982, 1985, 1987). Such automaticity reduces the attentional and memory load associated with the skill, freeing up cognitive capacity to attend to other features of the task or to talk or think about the task while doing it. For example, as Sheila becomes more proficient with the mechanics of using the computer for word processing, she can focus her attention on editing her work and crafting communications to fellow students.

Essentially the same process occurs with consolidating planning or application strategies. With increased experience in situations that call for planning, the student limits possible procedures to those potentially relevant, develops better planning guides or questions, and generally becomes more efficient.

In providing assistance, the teacher or assisting peer should provide the least assistance necessary. This can take the form of hints, strategic questions which prompt the student to recall needed procedures—e.g., "Do you think you need to add or subtract here?" or "What is Jane's problem in this story?" In both examples of assistance, teachers may provide needed procedures so that learners can complete tasks that they have undertaken. For example, they may read words so that learners can proceed with understanding a text, or may help calculate numbers so that learners can proceed with a math game. Thus, the teacher or peer role in relation to a consolidating student involves *scaffolding*, rather than instructing.

The term *scaffolding* was first applied to graduated prompts and carefully adjusted tasks by David Wood and his colleagues (Wood, 1988; Wood et al.,

1975, 1976). In the same way that a builder adds or removes the amount of scaffolding required to support a building as it is being constructed, the teacher can add or remove instructional supports as a student works to develop mastery. But in the case of teaching, the amount of necessary support is influenced by the student, as well as by the teacher. Scaffolding involves a dynamic interplay of teachers relinquishing task ownership and students actively appropriating task leadership. Self-directed learners are particularly active in influencing the nature of their instruction.

In consolidating roles, learners have shifted from a subordinate, other-directed role to a *mixed-directed* relationship with the teacher. The consolidating student directs the task when she can, but accepts assistance or guidance when necessary.

Thus, a second goal of teaching is *having students consolidate learned skills and task-planning strategies.* This occurs both through planned, deliberate practice on activities that highlight the skill to be performed or the task to be planned, and through carrying out meaningful or "consequential" tasks that require the use of specific learned skills or strategies. Such tasks may be games children wish to play, or larger-scale projects such as writing a newspaper or constructing a science project.

Consulting Role. When students have consolidated a skill or strategy, they assume *consulting* roles with others and with themselves regarding that skill or strategy. Consulting students not only can perform requisite skills and plan specified applications, but also can provide assistance to others as needed, collaborate effectively with others in planning large tasks (e.g., cooperative learning and Jigsaw Instruction), and consult with themselves when they encounter difficulties or problems in accomplishing tasks. In our example, Sheila not only needs to perform skills on the computer; if mastery is to occur, she must also be able to initiate and respond to requests for help from others. She must be able to teach others as she reflects on her own processes of learning.

The teacher's role at this point becomes largely one of *mentor*, and in some cases provider of relevant tasks. The teacher needs to be satisfied that the learner is successfully consulting about the requisite skills and strategies. With respect to this domain of tasks, the teacher-student relationship may end and be replaced by a collaborative relationship or an apprentice-mentor relationship. (For example, in elementary school, some of a third-grade teacher's former students may become assistants, helping the teacher with the current third-graders. Similarly, a university professor's graduate student may become a collaborator and eventually a colleague.)

Active consultation involves spontaneously using language (or some other form of mental representation, such as diagrams) to direct one's own or others' tasks. Consultation also occurs when responding to others' requests for such assistance. As we saw in Chapter 4, students who can successfully provide consultation to others about tasks can usually construct and accomplish tasks of similar complexity without assistance.

In summary, a third goal of teaching is to arrange conditions wherein students are able to consult and reflect on their learning processes as they assume more and more leadership. Leadership skills can be developed on simple, low-complexity academic tasks (e.g., spelling, math drills), or while carrying out more complex tasks. A child could be functioning at a consultation level on simple tasks in a domain, while remaining at a consolidation level on more complex or demanding tasks, and still working at the acquisition level on very challenging problems.

Self-Direction: Summary. The self-direction dimension has been characterized as an UP dimension (the Y axis in Figure 5.1). It is characterized as an UP dimension because as the student proceeds further UP the Y axis, the skill that is being learned becomes part of the student's own knowledge base and strategic repertoire. Movement along the UP dimension can occur at varying levels of skill demand and application complexity, depending upon which point the student is currently working at. As students move along the UP dimension, their role shifts from that of "followers" to that of "leaders."

In addressing the acquiring, consolidating, and consulting roles, it is important to realize that the same student can easily assume all three roles in the course of a day, as she works on different tasks at which she has different levels of competence. Likewise, a teacher may assume instructor, scaffolder, and mentor roles with the same student in the course of one day. We believe that truly effective educational programs provide opportunities for students to regularly assume acquirer, consolidator, and consultant roles with respect to each major curriculum focus in their program.

We have proposed that tasks can be described in terms of *skill demands, planning* or *application demands,* and *self-direction demands.* We have also proposed that students' educational progress towards increased mastery of a level of a domain occurs in the same three dimensions: (1) acquiring new skills; (2) applying those skills in increasingly complex authentic tasks; and (3) increasing self-direction by assuming responsibility for task accomplishment using learned skills. *Progress in all three dimensions is necessary for increasing real mastery of any academic area.*

The Interaction of Skill Demands, Planning/Application Complexity, and Self-Direction

The dimensions of skill demand, self-direction, and planning/application complexity are dynamically interdependent. Movement along one dimension influences student progress on the other dimensions. For example, if a task is too difficult on the X or Z dimensions, students may not be able to assume any additional task responsibility. However, if students are presented with tasks that fall within their range of competence, they may be able to teach these skills to others. The following sections further illustrate the nature of this dynamic interplay among the three dimensions of mastery.

Skill Demands and Planning Complexity

Skill demands and planning complexity combine to create what we subjectively experience as the ease or difficulty of tasks. When teaching a new skill, instructors usually try to limit the planning demands of tasks in which the child will be using the skill. For example, students who have just learned new math skills initially do "drill" work with simple computations, rather than solving complex math problems. (Note that such drill work may take the form of games that require repeated performance of a skill, rather than decontextualized drill sheets.) Similarly, students who have just learned new print vocabulary read relatively simple narratives in vocabulary-controlled readers.

Conversely, when we want students to deal with more complex problem solving, we are well advised to avoid confronting them with problems that require unfamiliar skills. (An exception to this occurs when tasks involving unfamiliar skills are introduced intentionally to *create the need* to learn those skills, as in the example of the teacher who used learning to fly an airplane as an impetus for students to learn elementary skills.)

The Impact of Skill Demands and Planning/Application Complexity on Self-Direction

When the skill demands of tasks are reduced through practice, adjustment of the task, or assistance with different skills (e.g., use of calculators or spelling assistance), then learners can demonstrate higher levels of self-direction. In other words, students can accomplish less demanding tasks with minimal assistance. With more practice, or on still less demanding tasks, they can take the lead, explaining to others how to perform needed skills and monitoring and correcting problems in their performance.

Similarly, when planning complexity or transfer demands are reduced, learners can also demonstrate higher levels of self-direction, using learned and self-generated strategies to plan solutions to problems with little help. On still simpler problems they can take a lead role in planning and accomplishing tasks. For example, as noted, we have found that fourth-grade children who are not performing at grade level in mathematics can be taught to assist second-grade children with their math tasks. Not only did this help the second-graders, but also, putting the low-achieving fourth-graders in a leadership role aided their own math performance (Inglis & Biemiller, submitted for publication).

Thus, reducing either skill demands or task planning complexity results in higher levels of self-direction. We suggest that having children routinely assume consultation roles with some tasks in each academic domain will improve their performance, their confidence, and their ability to bring verbal directive powers to bear on planning new tasks.

Why Self-Direction Fosters Mastery

A number of different terms have been used to label what we call self-direction: "appropriating task ownership," "engaging in self-regulated behavior," "demonstrating strategic learning," and "performing autonomously." Whatever the label, the central feature of developing self-direction is that the learner assumes responsibility for task accomplishment—specifying, planning, implementing, monitoring, and evaluating his or her task and task outcomes. As self-direction develops, the competent performer may be invited—or volunteer—to take responsibility for others' performance by providing advice and offering consultation. Individuals who develop self-direction should act as consultants not only to others, but also to themselves.

The ability to explain one's performance and to effectively assist others reflects a high level of self-direction, as noted in the description of self-directed students in Chapter 3. Recall that those students who thrive in school were characterized as "active, independent, self-directed learners." They were noted for their use of language to strategically elicit assistance, and to advise both others and themselves; they assumed leadership roles. Any model of instruction must consider the function of such motivational and language processes in the development of mastery.

Motivation. In motivational terms, moving from other-direction to self-direction means coming to actively identify, select, and plan tasks, to guide others and oneself to completion of tasks, to monitor progress, and to evaluate task outcomes. While not all of these task components can always be under the learner's direction, teachers need to keep in mind that an end result of successful education is successful independent task accomplishment in authentic contexts.

If we are to help more students to take active responsibility for tasks using learned academic skills, we must create for each learner some situations in which he or she is legitimately "in charge"—able to make decisions about selecting, planning, monitoring, and evaluating tasks. This means that teachers must sometimes relinquish control, and must engineer both individual and small-group situations in which each child can exercise legitimate direction and leadership. This also means that teachers need to engage their students in projects and activities in which they have opportunities to initiate, perform, and monitor complex authentic tasks that take some time and effort to accomplish. Cross-age tutoring and reciprocal teaching are examples of such activities. We will discuss these settings in Chapters 9 and 10.

Language. Language, particularly task-directive language, plays a crucial part in the process of self-direction. Although it is possible to accomplish many tasks without extensive verbal task direction, most academic skills and tasks involve verbal task direction or some other form of mental representation (e.g., diagrams, geography maps, semantic webs, graphic organizers, equations, mind maps, etc.). If students are to become independent learners, they must be able to use the power of language and other forms of mental representation to guide construction, adaptation, and correction of task performance, and to benefit from the assistance of others.

In order to construct one's own tasks in a domain, rather than seeking or waiting for instruction from others, one must have the confidence that one can effectively generate a solution, and the tools (task-relevant language and relevant consolidated skills and strategies) necessary to do so. Learners need experience in talking about tasks, and may benefit from helping others construct tasks, even before they can help themselves.

Since higher levels of self-direction are seen when skill and construction demands are reduced, we should not expect high levels of self-direction when children are working with just-learned skills. This conclusion is consistent with cognitive developmental theory and research.[2] If we want a wide range of children to exercise self-direction, we must be prepared to provide them with tasks that are less demanding than those on which advanced classmates demonstrate self-direction in the classroom. Students are more likely to employ task-directive speech when they are put in leadership consulting roles on tasks that are well within their skill and strategy repertoires. In subsequent chapters we will consider specific teaching procedures that teachers can use to nurture such self-regulatory learning activities in students.

In summary, verbal self-directive and motivational processes appear to be necessary for effective independent learning—mastery of academic skills—to take place. We turn now to a further consideration of the role of language and other forms of mental representation in the development of student mastery.

Why Is Mental Representation So Critical to the Development of Mastery and Expertise?

Throughout our descriptions of student roles and learning settings, we have highlighted the need for students not only to perform tasks, but also to engage in reflective activities in which they are called upon to describe, explain, and justify what they are doing—either orally or in writing—to others and to themselves. We propose that in order to master a curriculum area or unit and move toward expertise, students need to be able to consult and teach what they are doing to others. Students need to reflect upon the connections between what they are currently learning, what they have learned in the past, and what they will be learning in the future, and to consider how they can apply what they are learning to real authentic tasks and settings.

These reflective activities may be in the form of verbal productions (e.g., think-aloud samples, oral presentations, videotape demonstrations, teaching others), written productions (e.g., daily logs, diary entries, journals, portfolios), diagrammatic productions (e.g., graphic organizers, semantic webs, mind maps, artwork), or physical productions (e.g., mime, dance, sociodramatic skits). No matter what the form of mental representation, such reflective behaviors—especially in the form of language—are critical to the development of mastery and expertise.

What are the functions of language and other forms of mental representation that make them so essential to the learning process? Language and other forms of mental representation assist task accomplishment by acting as:

- a problem-solving device, a tool for learning, and a solution generator;
- a means for accessing and activating stored information and for enhancing conceptual understanding;
- a process that facilitates transfer;
- a way to seek and access assistance;
- a tool for sharing and consulting with others, as well as with oneself; and

- a means to becoming a member of a community of learners.

We will consider each of these functions, in turn.

Language as a problem-solving device, a tool for learning, and a solution generator. Humans can generate a virtually infinite range of messages to each other and to themselves regarding detailed task directions and contextual information, as well as emotional states. In the process of evolving a flexible language system, humans acquired a rapid problem-solving device. Every sentence we generate (rather than imitate) is a novel construction and, as such, represents a solution for expressing an intent/task/situation. The problem-solving process used in generating speech can be quite rapid: we can generate 10 to 20 sentences per minute when talking or thinking quickly.

In classrooms, students are called upon to generate rapid solutions—to put their ideas into words or into some other form of mental representation—on a routine basis. Such requests are designed to focus their attention and to lead them to clarify and symbolize their thought processes. Language is one medium for generating such solutions. This is illustrated in the common experience of students asking for assistance and, in the midst of explaining what they need help on, generating the solution themselves without any further aid. As students put what they know and what they don't know into words or into diagrams, they often generate solutions.

What is it about going public with one's thought processes (to others or to oneself) that helps to generate solutions? In the process of explaining oneself to others (or to oneself), executive processes such as planning, monitoring, self-regulating, and evaluating are invoked. In addition, one's thinking processes become the object of attention, as students are called upon to reflect on how and why they perform a task. These metacognitive processes were readily illustrated in a series of studies by Michelle Chi and her colleagues. The researchers found that when students were required to explain to themselves the problematic features of a task and the ways they worked them out, the higher-achieving students generated more complete self-explanations, utilized superior problem-solving protocols, and evidenced improved conceptual understanding on transfer tasks (Chi et al., 1989, 1994).

As language moves from being primarily a means of communicating with others to one of communicating with oneself, an additional means of reflection and explanation is developed. Research indicates that approximately 15% of students' verbalizations in class are to themselves (Meichenbaum & Biemiller, 1992), and as they progress from first to third grade, the students' self-talk becomes increasingly inaudible (Bivens & Berk, 1990). This transition permits students to construct hypothetical messages or responses before they are written or expressed. Such self-directed speech provides the means for description, self-questioning, and problem solving, as well as strategies for formulating rules. Out of such reflective behavior, students develop forethought.

Language as a means for accessing and activating stored information and for enhancing conceptual understanding. Language and imagery can help students activate and access stored information so they can take advantage of what they already know in order to construct new knowledge. Putting ideas into words or diagrams helps students to access prior knowledge (declarative, procedural, and conditional) and helps them construct solutions in ways that doing the same task covertly (quietly, to oneself) does not allow.

Such knowledge construction involves the development of abstract systems or solution strategies for organizing and accessing information. Whether the knowledge is in the form of a simple mnemonic (e.g., ROY G BIV to remember the colors of the spectrum), or more complicated self-generated procedural prompts, the linguistic and imaginal systems facilitate performance by acting as reminders to perform a task strategy. Without language, the learner would be severely handicapped in accomplishing tasks.[3] But if students are to develop mastery, language and other forms of mental representation must do more than act as retrieval cues. Language must help students gain conceptual understanding of subject domains.

Language provides a way to represent knowledge in a symbolic form that affords opportunities for abstract thinking. Language assists students in taking advantage of what they already know in order to construct new knowledge and strategies. When students are asked to reflect upon what they are learning, conceptual understanding is enhanced. As Brown and Campione (1996) observed:

> Understanding is more likely to occur when a student is required to explain, elaborate, or defend his or her position to others; the burden of explanation is often the push needed to make him or her evaluate, integrate, and elaborate knowledge in new ways (p. 306).

Language as a process that facilitates transfer. Language can be used to help identify patterns that occur across tasks and situations, and to help foster depth of processing so that students do not respond just to the surface features of a task. As students learn to summarize, self-interrogate, predict, and monitor their performance, the likelihood increases that transfer will occur (Borkowski & Muthakrishna, 1992; Palincsar & Brown, 1984). Language can be viewed as a series of "command actions" that permits students to control not only their behavior, but also their ideas, level of effort, motivation, and emotions. Language also provides the basis for producing novel, complex, goal-directed behaviors. Language and other forms of mental representation (e.g., diagramming relationships, or imagining possible barriers to transfer and ways they can be anticipated, avoided and handled) can foster generalization. Teachers need to create learning settings in which *all* students, both individually and in groups, have opportunities to regulate and apply what they have learned. At the heart of these pedagogical efforts, language plays a critical role, as students assume more and more responsibility for task accomplishment.

Language as a way to seek and access assistance. Language makes possible the seeking of assistance from others, as well as from oneself. Task-directive language permits the learner to access information from numerous sources (e.g., teachers, more competent peers, reference books, computers, videotape presentations). As students master skills, they also master the ability to access and use other people's minds very efficiently. Teaching and learning are two sides of the same coin and influence one another. For example, research indicates that asking questions can improve students' comprehension, internalization, and transfer of newly learned material (King, 1990, 1991; King & Rosenshine, 1993; Palincsar, 1986). Despite such evidence that asking questions is an important part of the learning process, students rarely use this tool in classrooms unless explicitly encouraged or taught to do so. As noted, high-achieving students tend to ask more questions, requesting more hints than solutions (Good & Brophy, 1994; Biemiller & Meichenbaum, 1992). Task-related language is the currency for such informational exchanges and is critical to the development of mastery.

Language as a tool for sharing and consulting with others and with oneself. Jean Piaget observed that we typically remain unaware of a large part of our actions and their mechanisms. However, by consciously and deliberately increasing his or her awareness, the learner can gain new conceptual understanding about performance (Piaget, 1964). One of the best ways to become more aware of how we perform tasks is to teach or consult with others. Such consultation may take various forms, including peer assistance, classwide peer teaching, reciprocal teaching, Jigsaw classroom instruction, e-mail communication, and many others. Such consultation contexts add to the development of self-direction and expertise.

   As noted earlier, students are more likely to learn when they are required to explain, elaborate, and defend their position to others. In the course of explaining an idea or procedure, students develop a better understanding of what they do and do not know. The strategies they teach become open to introspection and mindful self-observation, as they are often called upon to justify what they are teaching and why. In preparing for such consultation, students are usually taught what makes someone a good teacher and how to give hints and not answers, as described in Chapter 9. They are required to organize and rehearse information and strategies which reinforce memory representation and conceptual understanding. The need to explain also forces learners to integrate and elaborate their knowledge and strategies in new ways. Teachers need to create multiple opportunities for all students to use their language, writing, imaginal, and conceptual (diagramming) abilities for consultative purposes.

While it is most beneficial for students to be placed in a responsible teaching role, students also benefit from participating in peer groups where fellow students share what they are doing in their minds, as they engage in a task. Research indicates that the students who gain most from cooperative learning activities are those who provide the most elaborate explanations. Students who are merely exposed to such elaborations learn more than those who work alone, but not as much as the explainers. Peer teaching is one of the most effective ways to enhance student performance. Out of such social discourse, students develop the ability to conduct similar discussions with themselves, as they learn to self-regulate their own behavior (Berliner & Biddle, 1995; Silver & Cai, 1996).

Language as a means to become a member of a community of learners. As students learn to use the language (jargon, terminology) of a given discipline, they come to see themselves as members of a community of learners. As noted, students need to learn not only how to do mathematics, but also how to "talk mathematically" to each other. The same rule applies to every subject area. Students must learn how to communicate with each other about constructing poems, plays, artwork, and computer programs, and about sharing and getting along with each other. As students acquire and employ the language and accompanying concepts of a discipline, they develop greater ability to direct, control, and apply their knowledge and strategies.

In summary, the language used in classrooms shapes students' experiences and learning opportunities. Language provides the basis for student planning, self-awareness, personal control, and mastery.

Nurturing Student Mastery

Of the three dimensions of mastery, growth in the skill dimension is perhaps the most dependent on direct teacher action, and the easiest to assess. However, while the ability to perform academic skills and the possession of a large working vocabulary are *necessary* for long-term success in the modern world, they are not *sufficient*. Unless one has developed strategies for planning tasks and for using skills and information when constructing tasks in new situations, knowledge, skills, and strategies remain inert or nontransferable, and of little use to the student or to society. Unless one has become accustomed to being in charge and verbally directing tasks and task planning, one cannot be considered an independent master of those skills and strategies.

Teaching Learners To Become More Self-Directed

In general, the teaching process involves gradually transferring responsibility for planning and accomplishing tasks from the teacher to students. Increasing self-direction in planning applied tasks is usually seen when learners are made responsible for novel or unique tasks (e.g., writing a paper, planning a trip, creating a play, planning a lesson, making up a test, creating an exhibit to present to others)—often without demands for a new skill. Such tasks may be constructed collaboratively, with several individuals contributing to specifying, planning, monitoring progress, and evaluating results. However, in reality it is often the case that one must accomplish novel tasks on one's own, or that one individual in a group assumes much of the directive responsibility for a task with the assistance of several helpers.

Increasing self-direction with new skills is often first seen in the context of simplified or otherwise familiar tasks that allow a focus on a specific new skill. As the learner practices a skill on new tasks, the level of guidance by others can be reduced as the learner assumes more and more responsibility. Obviously, both the planning complexity and skill dimensions can be varied. As described earlier, the ways in which teachers calibrate task difficulty, titrate assistance, and relinquish task control as students become more competent at a given skill have been referred to as *scaffolding*.

Summary: The Nature of Mastery

We can now conceptualize the learning process as a journey from being a novice to mastering increasingly complex parts of a specific domain. This journey is marked by increasing independence in applying a growing range of skills to increasingly complex, novel, authentic tasks—in other words, moving along the X, Y and Z axes of the three-dimensional model of mastery (see Figure 5.1, p. 71).

In order to further clarify this model of mastery, consider any skill that you are trying to improve (e.g., tennis, using a computer, getting along with others), or a skill that you are trying to teach to someone else (e.g., math, reading comprehension, writing). Try to assess where the learner can be placed on the three dimensions with respect to a specific task, and ask what you, as a teacher, can do to move the learner (yourself or your student) OVER (along the X dimension of increasing skill), OUT (along the Z dimension of increasingly complex and authentic applications), and UP (along the Y dimension of increasing self-direction). As teachers of others, or of ourselves, we are confronted with a series of critical pedagogical questions.

- How far OVER (along the X dimension), in terms of new skills and new vocabulary, should we progress before we try to move a student UP in self-direction (along the Y-axis)?
- How can you ensure that students have practiced to the point of consolidation (moving UP the Y-axis)—so that their skills have become automated, freeing up cognitive resources to be directed to other features of the task?
- At what level of task difficulty (X dimension) on math, reading, etc., can students be put into a consultative (tutor) role (move along the Y-axis)?
- Should students be able to put into words the procedural steps involved in doing a task (the consultative level of self-direction) before you expect them to deal with more complex tasks on the OUT (Z) dimension?
- How can you employ authentic tasks that will motivate students to put out the effort to learn skills and practice (move OUT along the Z-axis so students put out effort to move UP the Y-axis)?
- How can you increase the likelihood that what students learn will be applied (transferred) to novel tasks in new settings (move OUT along Z-axis)?

The three-dimensional model of mastery also provides a framework for understanding why some students fail to thrive, while others succeed.

- Students who do not succeed in school are rarely asked to perform tasks that are just beyond their levels of competence. Instead, they are often presented with tasks that are too difficult, given their cumulative skill deficits, or that are too easy. Remedial schoolwork often consists of "busy work" and "baby-sitting activities," during which little learning takes place.

- Low-achieving students continually struggle to keep up with the more demanding tasks that are offered at an ever-increasing rate. Usually, when low-achieving students become proficient at a given skill, instead of being asked to reflect, describe, and teach what they have learned or to apply it to novel tasks, the curriculum-driven instruction requires them to acquire new material. As a result, they remain in "novice" (acquisition and consolidation) roles, without experiencing the role of being a consultant or an expert. Rather than becoming more "expert" on the self-direction (Y) dimension, low-achieving students are pressed to handle more and more difficult tasks on the skills (X) dimension. Low-achieving students are rarely put into leadership or consulting roles, and are rarely required to articulate the processes they employ to perform academic tasks. They rarely progress beyond the early consolidation phase on the self-direction dimension. The low-achieving student must race faster and faster to try to catch up, and in the end only falls further and further behind. It is as if there is an instructional treadmill—the belt of educational content goes faster and faster, to the point where 20 to 40 percent of students decide to drop out of school.

- Finally, low-achieving students rarely have an opportunity to perform their skills in authentic tasks, and seldom see the relevance of what they are learning to real-world task construction (limited movement on the planning-application [Z] dimension).

Contrast this pattern with those students who achieve in school. Those who thrive master academic skills by becoming increasingly self-directed when performing newly learned skills. High achievers receive multiple opportunities to develop and exercise their competencies and to employ their executive self-directive speech in consultative leadership roles. They actively plan and accomplish tasks that incorporate the academic skills they are learning; they are given projects to do, asked to teach others, asked to describe to the class how to do a task, and the like.

The challenge taken up in the next section of this book is to demonstrate how teachers can create learning settings in which most students can eventually do what the students who thrive do now. Quite simply, how can educators move students OVER, UP, and OUT? How can they help students move from being novices to becoming more and more expert? In order to answer these questions, we begin Chapter 6 with a consideration of the various learning settings and roles that teachers can use to nurture their students' mastery. We then consider how teachers can foster students' skill acquisition (Chapter 7) and consolidation (Chapter 8), nurture students' consultative abilities (Chapter 9), and bolster their constructive propensities (Chapter 10).

Endnotes

1. Technically, difficulty is a relative concept, referring to how an individual experiences a task. What is difficult for one person may be easy for another. As the term is commonly used, difficulty (or complexity) increases with skills that can be performed by older individuals. Thus, tasks routinely performed correctly by sixth-graders are more difficult than tasks routinely performed correctly by second-graders.

2. Both Case (1985) and Pressley and colleagues (1992) have observed the relationship between cognitive load, language production, and self-direction. Similarly, Gutentag (1984), Gutentag et al. (1987), and Paas and Van Merrienboer (1994) have demonstrated that high cognitive loads interfere with transfer or constructive processes.

3. See Loera and Meichenbaum (1994) for a discussion of how language plays a critical role in the development of higher-level metacognitive skills in deaf children.

Highlight Box 5.1
SUMMARY OF THE 3-D MODEL OF MASTERY

The three dimensions refer to:

   X = OVER — Skill Demand (including vocabulary)

   Y = UP — Self-Direction

   Z = OUT and BACK — Planning/Application Complexity

1. The X (OVER) dimension denotes the level of difficulty and familiarity of the skills required to do a task. Skills involve both procedures and vocabulary, and are organized hierarchically.

2. The Y (UP) dimension denotes the degree to which the performance of a task is self-directed—the degree to which the specification of the task outcome, planning, implementing, monitoring, and evaluating of performance is directed by the learner. There are three possible roles for the learner associated with different levels of support:

(a) *Acquiring Role*—the student is essentially a follower of the directions and instructions of others, usually during the introduction to a new task, skill, or strategy. The student may be at a beginning point or "clueless" about performing a task, and thus, highly dependent on others for direct instruction.

(b) *Consolidating Role*—the student performs tasks of controlled skill demand and planning complexity with reduced guidance and support. With repeated practice and corrective feedback, the student's skills are performed more automatically, becoming second nature, thus freeing up mental capacity so he or she can execute more than one skill or procedure at a time. With repeated practice in a domain, the student also becomes more effective at planning new tasks or applying familiar tasks and procedures in new contexts.

(c) *Consulting Role*—mastery requires taking a leadership role and becoming mindfully reflective with others and with oneself. The learner must come to spontaneously use language or some other form of mental representation (e.g., diagrams, graphic organizers, semantic webs) as a way to direct others and herself and to solve problems. Language plays a critical role in the development of mastery as students move from being a novice when doing a task to the point where they can now teach it to others.

While students assume acquiring, consolidating, and consulting roles, the corresponding teacher roles are *instructing*, *scaffolding*, and *mentoring*.

3. The Z (OUT) dimension denotes the planning and application complexity of a task, as students apply their knowledge and skills to new tasks in novel situations. The learners acquire or generate strategies for planning new tasks—transferring or generalizing their knowledge and skills. The tasks may vary from *near transfer* (tasks and contexts similar to training) to *far transfer* ("authentic" applied tasks that require high levels of skill integration and complex decision making). Students move from merely consuming knowledge to actually constructing knowledge, tasks, and procedures.

Students may move OUT from the initial simplified learning settings to complex "authentic" tasks. They may also move BACK from "authentic" complex tasks to focusing on the acquisition of needed skills and strategies. This bi-directional movement is a dynamic interactive process.

The instructional goals of the three-dimensional model of mastery are to explain how students can learn to perform *more and more difficult skills, on their own* (to the point of mastery where they can teach others), and to apply learned skills *when planning new tasks in different situations* (to the point of creating the new tasks and inventing new learning strategies).

Chapter Six

Creating Classroom Programs that Support Student Mastery: Learning Settings that Provide Appropriate Tasks and Roles for Students and Teachers

Introduction

The basic points of Chapters 4 and 5 can be summarized as follows:

1.   The learning environments of high- and low-achieving students are quite different from each other. For example, teachers often give able students tasks that are easy or challenging, while giving less able students tasks that are too difficult for them; in other words, teachers give able students tasks they can do independently, but give less able students tasks they cannot do without assistance.

2.   All students need a mix of *hard* tasks (tasks they require instruction or assistance to accomplish), *challenging* tasks (tasks they require deliberate mental effort to determine how to do), and *easy* tasks (good practice or consolidation tasks, on which they can act as consultants). At present, teachers approximate this mix of conditions for their advanced students, roughly one third of each class—but not for the other two thirds of students, who do not achieve at or above grade level. The failure to provide a similar mix of tasks for two thirds of students intensifies educational inequalities.

3.   If teachers could learn to treat the majority of students in the engaging

and challenging fashion in which they now treat high-achieving students, more students would develop academic expertise, and students would accomplish more tasks. When low-achieving students are explicitly taught to develop their self-directive capacities, and are provided with opportunities to help or consult with others, their own academic achievement improves.

This chapter provides a framework for understanding how educators can create learning settings with student roles that nurture their expertise—settings in which students *acquire, consolidate,* and *consult about* skills and concepts. We also consider how teachers can orchestrate learning settings in which students acquire, consolidate, and consult about *strategies for transferring or applying* learned skills and concepts. In addition, we consider how these settings can be organized within the constraints of classroom programs, and how classroom programs can address individual differences in student progress. In the next four chapters, we consider specific teaching practices to accomplish each of these objectives. Chapter 11 provides detailed descriptions of a number of educational experiments that have succeeded, emphasizing the ways they have created learning settings and student roles that nurture student expertise.

How can a single teacher bring students to high levels of self-direction in skill performance and task construction, when dealing with 25–30 students who differ markedly in the skills and strategies they have mastered? The simple answer is by constructing classroom programs in which most students can progress on all three dimensions (X, Y, and Z). Such programs should provide students with a variety of different learning roles in which they can (a) acquire and consolidate new skills, (b) acquire and consolidate strategies for solving problems or constructing increasingly complex tasks, and (c) extend the range of situations in which they can independently construct new tasks and guide both themselves and others in doing so.

Constructing programs that provide this range of learning roles for different academic domains is not simple! In order to understand how such programs can be developed, it is important to first consider the concepts of classroom programs, learning settings, learning roles, and learning tasks. We begin with an examination of *learning settings,* the basic building blocks of classroom programs. We then continue with a more detailed look at student and teacher *roles,* and at the students' *learning tasks* in these settings. Finally, we return to the problem of constructing *programs* that provide students with the necessary range of settings to develop mastery of curriculum content.

The Concept of Learning Settings

Let us begin with an example. The Language Arts component of Jane Smith's second-grade classroom takes up 6.3 hours a week, or 24% of the time her children are in school (omitting recesses and lunch). Over the course of a week, her 25 students participate in a number of different Language Arts learning settings:

- whole-class spelling testing (2 sessions, total 20 minutes per week)
- whole-class story (daily sessions, total 65 minutes per week)
- whole-class explanation of group activities (2 sessions, total 20 minutes per week)
- reading group with teacher (3 sessions, total 50 minutes per week per student)
- reading group: independent writing and art activities based on the book being read (4 sessions, total 2 hours and 30 minutes per week per student)
- individual or pairs story writing (1 session, 25 minutes per week per student)
- pairs story editing (1 session, avg. 20 minutes per week per student)
- individual conference with teacher about writing (8-minute session every 2 weeks, avg. 4 minutes per week per student)
- reading buddies with kindergarten (1 session, 30 minutes per week per student)

We present this list of settings not as an ideal language arts curriculum, but simply as an example of an actual program.

Each of these learning settings occurs with a specific group of children in a specific place at a specific time. In each setting, there is a *student academic task*, one or more *student roles*, and sometimes an explicit *teacher role*. (The teacher also has monitoring responsibilities over all settings in her classroom, and may have to interrupt a specific activity in one setting to assist or redirect children in another setting.) Below, we consider several of these learning settings in more detail.

Whole-Class Explanation of Group Activities. In this setting, the student task is to learn the task instructions that Ms. Smith provides, so that they can later carry out these tasks in their groups. (Thus, the "product" from this task is knowing what their assignments are.) The student role is acquiring task goals or specifications, as Ms. Smith specifies several different group tasks (e.g., writing a response to the story being read; writing and drawing a sketch of a character in the story; preparing a page of the book, including a relevant illustration; etc.). The teacher's role is providing direct instruction—explaining, modeling, and providing guidance on how each task is to be carried out.

Reading Group with the Teacher. In this setting, the main *student tasks* are reading aloud and understanding a story. In addition, students are expected to learn some phonics skills when Ms. Smith demonstrates them, and to learn to identify some unfamiliar words that cannot be identified using available phonics skills. The student roles involve *acquiring* skills and strategies as Ms. Smith provides phonics skill instruction and models and explains strategies for comprehending narratives, and *consolidating* skills and strategies, as students practice reading with guidance and assistance from the teacher. (In other reading classes, the teacher might try to move the students to *consultation* roles by having them help each other. That didn't happen here.) One teacher role is *instruction* in phonics skills, in the identity of specific sight words, and in comprehension strategies. Another teacher role is graduated assistance, or *scaffolding* of assistance, as students read. This involves providing the least assistance necessary to allow each student to complete his or her reading. Scaffolding may include reminding a student of a phonics skill or comprehension strategy, suggesting rereading of a misread sentence, or sometimes telling the student a word so he or she can proceed with understanding a story.

Independent Writing and Art Activities. In this setting, several different writing and illustration tasks are undertaken on different days. Each student is expected to complete his or her own writing—these are not cooperative assignments. The main student role is *consolidating* writing skills and strategies, as students attempt to apply writing skills in the process of planning and carrying out the specified tasks. One or two students in each group also have a *consulting* role as they assist fellow group members with spelling skills and writing content suggestions.

Reading Buddies with Kindergarten. In this setting, each second-grade child's tasks are (a) reading to a kindergarten child and (b) discussing what is being read. The second-grader's main role is *consulting* about the story. This student must be able to answer the kindergartner's questions about the story, pose appropriate questions about the story, and discuss possible directions the story could take. The kindergartner's role is *consolidating* comprehension of the story. (In many cases, the kindergartner will ask for the same story to be repeated.)

The teacher does not have an active role in this setting, but monitors the second-grade children's effectiveness and intervenes where necessary. Following the cross-age tutoring session, the teacher asks the tutors to reflect on how the session went and helps them put into words the teaching strategies they employed.

Learning Settings: Summary

These examples illustrate a number of different kinds of learning settings used in the classroom. Each learning setting involves at least one academic *task* for students, and at least one learning *role* which students can assume. As discussed in Chapter 5, student roles define a relationship between the student and the task (neophyte, novice, competent performer, consultant, expert), and a relationship between the student and other people (e.g., similarly competent students, more competent students, less competent students, the teacher, etc.) In addition, in some learning settings, the teacher assumes one or more roles (e.g., instructor, monitor, scaffolder, collaborator, mentor).

We now turn to a more detailed analysis of student learning roles and learning tasks.

Learning Roles and Teaching Roles

As we explained in Chapter 5, roles involve specific relationships between a person and a task and between a person and other persons. In most learning settings, students and teachers have complementary roles: roles that are defined in terms of how students and teachers relate to each other and in terms of student competence with the tasks to be carried out. These roles reflect different levels of self-direction as students gain mastery of particular skills or parts of curriculum domains. Below, we briefly describe two examples: one illustrating roles in relation to addition skills, the other illustrating roles in relation to a planning strategy for writing narratives. Both examples illustrate the three student roles outlined in Chapter 5—acquisition, consolidation, and consultation.

Acquiring, Consolidating, and Consulting about Multi-Digit Addition Skills

Consider the changing roles of students and teachers in a traditional math lesson in which students are learning to add multi-digit numbers.

Acquiring roles. At the outset of an initial lesson, the students are not competent at adding multi-digit numbers; they have the role of observing and listening to the teacher so they can carry out the steps of the procedure, and asking for assistance (from the teacher or a competent peer) when they do not understand what to do. Students then attempt to perform the task while the teacher (or peers) monitor their performance and correct steps when necessary.

In a complementary fashion, the teacher adopts the role of *instructor*, explaining the purpose of the new math procedure and demonstrating (modeling) how it is carried out. (Previous work with quantities may have demonstrated the usefulness of this procedure.) Following this initial instruction, the teacher's role includes guiding and monitoring the students' performance on the mathematical procedure, and strategically providing corrective feedback as needed.

Consolidating roles. In order to develop mastery of addition, students must not only acquire addition skills, but also consolidate them through repeated, deliberate, successful practice. To consolidate multi-digit addition skills, students need to practice the skills many times. As they do so, they will need some assistance and feedback; students typically work independently on such tasks, but they need access to assistance to avoid being "stuck" or repeating errors. A variety of different tasks could be used: (a) traditional drill sheets that simply present a number of numerical addition problems to be completed; (b) authentic activities that require repeated addition of large numbers (e.g., tallying Halloween UNICEF money); or (c) relatively simple word problems that involve adding large quantities.

The role of the teacher or more skilled peer is to provide assistance—the *least* assistance necessary to permit students to complete their tasks successfully. (If a great deal of assistance is needed, the student is effectively still in the acquiring role.) As noted in Chapter 5, providing the least assistance necessary for successful task accomplishment is described as a *scaffolding* role.

One does not become expert in anything without extensive practice. As we will consider in Chapter 8, educators have learned a great deal about what kinds of practice are most effective in skill development. For now, it is important to appreciate that teachers need to establish consolidating roles for students to practice skills and strategies, usually on planned tasks that the students are able to accomplish successfully.

When another student, rather than a teacher, assumes the consultation (scaffolding) role in this setting, the same setting provides both consolidation and consultation student roles. However, as we have stressed numerous times, among children in a specific grade, only those who are advanced in particular skills are likely to assume consultation roles with respect to tasks involving those skills. Encouraging others to consult requires learning settings that pair them with younger children, or with classmates whose skills are less advanced than their own.

Consulting roles. In order to become more expert at addition, students also need to assume direction in aiding others and in becoming more aware, self-reflective learners. This can be seen in classrooms as students who have become competent at adding begin to assist others. They assume the role of consultant, essentially doing what the teacher was doing as he or she assisted students in consolidating their addition skills. Students who do not shine at math in their own grade can act as effective assistants to those just learning to add. Other consulting roles in the addition context include supervising games that involve adding, working in teams to generate and check math worksheets and problems, and explaining math procedures to classmates and parents. Students may also reflectively record the procedures they used in daily logs, on their Tickets Out The Door, and in other writing formats, as described in Chapter 9.

Acquiring, Consolidating, and Consulting about Strategies for Writing Narratives

When students begin to write more than a sentence or two, we start to introduce writing strategies. Some teachers suggest the strategy of providing a "beginning," a "middle," and an "end" to stories. We prefer Anne McKeough's "problem," "barrier," and "solution" strategy (McKeough, 1992).

Acquiring a writing strategy. The teacher typically models the process of writing, asking herself *strategic questions* (e.g., "What problem will _____ have?"), and answering the questions (e.g., "I think she'll have trouble getting along with friends at school"). In the process of answering strategic questions, the narrative is generated. In this example, the students' initial role is to *acquire* the strategy—the sequence of strategic questions—so that they can guide themselves.

In other planning-focused tasks, strategic questions lead to generating a plan of action—a sequence of operations to be performed. For example, to solve a quantitative problem, a student would need to plan a sequence of calculations leading to a solution.

Consolidating a writing strategy. After this introduction to narrative writing, students *consolidate* narrative production by writing (or telling) a number of narratives. They may use strategy prompts to remind them of the steps to be completed in generating a narrative. These may simply be in the form of a list of questions or points to be addressed. With very young children, pictured strategic prompts and mnemonics have been used successfully (Harris & Graham, 1996; McKeough, 1992). The teacher or a more competent peer *scaffolds* the consolidating students' writing (or finished products) by monitoring their progress and, when necessary, asking students whether their character has a clear problem, whether the character has encountered difficulties (a barrier), or what happened (was the problem solved?). The scaffolding teacher or student may also give supportive hints and guidance, providing needed assistance with skills (spelling words, reminding students of punctuation, etc.). In essence, the teacher or competent peer acts as an editor.

Consulting about writing strategies. As students become more effective at using writing strategies, they may become editors themselves—asking others strategic questions, and providing supports when necessary. At this point, they have assumed a *consulting* role, actively directing their own and others' writing work. In order to become more expert at writing, students must become fluent in the vocabulary of a specific domain, as well as in appropriate language for explaining how they employ and apply these concepts and strategies. The use of this language permits students to become members of a community of fellow writers.

Complementarity of Roles in Learning Settings

In the various learning settings in which students acquire, consolidate, and consult about skills and strategies, the teacher's role must complement the students' roles for mastery to be achieved. For example, it is difficult for students to acquire skills if the teacher continually presents tasks for which the students do not have prerequisite skills, or if the students have not been adequately oriented and introduced to the task, or if the pace and level of difficulty is beyond all or many of the students' abilities. If the teacher's instruction is not sensitive to the students' current levels of ability and interest, and if the students don't see the relevance of what they are learning, the teacher has not adequately fulfilled his or her instructional role.

Similarly, it is difficult to have students consolidate their skills or strategies if the teacher or consulting student is too directive—not leaving the consolidating student ample control over the task—or if the tutor has failed to collaboratively establish learning goals and pace students' deliberate practice, with sensitivity and timeliness, on tasks they can perform with a high degree of success. It is also difficult to have students engage in consultation roles with others or with themselves in a setting where the teacher or assistant is reluctant to relinquish control of the task. For example, research indicates that students often discontinue consultative classroom discourse with peers when the teacher arrives on the scene to teach or to provide guidance (King, 1994; Langer, 1993). It is difficult for students to construct knowledge and strategies when the social discourse of the class and the questions and tests that the teacher employs only "pull for," assess, and reward the retrieval of facts and stored procedures (McGilly, 1994).

In order to develop mastery to the point of expertise, the teacher and students must fulfill several complementary roles. Table 6.1 provides a description of the respective roles for each learning setting. In subsequent chapters, we will provide detailed examples of how teachers can fulfill each role, as suggested by the research literature on teaching. For now, it is important to appreciate the *complementarity* of the teacher and student roles that are required to nurture student mastery. Our concern is that complementary relationships and opportunities should be available to all students, not just to the students who achieve above grade level. How this can be achieved is the focus of the rest of this book.

The continuum of acquiring, consolidating, and consulting roles should be thought of as just that—a continuum. These categories provide markers in the development of increased responsibility on the Y (self-direction) dimension, as students become their own teachers, as they take the voice of their instructor with them and transform it into their own.[1]

Learning Tasks

We have thus far considered the learning roles students have in different learning settings. For successful mastery in the X (skill/concept) and Z (planning/application) dimensions, learning settings with tasks focused on each dimension are needed. Students need to acquire, consolidate, and consult about task planning strategies just as they do about skills and concepts. Most areas of the curriculum are concerned both with skills and with applications or task planning. For example, students may be expected to construct language in the process of writing journals, stories, reports, etc. While writing, they continue to consolidate their basic writing skills (e.g., letter formation, spelling, punctuation), but also gain experience constructing stories, instructions, plans, and so on. In other content areas (e.g. social studies, natural sciences, etc.), there should be a similar sequence of acquisition, consolidation, and consultation roles, as students become progressively more independent in using acquired skills and concepts to construct new tasks or solve novel problems within the domain.

TABLE 6.1:
Teacher and Student Roles in Various Learning Settings

Setting	Teacher's Role	Student's Role
Acquisition Settings	Create an inviting learning environment. Prepare students for instruction. Use direct instruction (model, provide guidance, monitor, offer feedback). Calibrate the difficulty level (complexity) of tasks.	Be attentive and engaged. Observe and listen, and relate current instruction to what is already known. Learn instructional strategies.
Consolidation Settings	Carefully plan practice tasks on which students will have a 90% or higher success rate. Scaffold instruction (calibrate assistance and gradually fade supports). Use goal setting and praise student efforts. Monitor student performance and involve more competent peers as assistors. Reteach when necessary. Be sensitive to students' causal attributions. Bolster students' self-confidence.	Engage in repeated practice to the point of automaticity. Elicit and use feedback and supports. Monitor performance and engage in self-regulatory behaviors. Do homework (independent practice of skills already mastered). Accept and solicit help. Take credit for learning. Attribute improvement to effort and strategy use.
Consultation Settings	Use writing and have students engage in self-reflective thinking. Use peer teaching. Provide opportunities for students to explain to others how they perform a task. Use authentic tasks and assess students' metacognitive competence.	Be self-reflective (self-monitor, self-direct, self-evaluate). Consult with (assist) others. Assume more task responsibility and appropriate ownership. Plan and apply knowledge and strategies to new tasks and transfer skills to novel settings. Describe, explain, and justify approaches to others beyond the class. Display work publicly.

Students must be expected to assist others who are working on similar tasks, or to collaborate with others of similar competence with respect to the task. They may also be asked to reflect on their accomplishments, or on the work of others. The process of applying known skills to new tasks often involves much description, planning, problem solving, and construction. Being competent doesn't mean having all the answers—knowing all the right strategies and skills to use—in advance. It simply means being able to solve problems in a domain and to apply what is known to new tasks in novel settings.

There is a significant debate in the educational world concerning the relative priorities of skill-focused learning and planning- or application-focused learning. Without skills, students cannot construct tasks in new contexts; they cannot accomplish real-world tasks. If they cannot form letters and spell, they cannot write. If they cannot identify words, they cannot read. If they cannot carry out mathematical operations on large numbers, they cannot participate in activities that require such quantitative skills. On the other hand, if students are never expected to work on real problems—to plan tasks using these basic academic skills—we should not be surprised that they find much educational activity irrelevant, or that they fail to transfer their academic skills to the real world. Thus, learning tasks with an applied focus are also necessary to an effective educational environment. Students cannot be said to have mastered academic skills and concepts until they can, on their own, incorporate the skills and concepts in meaningful, authentic tasks. Students need to be given opportunities to apply what they have learned and to describe, explain, and justify their approaches.

Skill-Focused Tasks

Some school tasks are intended to highlight the performance and function of specific skills or concepts. Examples include exercises—both literal physical exercises, and written work—that highlight different skills, such as passages with cloze word alternatives, worksheets with many calculations of a specific type, educational games in which the competition (or cooperation) requires repeatedly performing target skills, and the like. Such tasks may be used both in aiding students to acquire new skills or concepts, and as a context for consolidation of skills and concepts. In addition, students who have become competent with a skill may consult about that skill by assisting others on such tasks, and by constructing similar tasks for others to use when consolidating the skill.

At present, skill-focused activities are often condemned in contrast to more applied activities, the latter being deemed more "relevant" or "authentic." While it is certainly true that a steady diet of skill-focused tasks can be mind-numbing, they do have their place as efficient, fairly quick methods for consolidating skills that can then be used in a variety of applied contexts. This is especially true if students are aware of the purpose and value of the skill-focused task. For example, many young learners can be observed spontaneously practicing baseball pitching, bicycle riding (when first learning), playing musical scales, etc. If this were all they ever did, bicycles, baseballs, and pianos would be very unpopular. However, for students with goals for using these skills, practice has its place.

Application-Focused Tasks

Not only must students acquire, consolidate, and consult about skills and concepts, they must also become able to apply what they know in the course of planning and accomplishing new tasks, and using similar tasks in different contexts (e.g., using dictionaries at home, not just at school). Teachers need to do more than just "train and hope" for generalization or transfer. They need to *explicitly instruct* how students can transfer what they have learned, and to reward students for engaging in transfer activities on authentic tasks.

Teachers also need to create learning settings where students develop "products" or public displays of their learning that will be of use beyond the classroom (having some aesthetic, utilitarian, or personal value) and that will be presented to an audience ("consumers") outside the classroom. Students must work on tasks that require them to integrate their skills and use strategies to construct and apply what they have learned. They need to work on some tasks that require authentic, real-life applications. In the context of presenting projects and portfolios of their work, students will be able to assume further consulting roles, as they are called upon to explain to people beyond the classroom what they have accomplished and how they carried out their task. As they plan tasks and apply skills, and as they assume consulting roles with regard to these applications, students develop mastery and expertise. In Chapter 10, we will consider the variety of ways in which teachers can engage students in application tasks, and why creating learning settings with application tasks is critical to success in schools.

Classroom Programs

At the beginning of this chapter, we asked how a teacher can foster high levels of self-direction on skills and strategies in several domains and with students of varying levels of achievement. Broadly speaking, our answer involves creating classroom programs that offer the range of tasks and roles that students need to build academic mastery.

A classroom *program* consists of the entire set of learning settings provided to students in a given classroom. The problem for teachers constructing classroom programs is moving students forward on skills and applications in several different academic domains, while ensuring that all or most students gain consultation experience leading to high self-direction. The basic solution involves designing learning settings in which most (if not all) students can consult about the skills they have learned, and settings in which most students apply consolidated skills in the process of planning and accomplishing new tasks. Most students should consult or take the lead on some of the tasks requiring planning or application to new settings. A second part of the solution involves providing tasks at varying levels of complexity (but *comparable levels of subjective difficulty*) for different students.

Now that we have described the various roles that students and teachers can assume, we can ask how teachers can create opportunities for students to adopt these varied roles. For example, if we visited your classroom, would we see you:

(a)   carefully engineering acquisition settings as you challenge and engage students to learn skills on calibrated tasks of varied difficulty?

(b)   thoughtfully orchestrating consolidation settings as you provide students with practice on tasks that they are able to perform?

(c)   challenging students to extend themselves to the edge of their abilities, while providing guidance and constructive feedback (i.e., actively monitoring students' performance and fading supports in response to students' increasing competence)?

(d)   skillfully setting up consultation settings (e.g., peer teaching tasks) and opportunities for self-reflection (e.g., student self-monitoring, journal writing about school tasks, keeping and presenting portfolios, involving parents, and the like)?

(e)   planfully ensuring that many of the preceding settings involve application-focused tasks generating authentic products for audiences other than those in the classroom?

Another way to ask these questions is to reflect on how you put together your program for the day, for the week, or for a unit of study. Do you think through ways you can create learning settings with varied roles for your students? Do you plan and monitor whether all your students have an ample mix of these various roles? Table 6.2 provides a lesson-plan outline we have used with teachers to help them reflect on their teaching practices in terms of the concepts of roles, tasks, and settings, and the ways they fit into the three-dimensional model of mastery.

It is important to recognize that in any classroom at any one time, various students may be in different roles. Some may be acquiring new skills or strategies under teacher guidance, and others may be in a consolidating role, practicing skills or application strategies. Still others may be in a consulting role, assisting classmates or younger students, or writing comments on how they performed tasks. Moreover, students will be assuming these roles with respect to

TABLE 6.2:
Analyzing The Potential of Learning Settings
to Nurture Student Mastery

1. **Name of Setting:** What do you call this setting (e.g., reading group, opening routine, gym class)?

2. **Purpose of Setting:** Why do you have this setting in your program? What student *skills*, *strategies*, and/or *self-directive roles* should change or become stronger as a result of students' participating in this setting? (We suspect that trying to foster change on all three areas at once for a given student may be ineffective.)

3. **Basic Academic Task in Setting:** The primary academic task at hand may be writing a journal, solving math problems, reading for comprehension, etc. (If some students are carrying out an assignment and others are helping, the basic academic task is the assignment itself.)

4. **Student Role(s) in the Setting:** Will students be *acquiring, consolidating,* or *consulting about* the skill or strategy being taught? Do different students have different roles?

5. **Prerequisite Skills:** What prerequisite skills are required for the students to perform the task in this setting? Consider what skills, knowledge and interests students possess that can be accessed and employed. Consider what missing skills seem to cause student problems. (These questions should be applied separately for each student role.)

6. **Prerequisite Strategies:** What prerequisite planning strategies are required for the students' task in this setting? Consider what missing strategies seem to cause student problems. (These questions should be applied separately for each student role.)

7. **Guidelines for Student Participation:** Will students be self-selected or teacher-selected? What basis will you use for selection?

8. **Teacher Role(s) in the Setting:** Are you primarily going to instruct, assist or scaffold, monitor, or collaboratively mentor? If you are instructing, how are you going to convey the skill, concept, or strategy being taught?

9. **Other Assistants:** Will anyone else be assisting or consulting in this setting? Who? What preparation do they have for this role?

10. **Mode of Interaction:** What will be the format for interactions (whole class, small groups, peer collaboration, independent seatwork)? If the interactions involve peer or cooperative work, indicate the type.

11. **Evaluation:** How (if at all) will the product or process be evaluated, and by whom (teacher, parent, peer, self)?

tasks of varying levels of skill required and varying levels of application or planning complexity.

As we have emphasized, *all* students need to experience teacher-directed (acquisition), mixed teacher-and-student-directed (consolidating), and primarily student-directed (consulting) learning settings. Each of these learning settings, with their accompanying teacher and student roles, have different educational objectives. Unfortunately, our review of the literature and our experience in schools indicates that in most schools, only the high-achieving students regularly experience these multiple roles. This pattern becomes more and more evident as students progress up the academic ladder. In many primary and intermediate grade schools, one can enter classrooms and see students assuming different learning roles in different learning settings, or see collaborative classwork and varied application tasks. But as students move into rotary programs, where grade-prescribed content drives the educational system, multiple learning settings and varied learning roles become quite infrequent. Often, in fact, multiple learning settings all but disappear when students reach the teacher-directed lecture formats of high school and college classes. (However, in college and university education there are frequently extra-classroom cooperative or laboratory activities that provide some framework for constructive tasks, and classroom seminars that foster genuine discussion. These discussions and the accompanying assignments focus less on skills and definitions and more on student application of skills and construction of knowledge.)

One way for teachers to foster student success is to cover less content, but to do so in more depth, and to ensure that many students have opportunities to describe, explain, teach, and apply what they have learned, rather than regurgitate this information in a form that has little value or meaning outside the classroom.

The three-dimensional model of mastery highlights the need for teachers to:

(a) provide students with a variety of diverse learning settings and roles in which they can acquire and consolidate increasingly complex skills, on their own;

(b) extend the range of tasks and situations in which students can independently apply what they have learned; and

(c) challenge students to plan and undertake new tasks, and to generate novel strategies of their own while doing so.

Table 6.3 illustrates a week in the classroom life of a third-grade student who is engaged in both skill-focused and application-focused tasks.

TABLE 6.3:
An Analysis of One Student's Learning Tasks and Roles

In the course of a week, Joan, a third-grade student, learned new reading and math skills, practiced drill exercises, had a lesson on writing newspaper stories, wrote a newspaper report of the previous week's class trip (with editorial assistance from a classmate), played a math game, helped a first-grade student read, read a story in her own reader (with assistance available from a fifth-grade "consultant"), discussed the story in a reciprocal teaching group, and worked collaboratively with a group on a science project. (Note that the total classroom time available was about 4.2 hours per day. The rest was taken up by transitions and out-of-classroom activities, not under the teacher's control.) Let us analyze Joan's week in terms of the concepts offered in this chapter. How much time did Joan spend acquiring, consolidating, consulting, and applying her skills?

Skill-Focused Tasks (learning and using new skills)		Sessions	Total Time
Acquisition Roles	Learned reading skills	2	0.7 hrs.
	Learned math skills	2	0.7 hrs.
	Learned spelling and vocabulary skills	2	1.0 hrs.
Consolidation Roles	Played math game	4	2.0 hrs.
	Practiced on math drills	4	1.3 hrs.
	Work on spelling/vocabulary with partner	4	1.0 hrs.
Consultation Roles	Helped a first-grade student read	2	1.0 hrs.
	Skill-Focused, Total:		**7.7 hrs.**

Application-Focused Tasks (learning and using strategies for planning tasks)			
Acquisition Roles	Learned strategies for writing newspaper stories	1	0.7 hrs.
	Learned reading comprehension strategies	2	1.0 hrs.
	Reviewed math problems, discussed and learned strategies for solving	2	1.0 hrs.
	Performed a science project task	2	0.7 hrs.
Consolidation Roles	Read independently	5	2.5 hrs.
	Read with a fifth-grade assistant	2	0.7 hrs.
	Wrote a newspaper article	2	2.0 hrs.
	Worked on math problems	3	1.3 hrs.
Consultation Roles	Discussed a story in a reciprocal teaching group	2	0.7 hrs.
	Worked collaboratively on science project	2	2.0 hrs.
	Application-Focused, Total:		**12.3 hrs.**

Implications of Mastery Development for Classroom Programs

It is virtually impossible for teachers to simultaneously address all of the educational needs we have discussed. Both teachers and students need to prioritize their instructional objectives and ensure a balanced distribution of learning roles for all students, regardless of their level of skill and strategy development. In order to accomplish these goals, teachers need to effectively distribute their efforts and time. Acquisition learning settings require a good deal of teacher participation, while consolidation and consultation settings require teachers to monitor students' performance and then provide constructive feedback as needed. A reasonable program solution is for teachers to spend much of their time (perhaps 50%) working with students in acquisition settings. Students, however, should probably spend no more than 25% of their working time in any one curriculum domain in acquisition settings, leaving time for consolidation and consultation in that domain. This means that much of the time, students will not be working directly with their teacher. Students can be taught and encouraged to assume more responsibilities, enlisting the help of peers and resources such as dictionaries, guidebooks, procedural prompts, computers, videotape modeling films, and the like. Students can also be given opportunities to work together on authentic tasks that require prolonged group problem-solving, and can be required to provide descriptions of the processes involved in performing academic tasks.

Classroom programs can have many learning settings, each with different tasks and roles, operating at one time. Teachers can use the support of others (resource teachers, peers, parents, computers) to create these varied settings. They can give students greater choice and responsibility by explaining to them the three-dimensional model of mastery, and indicating the *how, why,* and *when*— as well as the *what*—of the content being taught.

We believe it is logistically impossible to accomplish all of these teaching objectives for every student in every academic domain every day, or even every week. Having said this, we also believe that it *is* possible to ensure that more significant amounts of consulting and work on application tasks are incorporated into the classroom for all (or most) students each week, or at least over the course of a study unit.

We recognize that it would be extremely difficult to operate several different learning settings in the context of a rotary program with short periods (periods of than 60 to 75 minutes). Teachers working in rotary programs need to consider varying student roles on different days and creating out-of-class learning settings (e.g., homework groups)—and the school should probably consider modifying the schedule by making rotary periods longer.

How much time do students need in acquiring, consolidating, and consulting roles? How much time do they need applying skills on authentic tasks as opposed to learning new skills and concepts? We don't know, nor do we know how many mastery dimensions (skills, self-direction, and application) can be effectively addressed in a single setting for a particular child. As we discussed in Chapter 4, we do know that students who succeed in school receive and help create more opportunities to function in each of these diverse learning settings, and that they spend more time and expend more effort than other students fulfilling the acquiring, consolidating, and consulting roles. Successful students receive more opportunities to teach what they know to others, and more time to apply their knowledge on new authentic tasks. The high-achieving students not only acquire the skills and knowledge to perform academic activities, but most importantly, they also develop the self-confidence and feelings of self-efficacy needed to undertake new tasks that test and extend their knowledge and competence. In the absence of such a sense of mastery, the possession of skills is of limited value.

Implications of Individual Achievement Differences for Mastery-Oriented Programs

We have stressed that students' levels of skill achievement set a limit on the tasks that they can perform and consult about, and on the complexity of problems or novel tasks to which they can successfully generalize learned skills and strategies. Students cannot reach high levels of self-direction on tasks involving skills they can't perform, and cannot consult on or generalize skills that have not been consolidated. How can a teacher in a classroom of 25 to 30 students assure high levels of mastery experience for students who vary by three or four grade levels in skill and application achievement? One answer that has been offered is to assign students tasks that match or slightly exceed their performance levels and to provide them with scaffolded assistance. In the case of settings with consulting roles, however, we believe that the consulting students should be asked to perform tasks that fall well within their level of competence. One controversial way to match task demands to student achievement is ability grouping, which we address in the following section.

The Place of Ability Grouping

As noted in Chapter 4, a number of critics have emphasized the negative status effects of ability grouping, both within and between classes. These critics suggest that whole-class or heterogeneously grouped instruction is preferable. Critics including Mosteller et al. (1996) report that highly skilled students benefit the most from groupings, while medium- and low-ability students learn more from whole-class instruction than from skills-based groupings. On the positive side, Slavin and his colleagues (Slavin, 1987b; Gutierrez & Slavin, 1992) report that under conditions of careful monitoring and individual accountability, grouping can improve the performance of all students.

Reviews of the achievement research literature indicate that, at least at the elementary level, math and reading performance are enhanced by instruction that is geared to student ability levels. As Slavin notes, ability grouping has beneficial effects when students are (a) temporarily regrouped on the basis of specific assessed areas of skill, (b) taught at levels commensurate with their assessed skills, and (c) assessed in the specific skill areas that are being taught.

No similar achievement benefits of "streaming" have been demonstrated at the high school level—perhaps because in the context of high school subjects, instruction *truly geared to student achievement* has not been compared to non-ability-grouped instruction. Also, sometimes high school instruction is "streamed" by students dropping out and by use of different schools for different populations. These hidden types of streaming make comparisons of student progress in different instructional approaches very difficult.

Another fundamental issue in the ability grouping debate involves variations in the quality of instruction received by students of differing achievement levels. Unfortunately, there is evidence that streaming is often associated with poorer quality instruction for less-advanced students (Oakes, 1992). As noted, the heart of our argument is that *all* students should receive the range of acquisition, consolidation, and consultation roles now enjoyed by able students. We also believe that the quality of instruction should be equally distributed.

There are many ways of differentiating instruction to meet student needs. What remains clear to us is that confronting students with skills and tasks that they don't understand *cannot* result in independent mastery of academic skills. Neither can leaving many students in the position of continuously needing others' help to accomplish tasks. Critics of ability grouping have correctly identified problems associated with the quality of instruction offered to less-able students, and with the emotional consequences of being in the low group. They have yet to demonstrate that other more effective alternatives exist. As Oakes (1992) writes:

> Currently we have a growing body of anecdotes about detracking in schools that have reorganized into heterogeneous teams of teachers and students, developed integrated, thematic curricula, used mixed-ability cooperative learning strategies, experimented with more personalized assessment techniques, to name just a few techniques. Yet we need research that provides systematic accounts of these efforts and evidence about how each of these strategies works within a school's overall detracking effort (p. 17).

We do not wish to justify or perpetuate the poor instruction that now occurs in many streamed programs. But we do agree with Oakes that educators have yet to provide effective approaches for dealing with the half to two thirds of students who do not excel at academic skills.

Generally, we believe that the solution may lie in perceiving individual differences as differences in how long it takes students to reach real mastery of academic skills and strategies—at least those mastered by able students at the end of sixth to eighth grades.[2] We think it is possible that if we varied the age of entry into high-school programs and varied the course loads in high school, a large majority of students could complete high school with a high degree of academic mastery.[3] The net result would be more competent and expert graduates who would differ somewhat in age at graduation. This would be useful if what our society truly wants is a larger group of people who can use academic skills in a wide range of real situations. On the other hand, if what our society is seeking is a basis for excluding an increasing number of citizens from economic opportunities, our mastery-oriented approach would not be helpful!

The bleak picture of one half to two thirds of students not maximizing their academic potential *need not be the case.* If teachers could learn to treat this majority of students in the same engaging and challenging fashion that they now treat the high-achieving students, many students could more fully develop their expertise. We now have some understanding of how teachers can effectively help students acquire and consolidate skills, as described in Chapters 7 and 8; how they ensure that their students become self-reflective learners and can teach what they learn to others, as described in Chapter 9; and how they can arrange for their students to apply what they know to tasks beyond the classroom, as described in Chapter 10. In the following chapters, we turn our attention to specific, practical ways teachers can achieve these objectives.

Summary

Our call that all students be given learning opportunities to fulfill multiple roles of acquiring, consolidating, and consulting about skills and strategies, and to work on both skill-focused and authentic application-focused tasks, should be put into historical perspective. For the last 100 years, while some educators (e.g., William Bennett, Linda Darling-Hammond) have urged the merits of a "back-to-basics" curriculum, national tests of academic standards (especially in math and reading), grade-level benchmark performance measures, and accompanying calls for accountability, other educators have urged a holistic, relevance-oriented teaching approach in the tradition of John Dewey, John Goodlad, Jerome Bruner, and others. This latter group raises concerns that national testing will lead teachers to "teach to the test" so their students do not end up on the bottom of the comparative heap—with meaningful education falling victim to the chopping block of accountability. (There is substantial evidence of "teaching to the test" and other forms of dishonestly modifying test results; Biemiller, 1993.) They raise questions about what happens *after* the tests are administered and the results are in. How do test results help to close the educational gap between the high- and the low-achieving students? In response, those who focus on setting standards point to the fact that "holistic" education does not result in measurably improved performance (Cunningham & Allington, 1994; Engleman & Carnine, 1982).

Our proposed three-dimensional model of mastery and the related concepts of learning settings, learning tasks, and learning roles emphasize the need to combine and balance features of both the skill-focused and the holistic-focused positions. If students are going to achieve, they need to be able to perform learned skills and understand concepts, they need opportunities to apply skills while constructing tasks, and they need opportunities to guide others and themselves while performing these tasks. Progress in all of these areas can be assessed. When educators limit teaching and/or assessment to only one of these dimensions of academic progress, the others usually suffer, and student mastery of the domain is compromised. This loss is particularly pronounced when we enforce unrealistic expectations that all or most students should progress at the same rate on the skill, application, and self-direction dimensions.

Our preferred solution, as we emphasize in the remainder of this book, involves maintaining a focus both on skills development and on authentic, applied tasks in various academic domains. We also stress the importance of bringing students to high levels of self-direction with skills and application strategies they have learned. What are the best teaching approaches to help students acquire, consolidate, and consult about their new skills and application strategies? We now turn our attention to effective approaches for acquiring skills and strategies (Chapter 7), consolidating skills and strategies (Chapter 8), moving to consultative levels of self-direction (Chapter 9), and applying strategies to authentic tasks (Chapter 10).

Endnotes

1. This pedagogical suggestion about students becoming self-directed is consistent with the views of the Russian psychologist Lev Vygotsky, who proposed that the acquisition and mastery of skills and strategies is essentially a social process. As he observed, "the ways in which we talk and interact with other people become 'internalized' and change the ways we think and behave" (Vygotsky, 1962, 1978). Language and other reflective forms of mental representation provide the means by which such communal interactions take place.

2. This approach was first proposed by Carroll (1963) and elaborated by Benjamin Bloom in his book *Human Characteristics and Social Learning* (1976). It is the underlying premise of the "mastery learning movement" in education (Carnine, 1994). Unfortunately, proponents of mastery learning (1) have tended to be entirely skill-focused, ignoring other aspects of mastery, and (2) have, at least in Bloom's case, sought to equalize student performance *within a grade* by providing high levels of tutorial support and practice on skills. As Carroll (1989) notes, this attempt to equate students within grades contradicts the original concept, and no convincing evidence that it can be done has been put forward.

3. We must note that there is a limit to the degree that developmental differences can be equalized by time. At present, we estimate that roughly 60 to 80 percent of students could reach similar levels of academic mastery, given sufficient time and a full range of mastery settings. Students at the extremes of achievement, both high and low, may continue to differ significantly.

Chapter Seven

Planning and Implementing Acquisition Settings

In Chapter 5, we introduced our model of mastery, showing that as students master part of an area of curriculum, they move from *acquiring* new skills and new strategies, to *consolidating* those skills and strategies, and to *consulting* about the skills and strategies. In Chapter 6, we examined the settings in which students learn, including the tasks, student roles, and teacher roles in those settings. In some settings, students have acquiring roles; they learn new skills and strategies. Other settings provide students with consolidation roles—opportunities to practice recently acquired skills and strategies on tasks at which they are likely to succeed. Students should also participate in settings in which they have consulting roles—in which they can effectively assist others, collaborate with others to plan tasks, or "consult" with themselves by consciously reviewing their own work.

In this chapter, we focus on planning and implementing learning settings in which students learn new skills and strategies. We are concerned with skills and strategies that are unlikely to be acquired without direct instruction and intentional learning.[1] For example, few students learn to identify printed words, write words, count, calculate, or solve problems without some explicit instruction. We will consider how teachers can help students move from being essentially "clueless" about how to perform an academic task to being "informed novices" who engage in deliberate practice. We will focus on instructional strategies designed to help students develop skills and the accompanying vocabulary, concepts, and application or planning strategies. Educational researchers have learned a great deal about how teachers can use direct instruction to help students acquire skills and strategies. In this chapter, we consider what teachers should do:

a) *Before* working with children in an acquisition setting;
b) *At the outset* of a lesson—introducing content to be learned;
c) *During* the lesson—actual instruction;

d)   *When closing* the lesson—reflecting with students on what was learned;

e)   *After* working with children in an acquisition setting.

Before Working With Children in an Acquisition Setting

It is important that teachers be clear in their own minds about the objectives of the acquisition setting, and how those objectives relate to their students' progress in this component of the curriculum. If teachers can clearly define what is to be learned and why, they will be in a better position to explain this to their students, and to monitor their progress. In addition to defining their objectives for an acquisition setting or lesson, it is important that teachers be aware of relevant skills or knowledge that they are assuming students have (or know that they lack), and that they have decided how to organize students for instruction.

Defining What Is to Be Learned

Prior to engaging in instruction with students, teachers need to ask themselves two main questions:

* At the end of this period of instruction, what skills and concepts will students be able to perform or use, and what strategies will they be able to understand and apply that they are not able to understand and apply now?

* In what situations, in and out of school, should the learners use the new skills, concepts, and strategies?

This focus on end results will encourage teachers and students to highlight not only how and when to perform skills and strategies, but also why these skills and strategies are important to learn—how these skills and strategies fit into the bigger picture.

Relevant Previous Experience

Learning rarely occurs in a vacuum. Try to think of recent in-school or out-of-school experiences or tasks for which students needed the skills or strategies that are being taught. If it is difficult to come up with examples, or if many students lack such experiences, it may be important to create such experiences prior to teaching the skill or strategy. Teachers should review or create a problem which calls for the use of the skill to be acquired (e.g., reading passages that contain new words to be learned, math problems that involve larger numbers than the students have previously used, etc.).

Prerequisite Skills and Concepts

Frequently, lessons fail because students lack skills or terms that their teachers assume they possess. Teachers need to be aware of what their students know, as well as what they don't know. To a large degree, this is the point we are emphasizing in discussing differences in student ability. If some students can't profit from a lesson because it presupposes skills or knowledge they lack, those students will require an additional lesson to overcome their lack of knowledge. For example, observation of many mathematics lessons suggest that some students' lack of understanding of the number system and the place-value system contributes to their failures in learning new operations or using quantitative representation. Similarly, student vocabulary limitations contribute to comprehension failures and failures to build new vocabulary when reading challenging texts without assistance. Thus, it is important for teachers to be aware of the ways in which students' present skills and knowledge will affect their learning of the new skills or strategies that are going to be introduced.

In some cases, prior to introducing new skills, it may be possible to *preview* and *preteach* needed prerequisite skills. In other cases, it may be more appropriate to group students according to prior skills and knowledge, and to move each group forward as fast as possible. We recognize that such ability grouping is not currently popular. Often disadvantaged students wind up being taught too slowly or simply dismissed as not capable. However, our own extended observations and studies—summarized by Robert Slavin, Frederick Mosteller, and their colleagues—suggest that many students make slower progress than they might because instruction is not geared to what they know and can do (Slavin, 1987; Gutierrez & Slavin, 1992; Mosteller et al., 1996). Mosteller and his colleagues argue that

> Based on the extremely limited evidence now available, [cross-age ability grouping for reading] might work especially well for students with less developed skills. Similar remarks apply to within-class skill grouping. But again, the troubling reality is that the extensive research work has not yet been done (1996, p. 813).

Students differ in prior knowledge and in how fast they learn. We should make greater efforts to equalize prior knowledge early in schooling. Sharon Griffin and Robbie Case's *Rightstart* program illustrates how this can be done in kindergarten for mathematics (as discussed in Chapter 11). Similarly, Vellutino and Scanlon (1987) have illustrated how providing students with stronger phonemic awareness in kindergarten reduces reading difficulties for a large percentage of students predicted to have reading problems in first grade.

Even when greater efforts are made to equalize early experience, there will be continuing differences in student progress. If most students are to experience success in learning, there must be settings in which they can build on what they learn, rather than being dragged along by the pace of their faster-learning peers or by a preset curriculum.

Organization and Selection of Instructional Groups

Learning settings can involve instructional units ranging from whole-class instruction, to small groups, to one-on-one tutoring. In whole-class settings, teachers can rarely assume either that all students possess relevant prerequisite skills or strategies, or that all need to learn the skills or strategies being taught. And while tutorial methods are often effective for the individual being taught, they are not logistically feasible in the context of most classrooms. (For example, if a teacher has 20 students for roughly 20 hours a week, a purely tutorial approach would provide each student with one hour a week of instruction and 19 hours on his or her own.) Prior to beginning instruction, teachers must decide how to group their students (whole class or subgroups). If subgroups are to be formed, teachers must decide how students will be selected (e.g., on the basis of skill level or social compatibility).

In most cases, acquisition settings are best conducted with groups of students who have acquired the relevant prerequisite skills and knowledge and have some understanding of why they need the skills or strategies being taught (Slavin, 1996). This is particularly true when new skills or concepts are being taught. When new problem-solving strategies are being taught, it is important that students have the skills that will be used in the new tasks being planned, or that teachers or others provide assistance with missing skills. (These can involve words to be read or defined, math operations, procedures for using computers, etc.) In some cases, these needed skills will be learned in this problem-solving context (especially word recognition, definitions, and computer skills). In other cases, additional skill-focused instruction may be needed.

In order to achieve these objectives, teachers must also make decisions about what materials, tasks, and activities can be used most effectively to teach skills. Often students in the same classroom are working simultaneously on different tasks, or are working on the same task with varied learning objectives or supports.

At the Outset of a Lesson: Introducing Content to be Learned

The actual lesson begins with an introductory phase in which students are informed about what is to be learned, reminded of what they already know, and hopefully motivated to care about learning the new material. Teachers need to prepare students for the acquisition of new knowledge, skills, and strategies by:

a)   providing advance organizers (verbal, visual, and metaphorical);
b)   using informed instruction;
c)   accessing and activating the students' prior knowledge; and
d)   assessing the students' misconceptions that could interfere with their task engagement and performance.

We will briefly consider how teachers can incorporate each of these preparatory instructional steps, and why doing so is important.

Providing Advance Organizers

Advance organizers provide frameworks to help students recognize the relationships among concepts and procedures. Advance organizers help students better understand what they are about to learn and why, and provide the "big picture" of what will be taught. They also clarify how new knowledge, skills, and strategies follow from what students have learned in the past and how they will help students achieve future goals. Teachers need to provide a rationale, or to contextualize learning, so that students can see each lesson or unit as part of an evolving story.

Advance organizers should do more than convey mere facts about tasks and activities; they should also include information about motivational factors that influence performance. Research has indicated that teachers are most successful in facilitating learning when they present academic tasks as challenges and when they convey enthusiasm for what is being taught (Lepper, Aspinwall, Mumme, & Chabay, 1990). For example, teachers may convey to their students that a topic (or strategy) being taught is not usually taught until later in the school year, or until higher grade levels. While presenting students with challenges, the teacher needs to convey an optimism that with assistance, practice, and effort, the students will be able to make progress. The teacher can demonstrate or highlight what students should be able to do when they have mastered these skills and strategies. Such motivational statements set the stage for the students' task engagement, as described in Highlight Box 7.1.

Highlight Box 7.1
ADVANCE ORGANIZERS

Advance organizers can be verbal, visual, or metaphorical. Examples of verbal advance organizers include the following types of statements:

- "Let me begin by explaining what we are going to do today and why."
- "We are learning this because …"
- "Once we learn this we will be able to …"
- "Let me show you how what we are learning follows from [relates to, builds upon] what we have learned so far."
- "When you learn how to … you will be able to …"
- "It should look like this [show example]."

As students become more knowledgeable, teachers can ask *them* to provide various pieces of information, asking questions such as:

- "How is what we are learning like what we learned about …?"
- "Who can tell us why we are learning how to …?"
- "How will this help us to …?"

Students may be asked to work in small groups to prepare advance organizers to present during the next day's class. Teachers need to be careful to ensure that students of all levels of competence have an opportunity to answer such questions.

Teachers can also use visual advance organizers in the form of semantic webs, mind (concept) maps, procedural flow charts, time lines, and outlines, in order to help students diagram the relationships between various main ideas and procedures. The teacher can convey that "drawing certain types of pictures helps me see what I am thinking and helps me to understand better." In Chapter 9, we will consider various written forms of advance organizers that nurture students' reflective activities.

Whether the advance organizer is written or verbal, teachers need to be sensitive to the issue of *timing*. It is important that teachers not overwhelm students with too much information too early. Teachers need to tailor the use of advance organizers to the students' developmental stages of mastery.

Yet another way to provide students with advance organizers is to use metaphors. Research indicates that students often learn more and retain information longer if it is conveyed in the form of metaphors, analogies, or short, relevant, anecdotal stories, than if the same information is conveyed directly (Guthrie & Alao, 1997; Guthrie & Cox, 1996). We have observed teachers employ a number of metaphors to set the stage for learning. For example, math teachers have compared learning mathematics to learning a foreign language; this can help students understand the translation of word problems into the math symbol system, a different type of language. We have watched reading teachers encourage their students to view themselves as "detectives" who search for clues—e.g., telling students the information can be found right there in the story, by thinking and searching, or by using background information (Raphael & Pearson, 1985). We have watched writing teachers encourage their students to see themselves as "architects" or "builders" who follow a blueprint and have a tool kit with fix-up strategies (Duffy, 1993; Duffy & Roehler, 1987a, 1987b). Staying with the building metaphor, teachers have educated their students about their own instructional role by introducing the metaphor of scaffolding, to explain why it is important for the teacher to fade supports and assistance so students can become their own teachers or coaches. Some teachers even discuss with their classes what makes someone a good coach or helper. As we will consider in Chapter 9, such discussions provide the basis for students to learn how to become effective peer tutors and collaborators.

In preparing students to deal with possible setbacks and failures that are inherent in the learning process, teachers have asked students, "When do scientists learn the most?" Often, as the teachers explain, scientists learn the most when the experiments they perform don't work. In this way, teachers encourage students to view failures and setbacks as learning opportunities. In short, teachers can be good story tellers, as they spin tales of how students can prepare, plan, monitor, and cope with both failures and successes. Often teachers embellish their stories with personal anecdotal teaching stories.

In order for such metaphors to be useful, teachers need to employ them throughout the lesson (e.g., when praising a student for being a good detective who searches for clues, or for being a good coach who gives her partner hints and not just answers). The teacher should employ only a few metaphors, and then monitor whether students spontaneously use them.

Why should teachers make the effort to include verbal, visual, and metaphorical advance organizers as part of their instructions? There are several reasons:

- Advance organizers motivate students to engage in academic tasks by highlighting the relevance and value of what they are learning.

- Advance organizers help students link new information to existing knowledge and skills.

- Advance organizers put lessons and units into context (i.e., "This lesson follows from … and leads to …").

- Advance organizers convey both a challenge and optimism to students.

Using Informed Instruction

While advance organizers provide students with an overall framework (the "big picture"), *informed instruction* provides students with specific lesson details and explicitly conveys specific teacher expectations. Informed instruction can be provided at the outset of a lesson, but like advance organizers, key features of informed instruction can be repeated throughout the lesson as teachers monitor students' progress. Students may be encouraged to record this information in their daily journals (as described in Chapter 9). Informed instruction should include information about:

a) what will be taught and the reasons why it will be taught;
b) how it will be taught (e.g., independent seat work, homework, peer tutoring);
c) how and when to use a skill or strategy, and when not to use it; and
d) ways to identify, anticipate, avoid, and address difficulties that students may encounter.

As part of informed instruction, the teacher should translate unfamiliar vocabulary into language that students are familiar with, and should preview or preteach new concepts. The teacher can tell students, "I would like to teach you something that will help you help yourself ... (write good stories, solve math problems, spell better, etc.)."

In order for instruction to be "informed," teachers can preview the lesson with the following types of comments:

* "Our goal is ..."
* "Today we will be continuing with ..."
* "Let's get started with ... Then we will ..."
* "What we are learning is called ..."
* "What I expect you to do with this material is to ... (recall, use, apply, teach, etc.)"
* "Possible difficulties you might have are ..."

Each of these statements can eventually be reframed as a question that can be posed to students, e.g., "What difficulties [procedural bugs or tricky parts] do we have to watch out for?" "What are some things we might forget to do?" The importance of including such information in informed instruction was underscored by the research reported in Chapter 2 by Hegarty and Chi and their colleagues, who demonstrated that students who did poorly on math and physics problems failed to consider the deep structure of problems. Teachers need to anticipate these possible errors as part of the informed instruction.

Another way to provide informed instruction is to post organizational sentences on the blackboard or on a chart that students can help complete. Possible structures for these sentences include the following.

- "Today we are learning ..."
- "We are learning how to ... by ..."
- "We are learning this so that ..."
- "In order to ..., we need to learn how (when) to ..."
- "This fits in with what we learned about ..."
- "You will know you have learned this when you can ..."

Teachers need to sample from this list in order not to overwhelm students with too much information at one time, and they can review this information over the course of the lesson or the unit.

Access and Activate Students' Prior Knowledge

Learning is the result of the interplay between existing knowledge and new information gathered through interactions with the external world (teachers, peers, computer programs, resource material, etc.). Learning does not occur by passive absorption. Students approach new tasks with prior knowledge, expectations, and beliefs, and they assimilate new information and construct their own meaning. Therefore, it is necessary for teachers to determine what students know and believe about a topic, skill, or strategy to be taught. The teacher can obtain this information by means of paper and pencil tests (e.g., quizzes, questionnaires, solutions to simple problems) that indicate what students know and what they need to be taught. A second assessment approach is to use direct questions, such as:

- "What do you already know about ... ?"
- "Have you seen something like this before? When? Please give an example."
- "How do we know when we should ... ?"
- "How can you use what you learned about ... to ... ?"
- "Did anyone do this before? How is this like ... ?"
- "Based on what you know, what would you like to find out about ...?"

Research indicates that students are more likely to learn a skill when they can relate the material that is being presented to something they already know (Anderson et al., 1995, 1996). New material should be presented in familiar, concrete contexts that allows learners to draw on their experiential knowledge. For example, students are more likely to solve problems involving fractions when they are presented in the context of dividing up pizzas among friends than in the context of abstract questions regarding the sectioning of circles.

Teachers should routinely ask students to share what they already know about a given subject or strategy. In this way students can come to see the link between relevant background information and the lesson goals. This discussion is also useful in revealing any student misconceptions that might interfere with the acquisition and implementation of skills and strategies. Students' beliefs may inhibit them from task engagement and contribute to their abandoning tasks at the first signs of difficulties.

Assess Students' Potential Misconceptions

Another way to tap the students' possible misconceptions and attitudes is to ask students to explain the basis of their incorrect or unattempted work. For example, some students may hold beliefs (misconceptions) like the following:

- "Solving math problems should not take more than just a few minutes. If I don't get it right away, there is no sense on working on it further."
- "Some students have the ability to do math and others don't."

Sometimes students' misunderstandings are about specific concepts and are the result of gaps in students' conceptual knowledge. For example, some students think multiplication always means "more" and "bigger"—even when multiplying with decimals—or that if they see the word *more* in a word problem, they have to add. Teachers should address such misconceptions as they arise (if not beforehand), and help students identify and alter them. Teachers can have students perform personal experiments and use manipulatives in order to test their beliefs.

Teachers can also address students' misconceptions by conducting class discussions on specific topics, addressing questions such as the following:

- Why do some students do better on math (reading, writing) than others?
- Why is "I can" more important than IQ?
- Why does School Success = Knowledge + Strategy Use + Practice + Effort?

It is important for teachers to address students' beliefs explicitly, because providing them with new information usually does not replace their prior misconception; rather, students merely add new knowledge onto their already existing misconceptions (Bransford et al., 1991).

During the Lesson: Actual Instruction

A major adage in education is that if you want students to learn something, you should teach it to them directly. While this instructional principle may seem self-evident, it is surprising how often it is *not followed* in schools. As a prominent illustration, consider a classroom observational study conducted by Durkin (1978). She examined 4469 minutes of reading instruction in grade 4 classrooms. Of these 4469 minutes, how many minutes do you think teachers spent on comprehension instruction? Would you believe *only 20 minutes*? Most of the instructional time involved the teachers asking questions, but the teachers spent little time teaching students specific comprehension strategies that they could use to answer these questions. This instructional approach particularly penalizes those students who are struggling with reading. This finding takes on specific significance when we consider that by grade 5, most student reading is done silently, with little explicit reading instruction taking place. A similar pattern is evident at grade 3, where there is often inadequate direct instruction in word attack skills, which some slower students still require. Critics of classroom instruction have also noted the limited direct instruction in other academic areas, such as math and writing (Engleman & Carnine, 1982; Rosenshine & Meister, 1996).

In acquisition (direct instruction) settings, once the new skill or strategy has been introduced, the skill or strategy is *demonstrated*, task-relevant language is *modeled*, and students are *guided* to perform the skill or strategy and to participate in observing/guiding others. Finally, students are guided to evaluate their performance outcomes.

What features of direct instruction should teachers include as a part of their classroom routines? Direct instruction includes explicit, clear instructions, modeling, re-explanations, modeling again, goal setting, deliberate practice with teacher guidance, procedural prompts, continual teacher monitoring, corrective feedback, and the use of cognitive empathy, relapse prevention, and praise. Table 7.1 provides an overall procedural checklist of the steps involved in the direct instruction of skills, concepts, and strategies.

We will consider, in more detail, several of these procedures, namely:

a) cognitive modeling or think-aloud procedures;

TABLE 7.1: Procedural Steps Involved in Direct Instruction

1. *Provide clear instructions* of what the students will be asked to do and why. (Use advance organizers and informed instruction.)

2. *Relate* what students are being asked to do to what they have done in the past and to their future goals. (Access and activate students' prior knowledge.)

3. State *specific goals and subgoals* clearly, and *convey teacher expectations* explicitly.

4. Present the task or activity as a *challenge*.

5. *Cognitively model* (using think-alouds) the steps involved in performing simplified versions of the task. (Ensure that the think-aloud is in the form of an interactive dialogue, not a monologue.)

6. *Assess students' readiness* for instruction and preteach vocabulary and concepts (when feasible).

7. *Calibrate the level of difficulty* of the task so it matches or slightly exceeds the students' current level of competence.

8. *Manipulate the task difficulty level* directly or indirectly by providing hints, prompts, or supports, or by providing students with choices in the selection of tasks.

9. Continually *monitor the students' progress and efforts* and re-explain, model again, and reteach as needed. (During guided performance, you should roam—observe, probe, help students think through solutions, and cue them to use strategies.)

10. *Assess students' comprehension* to ensure that they understand how a specific skill or strategy works, when and under what circumstances it is most appropriate to use, what it requires of the student, and how it can be deployed on tasks and in contexts different from those in which it was first learned. Build in concerns for transfer from the outset.

11. *Use multiple exemplars and manipulatives* when providing instruction.

12. *Anticipate possible student errors,* and *correct any misunderstandings or misconceptions* immediately. Use relapse prevention in anticipation of how students can handle failures and setbacks and look upon them as learning opportunities.

13. *Solicit students' think-alouds* in order to identify when and where they are struggling. Provide graduated supports.

14. Engage students in deliberate *guided practice, goal setting,* and *self-monitoring.*

15. *Conduct reviews of learning and task accomplishment* after the task or activity and reteach necessary skills and strategies.

16. Ensure that students *take credit* for performance gains (attribute improvement to their strategy usage and their personal efforts).

17. Encourage and teach students to develop *self-evaluative skills* so they can become their own teachers.

b) strategy instruction;
c) self-instructional training;
d) procedural prompts; and
e) guided performance.

Cognitive Modeling: Think-Aloud Procedures

The actual demonstration component of an acquisition session usually involves both physically performing the skill or skills involved in the task, and verbally guiding oneself (thinking out loud—demonstrating self-regulation overtly) while carrying out the task. For example, in demonstrating a particular phonic skill, the teacher might read a piece of text, then illustrate "sounding out" a word (e.g., *bat*). She might then demonstrate sounding out several other words with the same letter-sound component (e.g., *mat*, *rat*, *hat*). In a well-planned lesson, she would continue with the text, soon encountering another -*at* word, and asking the students to sound out the word.

Teachers' think-alouds may be in the form of *self-questioning* ("What information do I need?"; "Have I checked my work?") or *self-instructional directive statements* ("My first step is ..."; "This is not the answer I expected; I'd better go back and recheck my steps"). Think-alouds can describe the various steps of the problem-solving process and highlight the importance of each step. Teachers should pace the modeling (so as not to overwhelm students) with what they think before, during, and after completing a task.

A think-aloud should be an interactive dialogue, rather then a monologue. While modeling, the teacher may request that students suggest the next step. For example, the teacher might say, "Well, what we might do now is ...", or "That does not work, so I'll try ..." then pause, allowing students to finish the statement, and then continue to model the parts of the task that students are unable to complete. The amount of teacher modeling is gradually diminished as students develop competence and take on greater responsibility.

In skill-focused lessons, "tasks" are typically highly simplified, involving little more than performance of the skill to be acquired. When task planning is involved, an overt self-dialogue—asking oneself and answering strategic questions—is necessary. For example, a teacher might illustrate a writing strategy, and eventually use an interactive dialogue with students:

> Let's see. I need a character—I'll call her Susie—who has a problem.
> What can Susie's problem be? I know—she lost her kitten.
> *[Teacher writes, "Once upon a time, there was a little girl named Susie.*

She loved to play with her kitten. But one day, she couldn't find the kitten."]

Now, Susie wants to find her kitten. So what does she do?

[Teacher solicits ideas from children at this point, and writes, "She looked in her room. But the kitten wasn't there."]

Now, in most stories, the character solves her problem. How is Susie going to solve her problem? Maybe this time the kitten will solve the problem.

[Teacher writes, "Then Susie heard something go 'Meow!' It came from her closet. She opened the door. There was her kitten!"]

At this point, the teacher could begin to talk about her strategy for writing a story. She could explain that she asked herself who could be a character—a person in her story—who has a problem (Susie). And she asked herself what the problem could be (a lost kitten). She asked herself what Susie did (looked for the kitten). And she asked herself how Susie's problem got solved (the kitten found Susie!). The teacher could list these questions, and begin to guide children in using these questions—the strategy—to make up stories.[2]

Possible areas of teacher think-alouds include the following:

(a) *Summarizing important information and planning*
   "Let me see if I understand what I have to do."
   "What additional information do I need?"
   "I need to do this one step at a time, and show all my work."
(b) *Accessing prior knowledge*
   "What do I already know about this?"
   "How is this like what I have done before?"
(c) *Self-monitoring*
   "How am I doing? What have I accomplished?"
   "Is this making sense?"
(d) *Accessing help*
   "Who should I ask for help?"
   "What is it I need to know?"
   "I only want her to give me hints, not solve the problem for me."
(e) *Self-reinforcement* (include self-attribution statements)
   "How did I do? Not bad; I used my strategy to...."
   "I didn't get it all done, but I tried hard. This was a challenging problem."

These general classes of modeled self-statements can be supplemented with domain-specific think-alouds that are tied to a specific task, such as reading or writing. For example, Davey and McBride (1986) have proposed that while reading a story aloud to their students, teachers should model making predictions ("From the title I predict ..."); monitoring comprehension ("This isn't what I pictured happening based on what I read so far"); and verbalizing a confusing point and accompanying fix-up strategies ("I'll keep on reading and see if it will make sense ... Hmm, maybe I should ask for help").

Educators have sometimes employed videotaped think-aloud modeling films of students demonstrating the desired strategy. No matter what the presentation format (teacher, peer, videotape), at the conclusion of the modeling demonstration the teacher should discuss with the class what statements and questions were modeled and why. The teacher can arrange for the students to practice them alone or in small groups. Teachers may provide students with pictures or procedural prompts to remind them to use their self-statements. The teacher can demonstrate how students can whisper these statements quietly to themselves, or just say them in their heads (covertly).

To help make think-alouds a shared activity, teachers can ask students:

- "What are you thinking as you solve that problem?"
- "I don't want just yes or no answers—can you explain how you got your answer?"
- "Can you explain your answer using a diagram?"
- "Could you explain that again? How did you know ...?"
- "Can you tell how you decided to ... and then what made you decide to ...?"
- "What are you trying to figure out right now?"

Students can be encouraged to ask each other questions that pull for thinking aloud and for social discourse about the cognitive processes involved in performing academic tasks.

A few caveats about think-aloud procedures:

1. Do not use a think-aloud if it is going to make the task more complicated than it needs to be. Don't make an intuitively obvious task into a complex introspective nightmare.
2. Don't try to model too much material at one time. Pace the amount of modeling while performing small, simple tasks.
3. Make sure students do not try to parrot or mimic your think-aloud.
4. Don't prescribe any specific technique as the only way to solve a prob-

lem or perform a task. Rather, teach students how to think on their own, and how to develop understanding.

Strategy Instruction

In order to help students learn to ask themselves such self-guiding questions, teachers can explicitly teach them how to use strategies. In order to be effective, strategy instruction should be long-term, ongoing, and integrated with the teaching of academic content throughout the curriculum. Teachers should not teach strategies in isolation or on a one-shot basis, and then expect generalization to occur (as we will consider in detail in Chapter 10). Moreover, mastery of strategy usage usually takes some time. For example, Harris and Graham (1996) suggest that most students require four to nine class sessions (acquisition and consolidation sessions) to learn a strategy well enough to use it independently. Table 7.2 provides a set of instructional guidelines for teaching strategies.

TABLE 7.2
Procedural Steps Involved in Strategy Instruction

1. Use *class discussions and demonstrations* to teach students what strategies are (plans for self-regulating performance and for sequencing if-then action rules or tactics) and why using strategies facilitates performance. You can help students appreciate what strategies they already use to guide their behavior, both in and out of school. What strategies have they already mastered? How do they combine, extend, and refine these strategies when solving new problems? Describe and model how you use strategies and why doing so proves helpful.

2. *Label or name the strategy* being introduced, and explain how and why it fits into the larger scheme of what is being taught. Ensure that students understand how the use of the strategy will help them achieve their goals (i.e., what students should expect to be able to do when they have mastered the strategy). Explain and demonstrate how the strategy works.

3. Use *direct explanations* and re-explanations, as necessitated by students' difficulties in carrying out and applying the strategy.

4. *Elicit students' commitment* to work on mastering the strategy, and help them recognize how *commitment* (will), *effort*, and *practice* are necessary for learning the strategy.

5. *Teach collaboratively*, involving students as much as possible in developing, piloting, and evaluating the strategies.

6. *Anticipate* with students *any glitches*—anything that may go wrong or prove difficult.

TABLE 7.2 (Continued)

7. *Gear the complexity* of the strategy instruction *to the students' capabilities.* (A rule of thumb is that a strategy should not include more than 3 to 6 steps.) Teach very few strategies at a time, but teach them well.

8. Develop and *teach a mnemonic of the strategy.*

9. Encourage students to *personalize the strategy* and make it their own.

10. Provide students with *practice* using the strategy in different contexts and on different tasks. Use the language of learning (terms like *strategy, self-monitoring, using your plan,* etc.) when you praise students.

11. *Monitor* the students' use of the strategy over time. Use student think-alouds and questioning to access students' thought processes.

12. *Reteach* components of the strategy, returning to any steps that need further attention.

13. Discuss with students how, when, and where to *self-monitor* the effectiveness of their strategy. Invite students to describe how the strategy is working. Have them graph the results, and discuss how they like using the strategy. Show interest in students' self-monitoring—but keep in mind that students' self-monitoring need not be highly accurate in order for positive benefits to occur. Don't quibble over the accuracy of the students' self-monitoring. It is the process that is important.

14. Provide opportunities for students to *deliberately practice strategies* with partners (peer pairing), without direct supervision, and opportunities for them to *describe, explain, demonstrate, and teach the strategy to others.*

15. Help the students determine how the strategy they are learning can be *applied across the curriculum.* Integrate the strategy and the content.

16. *Build the students' knowledge base* to supplement strategy instruction.

Self-Instructional Training

Another way to help students use strategies on their own is to teach them how to self-instruct. Discuss with the class the importance of what people say to themselves before, during, and after performing a task. With collaborative guidance, students can learn to generate and employ such self-statements as those included in Table 7.3. For younger children, teachers have used pictorial representations of these guiding self-statements (McKeough, 1992; Meichenbaum, 1977).

Some students find it helpful to put their self-talk on audiotapes, or to make individual and group cue cards that act as reminders to employ self-regulatory behaviors (e.g., signs that say *Goal, Plan, Do, Check*). Cue cards can be posted on the class bulletin board. Students should be encouraged to put the self-statements

TABLE 7.3
Examples of Self-Instructions Students Can Learn to Use

Defining the Problem (sizing up the nature and demands of the task)
- What is it I have to do here?
- Let me see if I understand what I have to do.
- What is the problem?
- What is my goal or the way I want it to be?

Accessing and Summarizing Relevant Information
- Have I seen a problem like this in the past?
- What do I already know about this?
- How is this like what I have done before?
- What additional information do I need?

Focusing Attention and Planning
- I have to … (pay attention, concentrate, think of different ways to solve this problem).
- First, I need to make a plan.
- My first step is …, then I will …

Self-Monitoring (evaluating performance, catching and correcting errors)
- Am I following my plan? Am I ready to take the next step?
- Have I used all my story parts?
- Can I think of more details?
- I need to go slowly and take my time.
- Is this making sense?
- How am I doing? Do I need to do anything differently?

Using Coping Self-Statements (handling difficulties and failures and the accompanying reactions)
- Oops! I missed one. That's okay, I can … (redo it, ask for help, etc.).
- So I made an error—that's okay. I can learn from my mistake.
- I can do this if I try.
- I'm not going to get mad. Mad makes me do bad.

Self-Reinforcing (including self-attribution statements)
- How did I do? Not bad! I used my strategy to …
- Although I didn't get it all done, I tried hard. This was a challenging problem.
- I am getting better at this.
- Wait until I show this to … (read this to …, etc.).
- I am proud of what I accomplished so far.

into their own words and to memorize and practice them. They can evaluate the usefulness of these self-instructions and revise them accordingly. It is critical that teachers ensure correspondence between what students *say* and what they *do*.

Procedural Prompts

One way to foster such correspondence is to use predetermined graduated prompts or memory aids. Students can learn how to give each other and themselves such prompts in order to initiate recall and to integrate present task demands with previously acquired declarative, procedural, and conditional knowledge. Teachers may provide procedural prompts at the outset of a task, or provide students with a procedural checklist—an exemplary model—against which they can compare their task approach.

The teachers' reminders can be in the form of *signal words* (e.g., Goal, Plan, Do, Check; Who, What, Where, When, Why, How) or *generic questions* (e.g., "How are ... and ... alike?"; "What is another example of ..."; "What conclusion can be drawn about ...? Why is this important?"). Teachers may also use diagrammatic reminders—such as procedural flow charts and concept or mind maps—to signal students' use of strategies.

Guided Performance

The next component of an acquisition session is having students perform the demonstrated skill or strategy while being monitored or guided by the teacher. The intent is to have each student experience successfully performing the new skill or strategy. The student acts while the teacher provides task direction (if necessary). As soon as possible, responsibility for verbal guidance should be shifted to the student or to his or her peers. In the case of strategies, peers can ask a student the questions that comprise the strategy. (See the story-generating example given above.) Soon, students should be able to ask themselves the strategic questions.

When Closing the Lesson: Reflecting With Students What Was Learned

Guided Evaluation

After demonstrating a skill or strategy and guiding students through performance, it is important to include an evaluation process. Students have to learn to ask themselves, "Have I learned what I set out to learn?" "How did learning this skill (or strategy) make a difference?" Teachers can foster this self-evaluative process by modeling and teaching ways to self-monitor performance (e.g., by graphing results) and by questioning students about the processes and steps they used to perform tasks. For example, teachers can ask students:

- "What are you thinking as you solve that problem?"
- "Can you explain how you got your answer?"
- "Can you explain your answer using a diagram?"
- "Could you tell how you decided to ...? Then what made you decide to ...?"

The discussion of these questions maintains the focus on intentional learning. Such discussion is critical to the learning process because students need to take credit for the improvements they experience (Dweck, 1986; Licht, 1993; Zimmerman, 1986). Students who attribute their learning to their own efforts and to the strategies they use are likely to put out more effort, persist longer when they encounter difficulties, and choose more challenging tasks and activities. In contrast, students who attribute their task difficulties and failures to factors beyond their control (e.g., lack of ability, chance) typically exert less effort, use less sophisticated strategies than they are capable of applying, and avoid and/or give up on difficult or challenging tasks.

Teachers cannot leave student attributions to chance; they must build into acquisition lessons class discussions on how students can handle any difficulties or setbacks they encounter. One way teachers can influence students' attributions is by teaching them how to anticipate difficulties and setbacks, and to view difficulties as "learning opportunities," occasions to pause and reflect. Failures should provide valuable feedback on what skills and strategies need to be reviewed, retaught, and practiced further. The class can discuss how making errors is a natural part of the learning process and how students often learn most when they encounter difficulties. As we will consider in the next chapter, teachers can even anticipate and illustrate specific types of errors ("snags" or "procedural bugs") that students should watch out for. However, they should not highlight these possible errors until students have begun to develop some proficiency.

After Acquisition of Skills and Strategies

Following an acquisition lesson, teachers should review progress, noting who is ready to move on to a consolidation setting with this skill or strategy, who needs more acquisition work, and who needs more prerequisite work. The teacher may also review (self-monitor) the effectiveness of the lesson as implemented.

The teacher can ask herself if she adequately:

1. Prepared students for instruction by using advance organizers and informed instruction;
2. Accessed and activated students' prior knowledge and reviewed possible student misconceptions;
3. Demonstrated a need and reason for learning this material;
4. Reviewed and, if necessary, pretaught prerequisite skills;
5. Used direct instruction procedures including cognitive modeling, procedural prompts, and guided practice;
6. Explicitly taught strategies; and
7. Ensured that students self-evaluated their performance, taking credit for improvements, and anticipating and learning from difficulties and failures.

Conclusion: Acquiring Skills and Strategies

Having students acquire skills, concepts, and strategies has been the objective of lessons for centuries. In this chapter, we have added a focus on intentional learning—on increasing students' awareness of learning goals, as well as performance goals. We have stressed the importance of teaching students from the start how to evaluate their own learning progress, as well as their actual performance. Only when students can take an active role in their own learning—their change in skill performance or strategy application—can they be said to be active partners in the learning process.

When acquiring new skills and strategies, it is essential that students understand *why* the skills or strategies are being learned—how new skills relate to contexts in which they will be applied, and how new strategies will help students on tasks they want or need to accomplish. It is also essential that from the start, students understand the role of language—both the specific vocabulary needed to talk to others and oneself about particular tasks, and the language used to direct or regulate tasks in any domain of activity (reading, mathematics, writing, science, etc.). Acquiring strategies, self-directed questions that facilitate task planning and task performance, is a major way of learning to use language to direct one's tasks.

A major theme in this chapter and the next is adjusting material to be learned to student achievement levels. We believe that students cannot master skills and strategies that they have not acquired and consolidated, and they cannot acquire and consolidate skills and strategies that presuppose other skills, concepts, or strategies that they lack. All students can learn, but they cannot all learn the same things at the same time.[3] For any teacher whose goal is student success and student progress, some differentiation of instruction is necessary.

In the next chapter, we will move our focus from *acquiring* new skills and strategies to *consolidating* them. This means creating settings in which students can gradually—and successfully—assume more responsibility for accomplishing tasks that require newly learned skills, concepts, and strategies. Planning effective opportunities for deliberate, intentional practice continues our emphasis on intentional learning, learning in which students take increasing responsibility for expanding their own competence.

Endnotes

1. Bereiter and Scardamalia (1986) have stressed the role of "intentional learning," as illustrated in their Computer-Supported Intentional Learning Environment (CSILE) program, described in Chapter 11.

2. This particular strategy is a variation on Anne McKeough's strategy for generating narratives. McKeough has used variations of this with children as young as four years old. She uses more elaborate strategies for older children's narratives (McKeough, 1992).

3. See "Lake Wobegon Revisited" (Biemiller, 1993) for a more extended discussion of this topic.

Chapter Eight

Creating Learning Settings with Student Consolidation Roles: Scaffolding Student Practice

In Chapter 7, we described learning settings in which students move from having no knowledge of a skill, concept, or planning strategy to being a "novice" with respect to the new learning. At this stage, they have some idea of what the skill or strategy is for, and of how to perform it. Usually, they have performed the skill or strategy under direct teacher guidance, but they are far from being ready to perform the skill or strategy successfully on their own—and even further from being able to independently consult about it or apply it in a new context. In this chapter, we focus on settings in which students can make the transition from performing skills or strategies with guidance to performing them without assistance on request. We call this process *consolidating* a skill or strategy. Consolidation of skills or strategies is prerequisite to being able to effectively consult about and apply them.

In consolidation settings, students are concerned both with improving their *performance* and with the *products* of their efforts. It begins to matter not just that they complete the task, but that they do it correctly. This means that teachers must give careful attention to the tasks they assign. Tasks must involve skills with which students have some competence. If the assignment involves planning or application (and strategies for these), students should have had some introduction to the type of task being planned, and should be competent with needed skills. In consolidation settings, students should be able to provide much or most of their own direction, and other students should be able to provide some of the needed assistance. Consequently, the teacher's role also changes. In the acquisition setting, we discussed guidance—the ongoing provision of direction regarding the task being performed. In consolidation settings, the teacher should no longer need to provide continuous support. Students who are consolidating skills or strategies need less direct assistance, and more in the way of *prompts* that lead them to generate their own task directions. Such assistance is often called *scaffolding*. We will elaborate on how to scaffold later in this chapter.

Learning settings in which students consolidate recently acquired skills or strategies occupy the largest proportion of school time, and thus comprise a very important part of the learning process. Surprisingly, such settings tend to receive relatively little attention in texts on teaching or lesson planning, relative to the attention given to direct instruction.[1] These settings are often called "independent work" periods. During such settings, the students are expected to complete as much as possible of an assigned task on their own. The role of the teacher or other assistant is to help students complete tasks successfully. In the past, much practice or seat work amounted to tests of independent performance. Students were not expected to help one another, and the teacher was usually busy with other groups of students. More modern practice reflects a recognition that getting and giving assistance can facilitate the consolidation process. However, that assistance needs to be given in a way that helps students become increasingly independent. (A student who needs *continuous* help is not yet ready to consolidate the skills or strategies required for the assigned task; more direct acquisition work or less demanding tasks are needed.)

There are two broad kinds of consolidation tasks:

- Those which emphasize repeated performance of the skill (e.g., "drill sheets" and educational computer programs, some drill games, etc.).
- More complex, applied tasks that incorporate the target skill (e.g., spelling and handwriting are practiced while writing, math is practiced while analyzing data or playing math games).

The first kind of consolidation task typically provides more concentrated practice than the latter, but can be off-putting. With the latter, the goal of skill consolidation can often be forgotten by both student and teacher.

If the primary focus is consolidation of new skills or concepts, it is important that the planning aspects of the task not be very demanding for the students. Conversely, if the primary focus is on a planning strategy, then it is important that the skill aspects of the task not be very demanding.

In the case of consolidating planning or application strategies, a problem must be introduced that specifies an outcome to be accomplished. The student is responsible for planning a course of action—the task plan—leading to the outcome, as well as for accomplishing the outcome. Thus, the student can be said to "construct" the task. Teachers must be clear that at least one objective of students' work in the setting is improvement in using specific strategies to plan new tasks. Examples of planning or application tasks include writing stories and reports, identifying and solving quantitative problems, generating work materials for other students, planning trips and events, etc.

Engaging Students in Deliberate Practice

Nobody masters a skill or strategy without extensive practice. With practice and feedback, as students' skills become automated or consolidated, their performance should become smoother, faster, and less error-prone. Once triggered, practiced skills (e.g., decoding words, performing computational skills, or generating story outlines) should unfold fully and with little or no pause to their conclusion, requiring a minimal outlay of cognitive resources. With proficiency, various skills should also become integrated functional units. For example, if we go back to our example of driving a car, with practice functional units develop (e.g., parking, defensive driving) that become routinized. With further deliberate practice these serially learned skills become integrated into a coherent whole. Table 8.1 summarizes research-based guidelines for deliberate practice.

Two examples of how practice has been successfully used to improve skills come from the area of reading. The first procedure, used by Samuels (1980), is called *repeated reading*. This method requires students to read the same passage or story over and over again until they reach proficiency. The difficulty of the selected passage or story should be slightly above the students' current reading level. In order to maintain the students' interest, the teacher may ask them to answer different types of questions each time they read the story (e.g., questions from the perspectives of different characters in the story).

A somewhat different approach to practicing story reading was offered by Shany and Biemiller (1995), who had students read each story while listening to an audiotape of the same story. They called this procedure *assisted reading*. The unique features of this study were that (1) the students (poor readers in grades 3 and 4) gradually worked up from materials they could read well (usually first-grade basal readers) to material that they were initially quite unable to read (third- or fourth-grade basal readers); and (2) students could control the rate at which the taped stories were read. In this way, they could tailor the practice reading sessions to their own skill levels. Over 16 weeks of practice (30 minutes a day), students improved their reading speed and became able to read grade-level texts without supporting prompts, while significantly improving their com-

TABLE 8.1: Guidelines for Deliberate Practice

1. Following the adage that nothing succeeds like success, students should be asked to practice tasks on which they can have a high degree of success (i.e., a success rate of 90% or more). Repeated failures can cause students to believe that they are lacking in ability and not able to overcome difficulties. High failure rates also result in the repetition of errors.

2. Practice should be conducted in small doses (e.g., around 20 minutes a day) over an extended period of time to the point of automaticity.

3. Students should be encouraged to proceed at their own pace, mastering prerequisite skills before moving on. Students should be viewed as collaborators and given choices in the selection of practice activities.

4. To receive maximum benefit from practice and accompanying feedback, students should monitor their progress with full concentration. The practice should be effortful and deliberate, as students monitor whether they achieved their preestablished goals or subgoals. Students need to be taught how to self-evaluate (e.g., graph) their progress.

5. Students also need to be taught how to establish a few short-term goals (one or two at first and three or four later on), as described further on in this chapter. Statements of goals should emerge out of class discussion on the purposes of practice.

6. During practice, the teacher and students should reinforce the meaning or purpose of the skill or strategy that is being worked on. Students must be able to describe verbally and/or diagrammatically what, how, and why they are practicing a particular skill or strategy. Such mental representation ensures that the practice is not performed in a mindless, rote fashion, but is deliberate and seen as connected to efforts at achieving future goals. Students should keep a log of their practice and results.

7. Students need to link their progress with both their increased use of strategies and their increased accompanying efforts. Teachers need to nurture students' sense of ownership and responsibility for their progress. Statements such as, "That's good. You are really working hard," illustrate *effort attributions.* In addition, teachers can and should use *strategy-usage attributions,* telling students, "That's correct. You got it right because you (used the solution steps in the right order, rechecked your answer, etc.)."

8. Teachers should incorporate into the practice sessions ways that students can handle any unexpected obstacles, snags, or procedural bugs. They can provide assistance for students who are having difficulties.

9. Another way to keep practice from becoming a rote and mindless activity is for teachers, textbook writers, and computer programmers to decontextualize the practice tasks as students become more proficient. For example, the practice problems that students are asked to work on should sample various skills and strategies, and not be overly cued.

10. Teachers should provide variety in practice. Students should be encouraged to work hard, but also to have fun at it!

prehension. The lesson from these studies is that it is better for students to make real progress on less difficult tasks than to continually struggle with overly complex tasks.

If a student's prerequisite skills and concepts are adequate, a single well-planned acquisition session may suffice for him or her to acquire a skill or strategy. However, students typically need many sessions in consolidation settings to reach a point of reasonably fluent and accurate performance or application. As the Russian psychologist Lev Vygotsky wrote:

> Our analysis alters the traditional view that at the moment a child assimilates the meaning of a word, or masters an operation such as addition or written language, her developmental processes are basically completed. In fact, they have only just begun at that moment (Vygotsky, 1978, p. 90).

The notion that teachers need to match instruction to the learners' emerging capabilities until the students can take charge is consistent with Vygotsky's ideas. Vygotsky proposed that tutees learn the most when instruction occurs within what he called their *Zone of Proximal Development* (ZPD). The ZPD describes the difference between tutees' *developmental levels*, as determined by their independent performance levels on progressively more complex tasks, and their *potential performance levels*. In other words, the ZPD is that part of a curriculum dimension that lies between what students can do alone and what they cannot do even with help. The instructional goal is to focus teaching efforts as much as possible in the student's ZPD. (The problem, of course, is successfully identifying this zone for different students.[2])

It should be noted that students are not passive recipients in this instructional process. They are active, reciprocal participants who influence the nature of the guidance and supports they receive. Through the questions they ask, their responses to assistance, and the effort and task persistence they evidence, students influence how much of their instruction falls within their ZPD. While teachers influence students, students also influence teachers. This bidirectional process has important implications for how teachers implement scaffolded instruction and engage students in a collaborative learning process. This is especially evident when we consider the variability of student abilities. Ann Brown has proposed that we view a classroom of students as consisting of a wide range of overlapping ZPDs. The challenge for teachers is how to conduct instruction so it is tailored as much as possible to each student's ZPD.

Scaffolding Assistance in Consolidation Settings

The term *scaffolding* refers to the practice of providing just enough assistance (not too much or too little) to help students succeed.[3] For example, if a student evidences a series of failures at a task, the teacher should provide more guidance, but following a series of successes, she should minimize her assistance and fade supports. Thus, the nature of the assistance is contingent on the student's performance. A key aspect of scaffolding student learning is that over several sessions, each student should come to need less assistance, and especially less direct assistance. The teacher must carefully monitor how students respond to assistance and strategically relinquish more and more task responsibility. This can be accomplished in a number of ways. The teacher can manipulate the task difficulty, pace instruction, gradually remove procedural prompts and prosthetic teaching supports (calculators, spelling assistance, etc.), enlist students as collaborators, and/or give students choices in self-selecting task difficulty levels. Table 8.2 summarizes research-based guidelines for scaffolded assistance.

We now turn to an examination of the teacher's responsibilities during the same five phases we used when discussing acquisition settings:

1. *Before* working with children in a consolidation setting;
2. *At the outset* of a session—introducing the skill or strategy to be consolidated, and the consolidation task;
3. *During* the session—scaffolding student practice;
4. *When closing* the session—reflecting with students on what was learned and what was accomplished; and
5. *After* working with children in a consolidation setting.

Before Working with Students in a Consolidation Setting

Defining Objectives

Teachers need to have a clear idea of what they expect to change as students carry out tasks in the consolidation setting. In most cases, what is sought is improved performance of a skill or, in the case of a strategy, improved effectiveness of task planning and implementation. With regard to skills, the teacher determines what she expects to result from the consolidation session(s)—e.g., increased speed and accuracy of performance, better understanding of concepts. Essentially, with skills what is sought is improved performance. In the case of consolidating a strategy, the teacher determines what change in task planning or

TABLE 8.2
Guidelines for Implementing Scaffolded Assistance

1. Ensure that students have sufficient background knowledge and prerequisite skills.

2. Begin with tasks at the level of the students' competence and gradually increase (by small steps) the level of task difficulty.

3. Focus on and pace instruction around students' emerging skills. Check students' comprehension and monitor their performance.

4. Shift supports (e.g., types of questions, predetermined graduated prompts, degrees of guidance) as students progress, making them contingent upon the students' levels of success.

5. Encourage students to take risks, to try working at the next higher level of task difficulty.

6. Involve students in guided deliberate practice and goal setting, and provide comprehensive and constructive feedback (as described further on in this chapter).

7. Cue students to assume more and more task responsibility by having them engage in self-regulatory behaviors (e.g., generating their own prompts, asking self-interrogative questions, giving self-instructions, and self-monitoring performance).

8. Cue students to verbalize or diagram strategies (e.g., "Do you think that repeating the rule would help?").

9. Have students review their present and past performance. Students need to see how their efforts and strategy usage translate into positive outcomes and performance gains. Initially, you can offer attributions for students' successes, but students should eventually make self-attributions.

10. Be sensitive to students' confusion and struggles. Employ cognitive empathy procedures to help students work through difficulties and anticipate, identify, and cope with future difficulties and failures.

11. Encourage students to create a community of learners who help each other.

strategy use should result from the consolidation session(s)—e.g., increased effectiveness at planning tasks to address problems in a domain (this may also include increased use of recently taught skills).

Many activities provide opportunities to consolidate several skills and strategies at once. It may be helpful to identify which consolidation outcomes (e.g., improved skill performance versus improved task planning and accomplishment) are particularly important for individual students or groups of students. Attempts to focus on all aspects of task performance simultaneously often leads to an overemphasis on skill performance (e.g., excessive attention to spelling at the expense of the overall content of a paper).

Selecting Consolidation Tasks

To accommodate students of varying ability levels in consolidation settings, a variety of tasks that range in difficulty or complexity may be needed. Teachers may assign specific tasks to different students, or may give students some freedom in choosing what tasks they work on. Our experience suggests that students are capable of choosing tasks at appropriate levels of difficulty, after they have had some experience and guidance in doing so. We have also found that students strongly prefer having some control over task difficulty (Meichenbaum & Biemiller, 1992; Biemiller & Morley, 1996).

Before students work in a consolidation setting, the teacher should be aware of the students' level(s) of achievement relative to the tasks at hand, and should consider the implications for group organization. How much assistance will students need to be able to perform the assigned tasks, or to plan tasks that address assigned problems? If some students are more skilled than others, are they expected to help others acquire needed skills—or to complete difficult parts of the task for others? If not, on what aspects of the task may they give assistance? (Reading words? Answering assigned questions?) Do students have access to dictionaries, or calculators? Are other assistants available? If so, do they know how to give scaffolded assistance?

It often seems easy to have an advanced student assist classmates. However, if this is done regularly, and other students rarely or never assume academic consulting roles, the other students may conclude that they really can't understand or do well in this domain. An alternative is to bring in older students as assistants, while providing consulting opportunities for your own students with younger children. (This idea is discussed at greater length in Chapter 9.)

Why is it important for teachers to calibrate and manipulate the difficulty levels of tasks? Any learning task can be viewed as falling along a dimension of skill demand (i.e., the X-axis, as described in Chapter 5) and application complexity (i.e., the Z-axis). The difficulty of a specific task for a specific student is determined by the student's familiarity with the skills involved in carrying out the task, and by the number of skills or cognitive operations that must be coordinated in planning the task. *Students learn the most when a task is slightly beyond their present level of competence, falling within their ZPD.* If the task they are working on is too easy or too hard, students are less likely to learn. In order to introduce this notion to teachers, we have used the following *Ski Hill metaphor:*

> Imagine that you want to improve your downhill skiing ability. You are somewhat experienced, but not an expert skier. You arrive on a pristine day and take the lift to the top of the hill. You discover that in your haste you somehow ended up on top of the beginners' hill. This slope is well within your ability level and presents little or no challenge whatsoever, so you descend quickly.
>
> The next time you take the ski lift to the top, you find that you are on the most difficult or challenging hill. You realize that this slope is too dangerous for you to ski, and your only goal is to get down the hill without injury. You do manage to make it down the hill, using familiar strategies of sliding, snow-plowing, or making slow, winding turns.
>
> Finally, you take the lift up to a hill that is slightly beyond your current level of competence. Now you know you are ready to learn. At the top of this hill you plan what it is you want to work on. You tell yourself, "I will work on correct form. Bend the knees!" You set goals, self-monitor, and self-evaluate your performance. You can ask fellow skiers for feedback on your performance, and so on. In short, you are more likely to be a self-directed learner and become your own teacher when the ski hill you have to negotiate is slightly beyond your level of competence.

We use the ski hill example to emphasize that if there is too great a mismatch between task demands and students' competence, the opportunities for learning are reduced. The same point can be made directly to students. If tasks are consistently too easy, boredom and disinterest set in. If tasks are initially too hard, fear and avoidance are evident. The goal of instruction is for the ski instructor (teacher) and the student to collaboratively select the correct ski hill (appropriate task difficulty) in order to create challenging opportunities. Below, when we discuss the concept of scaffolded instruction, we will consider how teachers can work with students so they operate as often as possible within their personal zone of proximal development.

In order to avoid large mismatches between task demands and student ability, teachers need to adjust tasks to appropriate levels of challenge. Highlight Box 8.1 summarizes methods for doing this.

Highlight Box 8.1
METHODS OF ADJUSTING TASK DIFFICULTY
TO STUDENT ABILITIES

If we leave the ski hill metaphor and enter the classroom setting, we can consider how teachers can help students maximize their opportunities to function within this optimal zone (or, metaphorically, find their right ski hill level). Teachers can:

1. Carefully analyze what is to be taught and determine what critical features contribute to the task difficulty level. In this way, you can dimensionalize the difficulty level. A good deal of research has been conducted on how to dimensionalize math problems (Jerman & Mirman, 1974).

2. Discuss the ski hill example with your students, or use other metaphors such as rungs on a ladder that should not be set too far apart. You can use the ski hill metaphor as a way to invite students to collaborate.

3. Discuss with students what makes tasks or problems easy or hard. For example, you can help students better understand that such task features as the number of if-then operations or decision rules, the number of memory searches, the level of vocabulary, time demands, and so on all contribute to the task difficulty level. The discussion of task features can help students learn how to decompose tasks—i.e., simplify the task (manipulate task demands, or do an easy version of the task), fractionate the task (break it into its natural units), or segment the task (divide it into temporal or spatial components).

4. Give students choices as to which task they wish to work on, challenging them to move up to tasks that are slightly above their current level. (As we noted in Table 8.1, when the instructional objective is to consolidate skills, students should work on tasks that will yield a 90% success rate.) Students can be taught how to self-monitor their performance in order to determine if they are working at the right ski hill level of task difficulty.

5. Manipulate the difficulty level of tasks by adjusting the learning demands to students' ability levels. On some occasions, you can alter the characteristics of the task (e.g., adjust the time limits or the quantity or length of the problems). You can also provide prosthetic supports that make the task easier for students (e.g., provide a tape recording of the text, give students directions in multiple media, provide students with a schematic flow chart of the directions or a copy of the class notes, or permit students to use calculators and spell checks). In addition, you may wish to enlist the aid of peer tutors, resource teachers, and parents in helping students develop the prerequisite skills for operating within their ZPD's.

6. Determine your students' ability levels—in terms of prerequisite knowledge, skills, application strategies, and motivation—at the outset of instruction, and carefully engineer learning opportunities. This engineering may involve:

    (a) breaking complex tasks into smaller units;

(b) reducing the memory load and cognitive demands;

(c) pacing instruction and reducing or altering time limits;

(d) using manipulatives to foster students' conceptual understanding; and

(e) providing supports, procedural prompts, and strategy cues (e.g., outlines of main ideas, skeletal notes, multiple examples of problem solutions, hints of possible procedural bugs). As students develop task competence, these supports can be gradually withdrawn.

Anticipating Student Problems and Appropriate Methods of Assistance

Teachers should consider difficulties their students are likely to have in carrying out the consolidation tasks (usually based on their past experience with these tasks). This will help them in warning students about potential difficulties, and in thinking about what kinds of assistance should be made available. Note that for consolidation tasks (as opposed to tests), it is appropriate to provide some assistance so that students can complete assignments. In the case of consolidating planning and comprehension strategies, teachers may want to be prepared to assist students with some skills so that they can succeed. For example, teachers may need to assist students (or allow assistance) with word recognition if the task objective is improving reading comprehension. Similarly, teachers may need to assist students with some computation if the objective is math problem solving. Before the task is assigned, it can be helpful for teachers and students to jointly make decisions about appropriate assistance.

Selecting the Organization of Students

Prior to operating a setting, it is also important for teachers to consider in what groupings (e.g., all students in the class, a particular working group, peer pairs, individual practice) and under what participation structure (e.g., cooperative, independent) students will work on the deliberate practice of this task. As we said before, consolidation settings will often involve more diverse groups of students than acquisition settings. However, it remains important that each student work with tasks of appropriate levels of difficulty for him or her to profit from the experience.

At the Outset of a Session: Introducing the Skill or Strategy to be Consolidated and the Consolidation Task

Explaining Task Goals

At the outset of a consolidation session, teachers should review the recently acquired skill or strategy, and introduce the current task. Teachers should make clear the overall purpose of the consolidation task—to improve the performance of a particular skill or to use particular strategies to plan new tasks or applications. (Often students are unaware of the purpose of consolidation activities and focus their attention on other, less important aspects of the task.) In many consolidation settings, both improved performance and the task product are important. For example, students may be playing a math game in which they care about winning. At the same time, they are practicing their adding skills. In such a situation, both the task product (winning the game) and the skill performance (adding correctly) matter.

Having students set explicit goals for consolidation activities can improve learning outcomes. Highlight Box 8.2 (pp. 148-149) describes ways of helping students set goals.

Preparing for Student Evaluation of Consolidation Progress

When setting goals, students should think about what success will "look like." How will they know if they have made progress in consolidating skills? (For example, will they read faster? Will they be able to read harder passages? Will they make fewer errors in computation?) How will they know if they have made progress in consolidating strategies? (For example, will they be able to solve more problems? Will they be able to generate richer stories, or generate stories more quickly? Will they have a better understanding of what they read?) Students need to put these goals into their own words.

Helping Students With Possible Difficulties and Failures: Cognitive Empathy

Inherent in the learning of any skill or strategy is the possibility of experiencing difficulties, setbacks, and failures, as well as successes. As noted in Chapter 7, the way students (and others) view success and failure is critical to the learning process. While teachers can help students anticipate and prepare for such difficulties, they also need to be able to respond to their students' struggles on the

Highlight Box 8.2
HELPING STUDENTS SET GOALS

When students are goal-oriented, they are much more likely to engage in deliberate practice, to intentionally plan and self-monitor their performance, and to
persist in the face of failure and frustration. When students have an interest in
and a reason for learning a specific topic or activity, and have made a commitment to achieve a set of goals, they are much more likely to put deliberate effort
into practice. Students need to be encouraged to have short-term, intermediate,
and long-term goals. As we noted in Chapter 3, when students (and their teachers
and parents) hold a positive image of their potential, they achieve academically
at higher levels. Teachers should not leave goal-setting processes to chance.

A *learning goal* is an individual's intention to attain a specific standard of
performance, usually within a specified time limit (Ames, 1992; Locke, 1990).
Performance goals may be initially established by the teacher, then collaboratively set with the students. Eventually, students need to determine their own
goals, as well as ways to plan, implement, self-monitor, and revise goals as they
proceed.

The teacher needs to educate students about different types of goals. A goal
may focus on a *product* or on a *process*. Product goals are usually established
when students are first acquiring a new skill or initiating deliberate practice. As
students develop some proficiency and begin to practice on their own, they are
likely to shift their focus to process goals (e.g., writing—or rewriting—a story to
describe each of the main characters' feelings and viewpoints, developing a
flow chart of how the student solved math word problems).

Students also need to know that goals differ in terms of several features:

1) *specificity*—the degree to which a clear, explicit, standard is established;
2) *difficulty level*—the degree to which the goal is seen by the student as a
   "doable" challenge; and
3) *proximity*—how close the goal is to being achieved.

Goals that are perceived as specific, proximal, and doable are more likely to
motivate students' performance than vague, distant, and potentially unachievable
goals. The setting of specific goals should be delayed until students have experienced enough practice that the relevant skills are beginning to be familiar and
automatic. Harder goals lead to better performance only when students have
made a commitment to attain the instructional goals, and when they have confidence that they can and will achieve the goals (Zimmerman & Schunk, 1994).
Students need to believe that the academic goals they are working toward are
attainable with assistance and guidance from others. Teachers should model
how to establish, plan, self-monitor, and periodically adjust goals. They can
post pictorial reminders of the instructional goals and refer to them throughout
the lesson.

Students must come to see why goals are important to the learning process. Teachers can ask students what they plan to do in order to achieve their goals. Students' abilities to represent (orally or diagrammatically) and convey their goals and plans will indicate the nature of the assistance they require. Another indication of students' progress is their ability to self-assess their goal attainment, as noted in their daily logs, diaries, portfolios, and Tickets Out The Door—each of which is described in Chapter 9.

Teachers need to remind students how achieving these short-term objectives relates to their long-term goals. John Borkowski and his colleagues have developed a metaphorical goal-planning activity called a *Possible-Me Tree*, in which students draw a tree and, with the teacher's guidance, indicate their possible long-term academic and occupational goals (Borkowski & Muthakrishna, 1992). They use the various branches of the tree to indicate the prerequisite skills and activities needed to achieve these long-term goals. As students move from their roots (what they bring to the learning settings), up the trunk, to the outlying branches and their offshoots, they come to see how working on current activities relates to the larger goal-attainment picture. Such explicit goal-setting is crucial, especially for inactive learners who are often passive and disengaged from the learning process. Students need to be reminded not only of what and how they learn, but also of why they are learning a specific skill, concept, or strategy. If students do not see the relevance of their school activities in terms of their personal experience or long-term goals, they are unlikely to put out the time and effort necessary to master skills and strategies. In order to succeed, students must have the necessary skills, but even more importantly, they must possess the will to learn.

Teachers can nurture such goal-setting behavior by inviting students to become their own self-advocates. Students can be given opportunities to inventory their learning strengths and weaknesses and to identify their goals and expectations. They can be given guidance in self-evaluating their classroom and at-home study behaviors, so they can work on achieving specific goals. Students need to be put into the role of shaping their educational program, so they feel empowered and can become self-directed independent learners.

In summary, if teachers want their students to develop skills and strategies to the point of automaticity and mastery, they have to be as thoughtfully skillful and strategic as they want their students to be. Teachers need to plan and prepare, implement and monitor, practice and evaluate. As we will consider in Chapter 12, for expert teachers, the procedural steps outlined in Chapters 7 and 8 on direct and scaffolded instruction, deliberate practice, and goal setting are integrated into a fluid, but intentional, teaching routine. With practice and constructive feedback, all teachers can become more expert.

spot. How teachers respond to students' failures can set the tone for how students view their efforts and abilities. Working backwards from students' errors to find out what students know and what is the source of their errors, teachers should evidence *cognitive empathy*. They should be sensitive to students' feelings about their performance (e.g., frustration, anxiety) and about their lack of understanding (which may persist even after much effort). Teachers should respond to students' nonverbal cues with the following types of comments:

- "I can see some puzzled faces. Let me explain that again."
- "It must be frustrating to work so hard and still have difficulty (not do as well as you expected)."
- "How many other students are having trouble with … ?"
- "I am glad you brought your difficulty to my attention. I am sure there are others who are having similar problems."

After this initial recognition of students' struggling, the teacher should *solicit the students' explanations*. For example, the teacher can ask,

- "What have you tried so far? What steps did you take?"
- "Please explain the last couple of steps that you tried. Help me understand how you got from … to …."

The teacher can also *build on the students' previous successes*, commenting,

- "I noticed an earlier problem that you were able to solve. Let's go back and have you take me through it."
- "Is the present problem like that one in any way?"
- "Have you seen this type of problem before? When? How did you go about solving that problem?"
- "Has there ever been a time when you were frustrated on a problem and you surprised yourself by solving it with the help of someone else?"

The teacher can provide *guided assistance* and *help students generate and test out alternative solution strategies*:

- "Are there any other ways we could go about solving this problem?"
- "What are all the possible ways you could …?"
- "What advice would you have for someone who is stuck (such as a younger student who needs help)?"

Some teachers use classroom tests in a constructive learning fashion to accomplish these objectives. For example, after grading students' exams, the teacher may review with the students the basis for their errors, then give them an opportunity to generate similar problems in order to demonstrate that they have learned the concepts and skills. Their final grade reflects a combination of their initial performance and their ability to become their own teacher. We will consider in Chapter 10 various ways that teachers can use assessment to help students become more self-reflective learners.

Discussing Available Assistance

Students should be aware of available sources of assistance (including "prosthetics" such as dictionaries and calculators, as well as people). If you want students to seek assistance from fellow students or "assistors" from another class, you must be clear about this expectation. You might also review using assistance effectively, so that the student becomes more competent in knowing how to ask for help (e.g., "Ask for hints, not answers. This means not having the assistant do more for you than you really need. Do what you can on your own!").

Telling Students What To Do When They Finish With a Consolidation Task

When students have completed and evaluated an assigned consolidation task, it is a good idea to have them be aware of what they should do next. Consolidation tasks will rarely be completed by everyone at the same time. Students must know whether to go on to another assignment (in which case, what?), or undertake specific "between-task tasks" (e.g., read a book, play a game with someone, work on journals, etc.). This is essentially a matter of good classroom management.

During Student Consolidation Sessions: Scaffolding Student Practice

The Teacher's Role

In an effective consolidation setting, the teacher's role should be that of a scaffolding assistant, not someone who is "on-line" all the time. This will allow the teacher to work in other settings with students who need her more. However, for this to be the case, either the tasks must be ones on which students need minimal assistance, or other students must be able to provide assistance. (In Chapter 9, we will discuss ways of preparing students to assist others, particularly to assist younger students.) Teachers must be prepared to monitor consolidation settings to ensure that all students are able to proceed with the assistance available, and that the assistors are not doing too much for the assistees.

Scaffolding Assistance

Assistance with skills typically involves reminding students of the steps in a skill (e.g., "What sound does *b* make?") or briefly re-demonstrating or reteaching the skill. Assistance with planning strategies may involve rephrasing strategic questions, or simply reminding students of the strategy. When providing assistance directly, teachers (and others) need to reduce supports as student competence increases, and encourage students to undertake increasingly difficult tasks. See Highlight Box 8.3 for examples of how teachers can reduce supports. Note that well-planned questions both cause the questioned student to generate relevant task-directive speech, and provide a means for making assistance more or less direct.

An example of the process of scaffolding assistance with respect to a strategy was offered by Harris and Graham (1996). They had students work in a peer pairing format to consolidate the strategy of revising their written work. (We will discuss other ways peers can be used in the next chapter.)

Before the peer pairing activities were implemented, the students first acquired revision strategies. The teacher engaged students in a classroom discussion of why writers revise and edit their written work (e.g., to ensure that their writing makes sense, to make their writing the best it can be, to make the story understandable and fun for the reader). The teacher also cognitively modeled the revision strategy ("Is this clear? Could my story use more detail? Is my story interesting?").

When introducing the peer pair task, the teacher discussed and modeled how students could offer suggestions and encouragement in a positive manner. As a reminder to give such feedback in a constructive fashion, students were given an accompanying cue card with a mnemonic summary of the strategy.[4]

With this as preparation, the teacher had students pair up, one student being the listener and the other being the writer. The listener would read along as the writer read her story aloud. The listener then had to tell in his own words what the story was about and what he liked about it. In providing this feedback, the listener had to answer several questions that were provided on a cue card:

Highlight Box 8.3
SCAFFOLDING ASSISTANCE: THE ART OF QUESTIONING

A critical feature of scaffolded instruction is the tutor's use of Socratic questioning. *Socratic questions* are designed to guide students to discover and invent solutions to problems. Specifically, these questions force students to generate language relevant to their tasks. The teacher's questions are designed to provide a framework for students to examine their knowledge and experience in new ways. The teacher should tailor the difficulty level of the questions to the learners' current understanding and ability levels. If a student is unable to answer open-ended questions, the teacher can use more specific, directed, and supportive questions. For example, the teacher should begin by asking general questions, such as, *Do you have all the information you need to solve the problem? What else do you need to know?* If these do not elicit an answer, the teacher can provide more guidance by asking, *What do you need to know about how to carefully read the question? What are the key words do you need to underline?* or *What diagram can we draw of what we know about the problem?* If this tactic does not elicit an answer, the teacher can provide even more guidance—reading the problem aloud with the student and pausing to ask specific questions, or beginning to model a solution and then asking questions about what should be done next. If these probes do *not* work, the tutor can provide explicit direct explanations and then probe for student comprehension. Sometimes students just want to be told what to do next or how to get unstuck in order to move on.

In short, the scaffolded process is like a dance: each partner needs to be attuned to the other, following the other's lead. But asking questions is only effective if teachers provide students with ample time to answer. Teachers often fail to do so, a failure which especially penalizes slower students. Research indicates that the average length of time between when a teacher calls on a student to answer a question, and when she provides the answer or calls on another student to answer, is *one second*. After just one second, teachers often redirect the question or answer it themselves. A number of educational researchers have demonstrated that when this wait-time interval is increased to 3 to 5 seconds, the quality of students' comprehension and answers is significantly improved (Riley, 1986; Rowe, 1974, 1986; Tobin, 1983). While the specific wait times may vary with the type of question that is being asked, the overall finding is that when teachers increase their wait times, students' learning rates improve. In short, the teacher needs to take the time not only to ask good questions, but also to provide ample wait times in order to allow students to respond reflectively.

Sometimes teachers ask questions of the whole class by employing *choral* or *group responding*. Choral responding is used most effectively when students evidence some degree of accuracy on the task and the primary teaching goal is to increase the fluency of their responses. While this method is an efficient way to increase the number of students who are responding, it makes it difficult for teachers to monitor individual students' performance. Choral responding can be supplemented with response cards on which students demonstrate their independent work.

1. Does the story have a good beginning, middle, and ending?
2. Is there anything that is not clear or is hard to understand about the story? Does the story make sense? (The listener was instructed to put a ? by any part that was hard to understand.)
3. Is there any place where more detail could be added?

The peer reviewer was also asked to make at least three suggestions for what the writer could say more about. In subsequent sessions the peers reversed roles.

We have stressed the *consolidation* aspect of this program. While students could *acquire* such strategies in one or two lessons, a number of sessions emphasizing student consolidation are necessary if students are to move from mimicking the teacher to using strategies to regulate their own writing. Such activities, whether conducted at the individual, group, or class level, help students become critical thinkers and strategic self-directed learners.

The benefits of teaching and consolidating such strategies is underscored by the results of Harris and Graham's intervention program. They employed this program with fourth-grade students (and sometimes successfully employed it even in grades 2 and 3). Prior to strategy instruction and consolidation, many students spent very little time planning in advance of beginning writing (often less than one minute). The students' writing was best described as *knowledge telling*—where they simply wrote down whatever they knew. Revision constituted simple proofreading, in which students merely substituted one word for another. Harris and Graham also report that prior to their skills and strategy instruction less than 10% of the students' essays contained all of the basic parts, and almost 50% included material that was unrelated to their arguments. After strategy intervention, 82% of the students included all basic parts of the essays, and reference to unrelated materials was reduced to 15%. The students who went through strategy instruction made 2 to 5 times as many revisions, and 3 out of 5 of these revisions changed the text in a meaningful way (prior to the strategy intervention, only 1 out of 3 students made such meaningful revisions). The strategy acquisition and consolidation also resulted in longer, more convincing essays, with fewer errors.

The success of explicitly teaching and consolidating domain-specific strategies highlights the potential value of teaching students generic strategies that can be applied across academic subjects. Teachers usually do not explicitly teach students strategies related to the processes of learning. Students rarely receive explicit instruction on how to take class notes, how to highlight a reading passage, how to study, how to use their time effectively, and the like. Teachers need to discuss, model, teach, and provide students with extended practice on how to apply such self-regulatory strategies. As noted in Chapter 3, students who succeed academically possess such strategies. Teachers need to explicitly teach *all* students how to use them and then provide extensive practice with feedback.

Monitoring Task-Directive Discourse

Teachers should also monitor or sample students' task-directive discourse. It is important that students become increasingly able to talk about their tasks. This can be promoted by placing students in responsible consulting roles (as discussed in Chapter 9). However, even before students have reached a point where they can effectively consult, edit, or collaborate, they can be expected to explain their goals clearly, and to respond intelligently to teacher questions. Teachers should note whether students are doing these things.

When Closing the Session: Reflecting With Students on What Was Learned and Accomplished

When a consolidation task is completed, students need to evaluate their progress toward efficient performance of skills, effective use of strategies to plan new tasks, and effective application of the skills in a domain (math, science, language, etc.). This process may require a more active teacher role. The teacher should highlight the original objective of the consolidation task (improved skill performance or task accomplishment) and discuss how students can tell whether it has been accomplished. (Note that such improvements may not be detectable in a day, but probably are detectable over a week.)

Students must also become responsible for evaluating the outcomes of tasks they accomplish in different domains, in addition to evaluating improvement in planning tasks and performing skills. Do you want children to check or evaluate each other's work? (This is often a good idea.) If not, do you want each child to make a final check of his or her work? Do you want them to discuss their work with you?

Maintaining a focus on student *progress*—rather than on student status or ranking in comparison to others—should enhance student motivation to become more competent in various domains. At the same time, examining barriers to progress should facilitate the teacher's planning for acquisition sessions. Review the section in Chapter 7 on Assessing Student Misconceptions (pp. 123-124) that discusses ways of dealing with learning problems and misconceptions.

After Consolidation Sessions

Although students should participate in evaluating performance and progress during consolidation settings, teachers are ultimately responsible for drawing and reporting conclusions about student progress. Not only must teachers be sure that evaluations are carried out by students (or in conjunction with the teacher)—they must also use these evaluations as the basis for planning both future consolidation sessions and additional skill or strategy acquisition work. Of equal importance is the need to recognize what consulting roles individual students are ready for. It is easy to draw conclusions about student successes and progress. Successful performance, independently accomplished, is evidence of growth. However, it is often important to understand student problems and failures. In listening to students, and in examining student work, teachers should attempt to understand how they arrived at unsatisfactory performances or wrong conclusions. This is another time to apply cognitive empathy—to try to see the task as the students saw it, and to understand problems students encountered. The outcome of such a review may be modified consolidation tasks, new acquisition lessons, or simply improved assistance. In the long run, the outcome should be more students who are ready to undertake increased responsibility in consulting roles and work on more authentic tasks.

Conclusion: Consolidating Skills and Strategies

Acquiring and consolidating skills and strategies has been the traditional objective of education. We—and many others—are seeking to expand these objectives to include real mastery of academic skills and subjects. However, before skills and strategies can be mastered, students must acquire and consolidate them.

Acquisition sessions are what educators have traditionally called "lessons." Consolidation sessions ("independent work" or "seat work") have been less emphasized in educational research and teacher preparation, although students typically spend far more time consolidating learned skills and strategies than acquiring them. The main goal of consolidation settings is improved student performance of skills and application of planning strategies leading to the successful accomplishment of tasks. We have stressed the importance of deliberate practice for improving performance. In this chapter, we have reviewed strategies for helping students consolidate new skills and strategies. These include issues teachers should consider prior to consolidation sessions, issues in the introduction of such sessions, issues to consider as consolidation sessions proceed, issues in closing consolidation settings, and issues to be considered after sessions are finished.

A major theme in Chapters 7 and 8 has been adjusting tasks to students' achievement levels. As we said in Chapter 7, we believe that students cannot master skills and strategies that they have not acquired and consolidated, and cannot acquire and consolidate skills and strategies that presuppose other skills, concepts, or strategies that they lack. While there remains some debate on this point in the educational literature, we have observed too many students struggling with "impossible" tasks. We have also observed many students whose work (or thinking) was essentially done for them by teachers or other students. This solves the student's and teacher's immediate problem of completing a task, but leaves the student unable to cope effectively with future academic challenges. Consequently, we stress the importance of establishing what skills students actually have, and adjusting instruction and consolidation activities to these realities. Students must move forward. Most of them can't leap chasms.

In subsequent chapters, we will address the creation of what we call *consulting roles* for students. These may occur in some of the same settings described in this chapter. They may also occur in unique "consultation settings." In addition, we will address the creation of "authentic" tasks and settings, in which students can apply learned skills and strategies in contexts where the quality of their performance matters. Both consulting experiences and authentic applications are necessary to truly master academic skills and strategies. However, students cannot master skills and strategies that have never been acquired or consolidated to some degree.

Endnotes

1. For example, in Good and Brophy's *Looking in Classrooms* (1994), an excellent text on teaching and classroom management, discussions of independent work or consolidation are appended to detailed guidelines for direct instruction, or attached to discussions of ways to deal with student diversity and management problems. There is little focus on the importance of such experiences for successful achievement.

   Similarly, Gagne and Briggs's classic book *Principles of Instructional Design* (1974) also provides comparatively little consideration of deliberate practice or consolidation, compared to the attention given to initial instruction of skills and strategies at a variety of levels of complexity.

2. Part of Vygotsky's point in describing the ZPD was that observed levels of performance may obscure differences between students. Two students may demonstrate the same level of "independent" achievement, but one may be capable of considerably more advanced performance than the other, given instruction and scaffolded assistance (Vygotsky, 1978). Brown and Ferrara (1985) describe a method of assessing the ZPD using a standard set of graduated questions regarding a specific task.

3. The term *scaffolding* was first used by David Wood and his colleagues (Wood & Middleton, 1975; Wood, Bruner, & Ross, 1976) in studies of parents and other tutors assisting young children who were building objects or solving a three-dimensional puzzle. In this work, the students were essentially novices. The scaffolders presented the task, but did not demonstrate how to do it. Rather, they supplied hints, the detail of which varied as a function of the child's progress.

4. Harris and Graham (1996) have taught students a variety of strategies to improve their writing skills. These strategies are summarized in the form of organizing mnemonics. For example, students were taught that story parts consist of "W-W-W, What=2, How=2." These stand for the following:

Who is the main character? Who else is in the story?

Where does the story take place?

What does the main character do or want to do? What do the characters do?

What happens to the main character and to the other characters?

How does the story end?

Another mnemonically based strategy to improve writing is TREE: note *Topic sentence* (tell what you believe), note *Reasons* (tell why you believe it), *Explain* reasons, note *Ending* (wrap up argument).

Math teachers often use mnemonics such as BEDMAS (*Brackets, Exponents, Divide, Multiply, Add, Subtract*) to solve algebraic bracket problems, while geography teachers teach students the mnemonic HOMES to recall the names of the five Great Lakes (*Huron, Ontario, Michigan, Erie, Superior*). The ultimate goal would be to teach students how to generate their own mnemonics.

Chapter Nine

Planning and Implementing Consultation Settings

If students are to master a set of skills and strategies, they must go beyond doing what the teacher says and merely responding to teachers' requests. Students must become *autonomous learners*. They must be able not only to perform a task on demand, but also to specify, plan, implement, monitor, and evaluate their performance. They must not only consume knowledge, but also be able to produce knowledge and invent strategies. They must be able to explain, teach, correct, and improve skills and task planning strategies—in short, to consult about skills and strategies.

Research has established a clear connection between students' use of elaborated explanations and their learning (Fuchs, Fuchs, et al., 1997; Swing & Peterson, 1982; Webb, 1989, 1991). As students strive to explain and defend what they have done and why—to others and to themselves—they tend to integrate and elaborate their knowledge in new ways and to develop mastery. As they become increasingly effective consultants to others, they also become increasingly effective consultants to themselves, resulting in improved independent and collaborative levels of accomplishment. This chapter is about how teachers and students can collaboratively co-create and implement settings in which students can effectively take charge of their performance and reflect on what they have learned.

What can teachers do to help students move from successful consolidation of skills and task-planning strategies to consulting about these skills and strategies with others, as well as with themselves? How can teachers create learning settings where students appropriate task ownership, demonstrate leadership, and mentally represent what, how, and why they perform tasks? This chapter will describe how teachers can explicitly teach and nurture students' consulting skills.

Creating Learning Settings with Consulting Roles

There are three kinds of consulting roles in which students take the lead in explaining skills, planning strategies, and tasks:

- *assisting or tutoring roles* in which students assist others who are less competent than themselves;
- *collaborative roles* in which two or more students plan and work on tasks together, jointly solving problems; and
- *self-consulting* roles in which students act independently as their own consultants in solving problems, evaluating task outcomes, and reflecting on possible alternatives or improvements.

Learning settings that provide consulting roles provide opportunities for students to:

1. take charge and be recognized as being competent (on tasks at which they actually *are* competent);
2. focus on strategies for planning tasks (e.g., be encouraged to ask strategic questions and to engage in think-aloud planning);
3. talk about task performance—to others (assisting, explaining), or to themselves (as in explicit reflection);
4. focus on skill performance, often in new contexts;
5. evaluate task performance and consulting abilities;
6. develop help-seeking behaviors and social supports;
7. learn sharing and cooperative behaviors; and
8. describe to others how to be a helper.

In order to lead to improved understanding and competence, such consulting roles should continue over a period of weeks or months. In planning an effective educational program, we cannot stress strongly enough the importance of ensuring that *most students participate in some consulting roles*. This must occur in each curriculum area in which students are expected to demonstrate mastery. We must reiterate that this consultative mastery will probably not be seen on tasks demanding recently acquired skills or construction competencies, but rather on tasks involving more consolidated skills, for which requisite skills are already in place.

The Teacher's Role in Consulting Settings

In order to achieve the educational objective of putting most students into consulting roles, the teacher needs to adopt a complementary, mentoring role. In this role, the teacher will:

1. plan, design, and initiate settings that include consulting roles for students;
2. strategically select appropriate tasks and define the setting as one requiring consultation;
3. ensure that consulting students have the prerequisite skills needed to perform the task;
4. teach and model (directly or using student videotapes) how to consult or how to be a good helper;
5. choose students who will work together effectively;
6. relinquish task responsibility, titrate assistance, and fade support—i.e., scaffold student consulting activity;
7. delegate authority and responsibility to students to teach others;
8. act as a resource to help student consultants as the need arises;
9. monitor peer consultation settings in order to ensure that consultants are effectively assisting less advanced students and that students who are working on cooperative projects are genuinely collaborating on a task;
10. provide students with an opportunity to self-evaluate and mentally represent (explain, diagram) both the procedural features of a task and their consultative efforts;
11. evaluate students' consultative skills and provide constructive feedback to students about their consultative abilities;
12. demonstrate to students that they can consult with themselves, as well as with others, and highlight how they use helping strategies with themselves, as well as with others.

Before Implementing a Consulting Setting

Some of these teacher responsibilities involve decisions made *before* a consulting setting is implemented. For example, teachers need to be strategic when choosing the tasks on which students are asked to consult. The consulting students should have the prerequisite skills needed to perform the task and should be placed in an assisting, editing, or teaching role. Teachers can also arrange for students to work together on constructive, authentic tasks with fellow students.

Illustrative planning or application activities might include collaboratively carrying out a science project, offering group presentations, developing a museum exhibit, producing a school (class) newspaper or television newscast, creating a class portfolio, preparing a lesson plan, or generating exam questions. Students are more likely to become engaged in such collaborative tasks when a valued real-life product is being created. These activities should require problem-solving over an extended period of time.[1] Students' consulting roles can be strengthened further if they are asked to present and describe their products to an audience beyond the classroom, so that they are called upon to explain what they did, how they did it, and what they learned from helping or working with others.

Just as teachers need to strategically select and discuss consulting tasks, they must also be strategic in deciding which students should work together in consulting situations. As one teacher commented,

> I put a lot of thought into the groupings. I do not just "throw" students together. When the group has a problem, I try hard to have them solve the conflict on their own. It is extremely rare that I allow a student to change from one group to another. Instead, I give them "problem solving time" to work out problems, and then when we come back together as a group, I ask students to talk to each other about what worked and what didn't and why (Guthrie & Cox, 1995, pp. 31-32).

It is unlikely that all students will be able to participate as consultants simultaneously. Hence, a consultation setting cannot usually be a whole-class event. Students at the consultation level should not require a lot of teacher support to carry out their role. In addition, the students should have some competence at instructing on the types of tasks on which they are expected to consult. If other students are to be put into tutee roles, the teacher should know that they are less competent than the student consultants who will act as tutors.

These decisions about selecting tasks and students, preparing materials, planning and designing consulting activities, each occur before the consultation setting begins.

During Implementation of Consultation Settings

The teacher should discuss with the students the importance of undertaking consulting roles—relating this type of role to previous work and to previous consulting. When consulting students are assisting others, the teacher should clearly specify both the tasks and the consulting roles, being clear about which students are responsible for accomplishing the academic task and how each role will be evaluated.

In the case of academic tasks with an applied focus, there will be a planning process. It is desirable that this process be as overt and public as possible. Consulting or collaborating students should be prepared to *assist* with planning, not to simply do the task for others. This means being able to ask leading questions, and to step back if the assistee is on the right track.

As the academic task is carried out, consulting students should monitor the progress of those whom they assist. They should receive guidance about when and how to intervene if they see a problem. It is worth noting for both teachers and consulting students that there is evidence that unrequested assistance is not incorporated into student work as much as requested assistance (Beyer, 1988).

The teacher should be prepared to monitor student consulting. This may mean listening from a distance. It may mean checking with consultees after the fact. Two key features to attend to are whether the student consultant is able to put aspects of the academic task into words as needed, and whether he or she is providing effective assistance or consultation to peers.

Johnson and Johnson observe that assigning students the specific roles of tutor and tutees by no means guarantees that a consulting experience will occur.[2] Cooperative group activities cannot simply be assumed to provide consultation experience. Our research has demonstrated that although children of varying ability levels can verbalize tasks sufficiently to act as helpers, they do not always demonstrate good helping skills. For example, some of the children we observed were inattentive, somewhat rude, easily frustrated, too directive, not directive enough, and/or too rushed. Consultative skills need to be taught, nurtured, and reinforced on a continual basis.

At the Close of a Consultation Setting

When the task in the consulting setting is finished, evaluation of both the completed task and the consulting role is crucial. Student consultants should be actively involved in evaluating the success of the academic work (their own and that of others). Part of becoming an effective consultant—a master of a topic—is being able to judge the quality of work at the academic level. Consultants need to know what a "good job" is. Student consultants should also evaluate their own consulting efforts. Were they able to effectively help others or effectively collaborate on a project? The teacher should provide students with feedback on their consulting ability. Students should be given opportunities to make presentations to others (peers, parents) about their collaborating, helping, and tutoring activities. This may be in the form of oral or written presentations. They might be asked to work on publishing books on how to be a good helper. Students may also give presentations or videotape demonstrations on the differences between effective and ineffective tutors.

After Implementation of a Consulting Setting

The teacher should review with students, asking questions about the interactions. Did they understand what to do? Were they able to help each other? What evidence is there that effective consultation took place? If the teacher lacks direct information on these points, she should plan closer monitoring in the future or interview the participants during the consulting activity. Consulting accomplishments should be recorded by students and teachers, just as consolidating accomplishments are recorded and acknowledged.

Ways Students Can Engage in Consulting Roles

There are several different ways in which students can consult.

- *As helpers, assistants or tutors.* Students must be taught how to assist, not do for others.
- *As generators of tasks and feedback for other students.* Students can develop consulting skills by learning to identify and determine patterns of problems which they or the teacher might help with. Based on their observations, consultants can generate lesson plans, help select tasks and manipulatives, and create tests for assessing an assistee's level of comprehension. This consulting process will work best with student tutees for whom the skills in question are a problem. If the tutor's editing leads to helpful dialogue with the tutee, a consultation setting is created.
- *As collaborators in constructing tasks or complex products.* For true collaboration, students' abilities must be similar, or at least complementary. Consultation is most likely to occur when students are called upon to apply, invent, and construct—not just consume—knowledge and skills.
- *As participants in structured cooperative learning.* The students' roles may be rotated, as in Jigsaw instruction and reciprocal teaching. In these and other cooperative learning roles, each student has a defined sub-task responsibility within an overall task. When it is a particular student's

turn to serve as a more knowledgeable participant, he or she is called upon to consult.

- *As reflectors after accomplishing individual and collaborative tasks.* Students can be asked to review their own work and comment on it orally or in print. To a large extent, reflection amounts to self-editing and self-evaluation. If this process is focused on improvement, rather than criticism, it can be a positive consulting experience.

We are sure that this is not an exhaustive list of possible consulting roles for students, and that creative teachers develop many other effective consultation roles. Before we consider two of these consulting contexts (peer teaching and writing) in more detail, we will first examine several examples of how educators have successfully developed consulting roles for students. We will briefly describe them at this point and provide a more detailed account and analysis in Chapter 11.

Educational Projects Designed To Facilitate Students' Consulting Roles

1. Ruth Mertens has developed a parent involvement program called the *IMPACT Project*, which now runs in 5000 schools across England, Scotland, Wales, and parts of Europe. The project is being conducted in elementary schools (grades 1 to 7) and involves assigning students tasks that require them to talk to, play a mathematics game with, or collect data with a family member (a parent, sibling, or other relative). The student is taught how to be a "tutor" at home, guiding the relative through an activity. For example, the student may ask the relative to help figure out how tall each of them is, measured in lengths of spoons, or how many birthday candles each of them has blown out in their lives. The results of these home-based, student-initiated activities are incorporated the next day in the mathematics classroom. The goal of the IMPACT Project is to arrange for the students to act as tutors for task-ignorant adults (relatives), to increase both their acquisition skills and their enthusiasm for mathematics. As Mertens observes,

    > It is the process of verbalizing a procedure which enables [children] to make sense for themselves. In Vygotskian terms, the mediation of another's [mathematical] activity is predicated upon the self-regulatory functions of language learning. Thus, through verbalization the

[children are] able to regulate their own and another's mathematical actions (1996, p. 419).

2. Palincsar and Brown's *Reciprocal Teaching* (RT) program explicitly uses consulting roles to improve reading comprehension—specifically, strategies for summarizing, clarifying, questioning texts, and predicting future content. The original RT program involved creating consultation roles for seventh-grade poor readers by moving learners into teaching roles, as small groups of children learned and applied strategies for constructing the meaning of texts. Within the group, students took turns acting as the teacher (Brown & Palincsar, 1989; Palincsar & Brown, 1984, 1986). (More recent developments of the RT program will be discussed in Chapter 11.)

3. Pressley and colleagues' *Transactional Strategies Instruction* program also focuses on improving reading comprehension (Brown, Pressley, Van Meter, & Schuder, 1996). In this program, there is a strong emphasis on teacher-explained and teacher-modeled comprehension strategies. However, the program also provides consultation settings in the form of extended interpretive classroom discussions of text, which emphasize student application of strategies to text. These discussions include having students think aloud as they practice applying comprehension strategies during reading group instruction (Pressley et al., 1990).

4. Scardamalia, Bereiter, and Lamon's *CSILE* (Computer-Supported Intentional Learning Environment) focuses on students' knowledge generation and writing skills (Scardamalia, Bereiter, & Lamon, 1994). Using online dialogue on computers, rather than direct face-to-face discussion, students consult with each other and with the teacher about what is being learned and about problems encountered. (Obviously, CSILE requires some degree of literacy skills before it can be fully implemented.)

5. Inglis and Biemiller's *cross-age mathematics peer tutoring* program attempts to create for less advanced students the informal assistance setting in which advanced students are observed to participate (Inglis & Biemiller, submitted for publication). This is accomplished in a cross-age helping context, preceded by training (acquisition and consolidation) of helping strategies. Their program ensures that all students, regardless of their level of performance, have an opportunity to be tutors.

Each of these examples illustrates what we call "consulting" roles, although their authors do not use this term. Each emphasizes informed dialogue with others as a route to improving understanding and performance. Each involves situations in which students have "in-charge" roles. In addition, each reflects a realization that participation in such settings must occur over extended time periods (weeks, months, or years) to have any measurable effect on autonomous task construction or problem-solving ability.

To summarize, learning settings with consulting roles are the components of a school program in which students can successfully "take charge" of tasks using consolidated skills and consolidated task construction strategies. The consulting aspect is the students' overt verbal direction of task construction and skill performance. As noted earlier, there are a variety of different roles and settings in which consulting can occur. Two that are worth special attention are peer tutoring and writing.

Peer-Based Instruction as Consulting

In national surveys, 79% of elementary teachers and 62% of middle school teachers report some sustained use of peer-based instruction such as cooperative learning (Berliner & Biddle, 1995). In fact, in California, the inclusion of cooperative learning has been mandated for all schools. The interest in cooperative learning is justified by research findings. As Robert Slavin (1978) observes, "Research on cooperative learning is one of the greatest success stories in the history of educational research" (p. 43).

Slavin reports that the large majority of cooperative learning studies in which group goals were combined with individual accountability led to significant positive achievement. (Cooperative learning studies in which there was no individual accountability for task performance were typically much less effective.) Moreover, there is little evidence that gifted students are shortchanged by cooperative learning arrangements. In fact, the students who benefit most are those who provide elaborated explanations to others. While those who serve as explainers learn the most, the others who are more passive learners but are nevertheless exposed to high-level reasoning also benefit. Peer tutoring has also been found to increase academic gains for both tutors and tutees, especially for students with learning disabilities. Additional benefits occur in terms of self-esteem, sense of belonging, and identity with the group (Osguthorpe & Scruggs, 1986; Scruggs & Richter, 1985; Yasutake, Bryan, & Dohrn, 1996).

Two additional studies illustrate the potential value of peer tutoring. Perkins (1992) reported that when students were asked to read a story in order to teach this material to someone who didn't understand it, they extended more effort, retained more, and evidenced greater conceptual understanding than students who received only direct praise and rewards for their efforts. But these effects are not limited to high-achieving students. Inglis and Biemiller (submitted for publication) demonstrated that low-performing math students can also benefit from the opportunity to be a cross-age tutor. They taught low-performing grade 4 students how to be effective tutors for grade 2 math students, thus putting the grade 4 students into the role of expert consultants. This tutoring experience improved math performance for the grade 4 tutors.

These results indicate that all students, no matter what their initial level of performance, can benefit from being put into consulting roles. As the adage notes, "The best way to learn something is to teach it someone else." As Fisher and Berliner (1995) report:

> In fact, some scholars have argued that of all the methods recommended in the last decade for improving education, cross-age tutoring generates the *largest gains* in learning for the *least financial cost*. When it comes to cost-benefit analysis and seeking the biggest bang for the educational buck, peer and cross-age tutoring programs may be the clear winners (p. 308, emphasis added).

Why does peer teaching have such beneficial effects? Having students engage in peer tutoring, in one form or another, requires the peer tutors to:

1. externalize their thought processes, making their ideas explicit and accessible both to others and to themselves;
2. elaborate an idea or skill to other students, resulting in an increased awareness and understanding of what the tutors do and do not know (students are more likely to ask each other questions that they are too embarrassed or uncertain to ask the teacher);
3. share, explain and defend ideas and opinions, thus making their thinking clearer;
4. act as role models of thinking, reasoning, and reflection;
5. take on the perspectives of others and offer explanations so others can understand them, thus cultivating a language of thinking;
6. cooperate and collaborate with peers in problem solving on joint tasks, resulting in students' taking more responsibility for and ownership of a task;
7. provide other students with opportunities to talk about learning and helping; and
8. encourage other students to help each other succeed academically.

In addition, peer tutoring requires that students attend to the task, generate a plan, self-question and self-monitor, access prior knowledge, define and translate technical terms, note relationships, generate multiple examples, clarify concepts, reorganize information, and resolve inconsistencies, since higher forms of understanding emerge out of cognitive conflicts. Students who engage in peer tutoring also learn how to provide hints (as compared to offering answers or solutions), how to help tutees cope with setbacks and failures, and how to provide them with encouragement and praise. As a result, students in the role of tutor develop a deeper conceptual understanding of the task and of the learning process. Tutoring skills do not arise naturally, however. Students need to be taught how to be an effective tutor and a good helper, as described in Highlight Box 9.1.

Forms of Peer Teaching

Educators have developed a number of different ways peer teaching can be used. We will comment on only a handful of these instructional procedures. We know of no research that has established the relative effectiveness of one peer tutoring procedure versus another procedure across subject areas and across grade levels. At this point, classroom teachers are left to their own preferences in choosing among these procedures. Following a brief description of these techniques, we will conclude with a consideration of some practical guidelines to follow when implementing peer tutoring procedures. (See Appendix 9-A.) The specific tutoring formats we will describe in detail include the following:

1. Cross-age tutoring
2. Collaborative learning
    a. Informal exchanges
    b. Paired learning (Think-Pair-Share)
    c. Classwide Peer Tutoring
3. Jigsaw Instruction
4. Reciprocal Teaching
5. Shared videotaping
6. Community of learners

Cross-age tutoring occurs when older students are assigned to work with younger students or students at lower grade levels. For this method to be most effective, we recommend that the tutor and the tutee be at least two grade levels apart. The assigned tutor may work one-on-one or on a small-group basis. The tutors

Highlight Box 9.1
HOW TO TEACH STUDENTS TO BECOME
EFFECTIVE TUTORS

Educators have learned a great deal about how to help students become more effective peer tutors and collaborators. A number of guidebooks on peer teaching highlight that *it is the quality of interactions during peer-mediated learning activities that is critical in determining how much students learn.* The research highlights the importance of students' providing *elaborated assistance*—giving and receiving explanations as part of the helping process. Researchers also highlight the importance of teachers' *structuring, guiding,* and providing *ongoing monitoring* of peer interactions. Students need to be prepared for peer work and explicitly taught how to be good helpers and collaborators. Following peer activities, teachers need to hold debriefing sessions with students on the effectiveness of their peer experience. Finally, there is increasing recognition that students who have learning problems and learning disabilities require additional adult-directed lessons to supplement the peer-mediated instructional opportunities (Yasutake et al., 1996).

In order to become effective peer tutors, students need to learn how to:

1. **offer elaborated help** (i.e., pay careful attention, actively listening to the partner; monitor the partner's comprehension, and offer help in the form of hints; explain to the partner (tutee) how to find an answer, without giving the answer; provide another explanation if the initial explanation does not work; and ask the partner to explain the tutor's explanation back to her, in order to find out if he understands);

2. **ask step-by-step questions** to assess the tutee's comprehension and to elicit the tutee's explanation of how he goes about performing the task (e.g., use *what, where, when, how,* and *why* questions—"What is the first step ...?"; "How did you know how to ...?"; "What if they asked ...?"), allowing ample waiting time before providing hints and answers;

3. **respond to requests for assistance** by relating the current problem to something familiar to the tutee; explain something in different ways; reread with emphasis; simplify a task (breaking it into its natural units); start with easier tasks and gradually increase the difficulty level; and model a solution slowly (think aloud and demonstrate), while checking for the tutee's comprehension;

4. help the tutee **anticipate problems and possible obstacles**, and demonstrate how to **use procedural prompts** (reminders, cue cards, procedural checklists, manipulatives) and how to ask for help (encourage the tutee to keep asking until she fully understands);

5. **monitor the tutee's progress** (e.g., take notes and fill out a tutor's journal page on each session);

6. **compliment the tutee for her efforts**, and not just for getting the answer; encourage the tutee to keep trying and take pride in her work.

This list indicates that being a peer tutor is a demanding role that requires discussion, training, and practice with feedback. If students can master these helping skills, they should be able to use them on their own learning activities to help themselves. In order to accomplish these ambitious objectives, teachers need to take an active role before, during, and after the peer-mediating activity.

Before the peer activity, the teacher can employ a number of activities to instruct students on how to help each other, and as a result, how to help themselves. To explain to students why giving and receiving explanations can prove helpful, Fuchs and her colleagues (1994) use a baseball analogy. They describe how a struggling player requested help from a better hitter. The better hitter analyzed both their hitting techniques and offered an explanation and assistance. As a result, *both* players were able to hit the ball more successfully.

The teacher can use a number of activities, such as a questions circle in which students practice asking good questions, a blindfold game in which students practice giving "good hints" without telling the answer and without solving the problem for the blindfolded student, or an analysis of modeling films that show two students helping each other. The teacher can model and have the students practice different levels of hints and questions. These can go from the general ("Do you need help?") to the more specific ("Are you sure you counted right? You're close, but count again. Try using your fingers."). Students need to learn how to give help, but not make the task too easy. The students can record their observations on how it feels to give and receive hints in their "Helper's Workbook."

In addition to these generic helping behaviors, the teacher needs to ensure that the student tutor has mastered the skills that will be taught, especially when cross-age tutoring is used. It is critical for the tutor to know how to perform the academic task and to possess the necessary prerequisite skills, so that she can focus on the mentoring process. In order to facilitate this consolidation process, the teacher can ask the tutor to help develop a procedural flow chart, worksheets, reminder cards, and so on, that can be used in the tutoring process. Tutors and collaborators need practice and feedback to develop these skills.

During the peer activities, the teacher needs to actively monitor the peer interactions and provide assistance as needed and requested. Following the tutoring session, the teacher needs to review the peer experience with both the tutees and the tutors (or with the peer collaborators). The teacher can ask the tutors to describe how they decided what their tutees needed help with, how they helped them, and how they dealt with things that were difficult for them (e.g., keeping the tutee's interest and handling any discipline problems). The teacher can ask the tutees if they received explanations that helped and what the tutors did well. The teacher can ask both the tutors and the tutees what they learned from their peer experience, and whether they can use these same skills in helping themselves.

Appendix 9-A provides even more specific guidelines for using peer teaching. Teaching students to be good helpers and to work collaboratively in groups takes time. The teacher needs to be patient and not get discouraged if things do not go smoothly at first. Teaching students to develop tutoring and helping skills will pay off, as the research literature indicates.

should work at a performance level where their skills have been consolidated, so they can readily develop consultative skills. The tutor is trained on how to be a helper (as described in Highlight Box 9.1). The teacher provides students with procedural prompts on how to tutor, which are complemented by a post-tutorial process session with both the tutors and tutees. For example, Inglis and Biemiller (submitted for publication) had cross-age peer tutors keep a Helper's Workbook to record the helping skills they were learning. The workbook was divided into five sections that highlighted the *what*, *how*, and *why* of tutoring:

1. *Look and Listen*—so you know who needs help and the kind of help that is needed.
2. *Ask Questions*—so you know what kind of help is needed.
3. *Give Hints*—instead of answers, when you help. This leads the other person to the answer without doing the work for her. Help only when necessary.
4. *Give Pats On The Back*—encouraging the other person. Notice good effort or a job well done, and say so.
5. *Check It Out*—means looking to see if the work has been done correctly. "Checking it out" also involves asking yourself, "Did I do a good job helping?"

(Each skill was represented in the Helper's Workbook by a picture.) In subsequent sessions, the teacher had peer tutors also fill out sections on "What I Learned Today" and "What is Fun and Hard About Helping."

These types of reflective student behaviors gave teachers a way to monitor their students' progress. They also provided guidance for addressing tutoring gaps and misconceptions by means of direct instruction and hands-on supervision of good helping skills.

The benefits of putting students in a knowledgeable position, in charge of teaching an academic task to others, was reflected in the comments of the grade 4 tutors:

- "I like to make up math problems for them [the grade 2 students] to figure out. I liked to help them with their math. It's important to learn to help so you get smarter."
- "I learned how to look and listen, ask questions, help grade 2 how to do math."
- "I like to help so they learn and we learn. It's like both of us are learning."

- "I learned to read hard words, dividing and time tables. I learned to help grade 2's to say 'wait a minute,' tell them to read the problem again and check it."

These grade 4 tutors were predominantly from a low-SES urban immigrant population; they displayed average to low math performance, relative to their classmates. Putting these high-risk students into legitimate leadership roles had a positive impact on both their attitudes and their performance.

Yet another form of cross-age tutoring involves having students act as "big brothers" or "big sisters," providing guidance for younger students. Whether it is in the form of tutoring or peer counseling, it is critical that students at all levels of competence be put into these consultative "helper" roles. At present, it is usually only the "smart" students who are given these tutorial opportunities and responsibilities. Such selectivity in instructional opportunities exacerbates individual differences and widens the gap between high- and low-achieving students.

Collaborative learning occurs when pairs or groups of students have approximately equal knowledge and skills. Collaborative learning may be quite informal, with the teacher asking pairs of students to share ideas, to exchange answer sheets, and to check each other's writing, classwork, homework, journals, Tickets Out The Door, mind maps, or portfolios. Students can also work in what are called "thinking pairs," in which one student does work on a task while thinking aloud. The other student follows the procedural guidelines to make sure the partner does not skip steps without some justification. The students then switch roles. Before having students work in thinking pairs, the teacher should first model such thinking-aloud procedures, or use a diagram to explain an answer.

Students can also be given questions to ask each other as they conduct and discuss tasks. For example, in discussing their classroom projects, students can be encouraged to ask each other,

- "Where did you get the idea for this project?"
- "Did you have difficulties completing this project?"
- "How did you resolve your difficulties?"
- "What did you learn?"
- "Would you do this project again?"
- "Would you recommend this project to others?"

Following these paired or small-group discussions, the students can be asked to share their answers with the whole class.

In a variation of this tutoring process, called Think–Pair–Share, students are asked to read a passage or to listen to a student presentation. The pairs of students are given an opportunity to think individually about the task (e.g., what they have just read or listened to). The students can discuss with their partners what they have learned and any questions they have. Each pair can diagram solutions to preassigned questions that were provided by the teacher or collaboratively generated.

Another variation, called Classwide Peer Tutoring (CWPT), is a more formal way of conducting collaborative peer learning. CWPT combines peer-mediated practice with teacher-orchestrated procedures and with whole-class participation. CWPT requires that each student be paired with a partner. The partners are then assigned to a team to which the pair must report, and eventually the team shares with the whole class. One student in each pair serves as a tutor for a fixed period of time, and then the partners switch roles (Fantuzzo, King, & Heller, 1992; Fuchs, Fuchs, Mathes, & Simmons, 1997; Greenwood et al., 1987, 1988, 1989). For example, when reading comprehension is being taught, one student (usually the slower student) acts as the teacher first. For 10 minutes, he reads out loud, and then for 5 minutes, the other student has to answer procedural questions. They then reverse roles for 15 minutes. CWPT is designed to provide students with an opportunity to talk through problems. In the area of writing, CWPT may be used with "writing buddies" as they work their way through the phases of planning, drafting, editing, revising, and publishing their work. Students can be taken through various phases in the production of a report or essay. Students' experiences in the peer groups can be written up and added to their journals and portfolios.

Barone and Taylor (1996) suggest that students participating in cross-age tutoring and cooperative learning should be asked to fill out a Tutor Journal Page (see Figure 9.1) that asks for a few main details about their consultation experiences. Similarly, the tutee can be asked to fill out information on a Tutee Journal Page (see Figure 9.2).

The collaborative learning process can also involve providing time for small groups of students to talk about specific topics or issues. Have students discuss a book they recommend, or share material from their journal or portfolio, or engage in a debate on a specific topic where they have to write out their respective positions and exchange back and forth the list of pros and cons before having an oral exchange.

Guthrie and McCann (1996) have proposed giving students opportunities to

FIGURE 9.1: Tutor Journal Page

Name _____ Buddy's name _____

What activity did you teach or work on together? _____

_____

Explain how you did it. _____

_____

What did your buddy do well? _____

_____

What does your buddy need to improve? _____

_____

Tell one thing you did well as a tutor or as a helper. _____

_____

Tell one thing you will work on as a tutor or as a helper. _____

_____

Do you want to do this again (with the same or a different partner?) _____

From Barone and Taylor (1996).

FIGURE 9.2: Tutee Journal Page

Name _____

Describe what you did. _____

_____

Tell one thing you did well. _____

_____

Tell one thing you want to work on. _____

_____

Tell one thing you liked about your tutor. _____

_____

Tell one thing you would like your tutor to improve when he or she works with
you. _____

_____

From Barone and Taylor (1996).

form Idea Circles, small groups in which students share their expertise and brain-storm on a given topic. They also suggest that students be given an opportunity to provide feedback on their classmates' school work. For example, they offer a Peer Response Form (see Figure 9.3) that can be used to help students evaluate each other's rough drafts of papers. Such collaboration can facilitate learning.

Jigsaw Instruction is a somewhat different instructional procedure that is designed to put students in an expert role. The teacher divides a task or a topic into different segments or subtopics (metaphorically constituting pieces of a puzzle), and then asks each student to assume responsibility for—or become an expert in—a different aspect of the joint task. Usually the topic is divided into four or five subtopics, each of which is distributed to an individual student or group of students. In order to cover the full topic, students are dependent on each other for information. The teacher should convey that since everyone is expert at something, and nobody—not even the classroom teacher—knows it all, students need to learn to share information. Each student is responsible for sharing his or her knowledge with the other members of the group, and everyone is responsible for the whole unit. The quality of the final product depends on the contribution of each participant (Aronson, 1978).

Stevens and Slavin's (1995) evaluation of various forms of peer teaching has raised some questions about the effectiveness of Jigsaw Instruction. They pro-

---

FIGURE 9.3: Peer Response Form

1. Ask your partners to listen carefully as you read your rough draft out loud.
2. Ask you partners to help you improve your writing by telling you the answers to the following questions. Write down their answers (or have them help you write down the answers).

   What did you like best about my rough draft? _____

   _____

   What did you have the hardest time understanding about my rough draft?

   _____

   _____

   What else can you suggest that I do to improve my rough draft?

   _____

   _____

   From Guthrie and Cox (1995).

pose that group rewards and outcomes, as well as individual accountability, should be added to the Jigsaw procedure.[3]

Reciprocal Teaching (RT), as described earlier, was developed to enhance students' oral reading comprehension. Students are trained to assume leadership roles in a turn-taking procedure. They are taught how to formulate questions for one another around the text. They are taught additional metacognitive skills such as summarizing, predicting, clarifying, and monitoring comprehension. The participants take turns fulfilling the role of student and teacher (Palincsar & Brown, 1984). RT will be considered in more detail in Chapter 11.

Videotaped peer modeling has been used to teach students mathematical skills. Students are videotaped thinking aloud while solving math problems, and these tips are shared with the students in the class who critique and discuss the students' problem solving approaches. The videotapes are not of students from the same school (Schoenfeld, 1985, 1987).

Community of learners is an approach in which students are encouraged to communicate with others who can act as resources (Brown & Campione, 1994, in press). These *resource people* may be fellow classmates who have mastered a particular subtopic as part of Jigsaw Instruction, or others available by means of e-mail or pen pal communication. Knowledge may also be accessed on classroom computers or videotape films. The community of learners model broadens the definition of who may act as peer tutor. Further examples of this teaching approach are considered in Chapter 11. Such social exchanges encourage students to engage in dialogue in the language system of a particular discipline.

Writing as a Means to Consulting Competence

In addition to peer instruction, another way to nurture students' consulting skills is to have them reflect on their performance, orally or in print. Typically, little time is set aside in the curriculum for writing or for other written forms of mental representation (e.g., diagramming in the form of graphic organizers, semantic webs, mind maps, drawing, photography). Why is this a mistake? Why should students not only be required to perform tasks in academic areas (mathematics, science, etc.), but also be required to write and speak in the language system particular to each discipline (mathematically, scientifically, etc.)? Why should students be asked not only what they know, but also how they came to know it? And why is it critical for students' mastery that they use language to describe and discuss what they are doing to learn a task?

Evidence for the importance of engaging in reflective and planful activities comes from two major sources. First, as we noted in Chapter 4, those students who are high achievers in school have been observed to engage in more elaborate self-explanations and self-reflective regulating activities. This pattern of heightened self-awareness and metacognitive competence is also evident in laboratory studies in which high- and low-achieving students are asked to think aloud while performing tasks (math and physics problem solving). Evidence indicates that expressing problem-solving strategies aloud promotes learning (Chi & Van Leehn, 1991; Pressley et al., 1987, 1990, 1995; Rosenshine et al., 1996).

A second source of evidence comes from training studies in which students are asked to write down a sequence of logical steps for solving problems and to explain them to their classmates. Cobb and his colleagues (Cobb, 1994; Cobb et al., 1993, 1996) found that such reflective writing and shared discourse helped first-, second-, and third-grade students consider multiple ways of solving math problems. Similar findings have been reported in other subject areas such as English, physical science, and social science. When students are challenged to explain the reasons behind their solutions, they engage in deeper, more reflective, integrative thinking (see Harris & Graham, 1996).

What is it about writing that facilitates academic mastery? Writing is a tool that serves several functions—including communication, knowledge building, self-expression, personal reflection, and self-evaluation of one's state of understanding. Writing also serves several useful self-regulating functions, helping students organize, reflect on, and refine their thinking. Writing can be viewed as a platform which students can build upon their ideas. Writing also provides a window into students' thinking and a vehicle for assessment, both for the teacher and for the students. Writing provides a record of students' thinking; they can come back to their written accounts in order to see the progress they have made. Writing helps students process information more deeply, improve their organizational skills, and better assess their level of understanding. In addition, revising their writing provides a way for students to further develop their self-regulatory skills, especially when the skills and strategies of revision are explicitly taught and practiced.

Types of Writing Used to Improve Consultation Skills

Teachers have been very creative in developing ways to use writing activities in their classroom on both an individual and a group basis. The exact form of these writing activities will vary depending on each student's age and upon the subject domain. The following list, which is not exhaustive and is particularly applicable to middle and secondary school students, illustrates ways teachers have used writing as part of their pedagogy. The proposed writing activities are not limited to English classes; we are proposing that writing should be used through the entire curriculum, across all academic subjects. Students may be asked to:

1. *Make entries in daily logs, weekly diaries, or journals* of their learning activities. The teacher can prime students' responses by providing them with leading questions (or question stems) to answer in their logs, and continually referring to what has been called a KWL poster. The abbreviation KWL refers to the students' need to answer three questions:

   - What I *know*. (K)
   - What I *want* to know. (W)
   - What I *learned*. (L)

   The teacher can model the use of these probes in the instructional lesson. Figure 9.4 lists additional questions that teachers can offer, or that students can choose from in filling out their written entries.

   Tsurunda (1994) wrote a fine book on how to use writing in math class. He proposes that students record their in-class learning experiences on a Math Journal sheet. The students' entries encourage them to think about their own learning and provide the teacher with feedback on what students think about various learning activities. The students' Math Journal entries have three parts:

   - what the class did (a detailed description of class activity);
   - what the student thought of the activity; and
   - what the student learned (about math and about him- or herself).

   Teachers collect these entries at the end of each week and provide constructive feedback. Peers can also be asked to review each other's entries.

2. *Fill out a Ticket Out The Door*, which asks students to answer specific questions concerning what they have learned in a particular lesson. The questions that teachers use may vary, and the Ticket Out The Door procedure may be used selectively for specific topics or lessons. As in the case of the learning journal, students can be given a choice as to which questions they wish to answer. Figure 9.5 provides examples of the questions students can be asked to answer when using the Ticket Out The Door procedure. Note that most of the items in Figure 9.5 ask *what* and *how* questions that pull for procedural and conditional knowledge.

FIGURE 9.4: Daily Learning Log

Students may be given or asked to *choose questions* from the following array. Their parents can review their logs and then sign off on them.

Date: _____

I think _____

I wonder _____

I saw _____

I want to know _____

What we are doing is called _____

What we are learning today is _____

The goal of the lesson (unit) is _____

Before I begin I must know (be able to do) _____

What we are doing today follows from _____

The task I worked on is _____

What I did first to accomplish this task was _____

     Next I _____

     Next I _____

Some of the strategies I used were _____

Some of the strategies I plan to use are _____

A sign I am understanding this is _____

A sign I am making progress is _____

What did I know that helped me do these things? _____

How did I know I was doing it correctly? _____

What kind of obstacles did I encounter? _____

How did I deal with them? _____

What I still need to work on is _____

What I still don't understand is _____

I'm not sure about _____

I am most proud about _____

Filling out this Learning Log helped me better understand _____

3. Schematically diagram the main concepts they learned or what they took away from a specific lesson. Students can be taught (through teacher modeling, demonstration, instruction, guidance) how to fill out mind maps, graphic organizers, and semantic webs. An example of how teachers can teach Mind Mapping as a form of advance organizer, and as a way to have students reflect and explain what they have learned, is illustrated in Highlight Box 9.2 (p. 182).

Teachers have developed quite creative ways to incorporate independent and collaborative writing into their curriculum. For example, student writing activities may include:

FIGURE 9.5: Ticket Out The Door

At the end of a lesson, students may be given or asked to *choose* a few (perhaps 3 or 4) questions from the following list.

1. What was one thing you learned (or found out about) today?
2. What do you want to remember?
3. When can you use what you learned today?
4. What is one thing you are still not sure about?
5. What did you like *best* about today's class?
6. What did you like *least* about today's class?
7. What would you suggest changing?
8. What do you *know* you know?
9. What do you *think* you know?
10. What did you find difficult to do?
11. How did you try to figure that out?
12. What did you learn from this?
13. What did you expect you would learn from doing this?
14. What surprised you the most in doing this lesson/project/unit?
15. What did you find easy to do? Why?
16. What don't you understand and need help in?
17. What did you work on in class? What did you think about it?
18. How did you help someone today?
19. What do you plan to do tomorrow?
20. What did filling out this Ticket Out The Door help you understand better?

Highlight Box 9.2: MIND MAPPING

One way to foster students' self-reflective thinking, conceptual understanding, and consultation abilities is to teach them how to graphically and schematically summarize what is being taught. There are a number of pedagogical tools available to accomplish this task (e.g., graphic organizers, semantic webs, family trees, concept mapping). These procedures can be used at the outset of a lesson or unit as advance organizers, or at the end of a lesson, in the form of a Ticket Out the Door, as a way to review what was taught. Teachers and students can use these conceptual mapping procedures to assess what students do and do not understand.

An example of how Mind Mapping can be used was offered by a teacher, Virginia Entrikin (1992). She proposed that instead of beginning class with the usual question, "Are there any questions from yesterday's homework?", the teacher can ask students to provide one word or phrase that best describes the main topic of the new material presented the previous day. The teacher then places this word or phrase in the middle of a transparency or on the blackboard. (A transparency is preferred so the teacher can maintain continuous eye contact with students.) Finally, the teacher asks the students what they have discovered about this concept, posing leading questions, and draws a concept map.

The Mind Map provides a picture of the whole subject and shows how the separate points are related to the new topic. By using boxes, circles, arrows, and line segments, the class can come to see and remember the connections between various concepts and operations.

After the class has practiced Mind Mapping, students can be given an opportunity to work in pairs or small groups to generate their own Mind Maps. It is critical that students be required to explain their Mind Maps and to describe to each other how they put the Maps together. The teacher can compare her own Mind Map with those of the students, and all of them can be posted. Subsequently, students can be asked to create their own Mind Maps independently, and to include them in their daily Learning Logs or use them as their Tickets Out The Door. The students' Mind Maps provide an indication of their levels of comprehension.

The teacher can also model and discuss how the Mind Map serves as a useful tool in planning lessons and creating tests. Students can be taught how to use their Mind Map to put together study guides or "cheat" sheets to take into an exam. Mind Maps should be viewed as "living documents" that grow over the course of a lesson, or even over the course of a term, as the students and teachers come to see how what they are learning fits into the "big picture." A teacher may liken the Mind Mapping process to that of rolling a snowball that gets bigger and bigger as it rolls along, and eventually continues rolling under its own momentum.

The visual presentation helps students relate unknown concepts to known concepts and to organize ideas, concepts, and procedures around essential similarities. The Map acts as an anchor or scaffold for adding additional information. In this way, key concepts and procedures are linked to each other by means of a mental picture. Students are encouraged to not only create Mind Maps, but to talk and write about how the Mind Maps helped them learn. They can be asked to explain their Mind Map to their parents, to a student from a different grade, to the teacher, and others.

1. a mini-essay or letter to others (e.g., an absent student, student teachers, parents) about the procedural steps involved in performing a task;
2. a student resource guide on possible procedural bugs to watch out for, "crib" or "cheat" sheets, or possible exam questions;
3. a self-advocating essay indicating their strengths and the areas that need help, what they have learned from previous teachers, and a list of possible resources;
4. note-taking and note-making activities, generating reports on interviews with significant others on how they use specific academic skills, or helping to produce a class newspaper;
5. a portfolio or chronological collection of their work.

Karen Harris and Steve Graham have proposed that students' portfolios may take a variety of forms, including (a) a biography of their work, including pieces that portray different developmental stages of their writing; (b) a diverse range of works (e.g., stories, essays, journal entries, videotape demonstrations); (c) critiques of their work over a period of time, noting changes, areas that require further development, etc. (Harris & Graham, 1996).

Students can be required to present their portfolios to peers or parents. In preparation for such presentations, they can learn how to answer a number of *what* and *how* questions about their portfolio, such as the following:

- What is your favorite piece in your portfolio? Why is this your favorite?
- How did you choose to include these pieces?
- What goals did you set for yourself? How well did you accomplish them?
- What are you now able to do as a (writer, math problem solver, artist) that you couldn't do before?
- How has your approach changed?
- What are your goals for the next (unit, class, term, project)?
- What is it about this topic that interests you?
- What would you say is the easiest thing to do to be successful?
- As you look back at your work, what changes do you see?
- How has your performance changed since the beginning of the year?
- Let's compare a page you are (reading, writing, etc.) now to what you were (reading, writing, etc.) then.
- What would you like your parents to understand about your portfolio?
- What did you learn about yourself?
- How can teachers help you improve your (writing, math problem solving, etc.)?

Clearly, the intent is not to have students answer all of these questions at one time. Students should have opportunities to practice their answers to these questions over a number of sessions. Such practice will enhance their consultative abilities and help them become more reflective, self-directed, and accomplished students (Bergeron, Wermuth, & Hammer, 1997). Having students regularly answer questions such as these will also encourage students to use thinking-related terms as they offer descriptions, explanations, reasons, plans, predictions, and conjectures. Thus, students have an opportunity to exert executive control and ownership of their learning processes as they address the *what*, the *how*, and most importantly, the *why* of their activities.

Recall that students should only be expected to answer these questions on skills and procedures that they have consolidated and on which they have demonstrated some mastery. Not all students will be discussing the same level of material in their portfolios. The teacher should carefully monitor whether the students spontaneously incorporate in their descriptions of their portfolios the language of thinking and instruction. How much have the students internalized the voice of their teacher? As one teacher asked her students,

> Do you ever find yourself, while doing your work, asking yourself
> the kind of questions we ask each other? Do you ever find yourself
> becoming your own teacher?

By repeatedly asking such questions of her students, this teacher conveyed an expectation that they will become their own teachers or consultants. But teachers must go beyond conveying such expectations if their students are going to develop consultative skills. Students must be taught both how to help others and how to help themselves, and then be given multiple opportunities for and feedback on practicing consulting skills. Peer teaching, in its various forms, is the most effective way to help students develop their consulting skills. Writing and other forms of mental representation (diagramming, presenting to others) are also effective ways to nurture students' self-reflective abilities. Appendices 9-A and 9-B (pp. 185-190) provide suggested guidelines on how teachers can implement peer tutoring and writing in their classrooms.

Summary

Teachers should include in their curriculum more language-based activities and highlight other forms of mental representation. Putting students in a consulting mode is a critical step in developing their mastery and expertise. Language serves a number of functions, acting as a problem-solving device, as a way of accessing and activating knowledge in its various forms, as a self-regulating device, and as a means of accessing help. Two activities teachers can use to effectively nurture such self-reflective, self-directed behaviors in all classroom activities are peer tutoring and writing. We have described the various ways in which teachers have creatively used these educational procedures. We also provided practical guidelines on how to implement these teaching practices. Whether it is teaching students how to be good helpers or how to do Mind Mapping, the object of instruction is to help students become their own teachers. We now turn our attention to the challenging issues of transfer and generalization—to how students can engage in consultation on new tasks in novel situations.

Appendix 9-A: Guidelines for Using Peer Teaching

As noted in Highlight Box 9.1, a number of practical procedural steps for implementing peer teaching have been offered. Clearly, these guidelines will vary somewhat depending upon the specific form of peer teaching (e.g., cross-age peer tutoring, Jigsaw Instruction, etc.) and on the age group one is working with. There are, however, certain common guidelines that cut across these diverse instructional procedures. Following these guidelines will increase the likelihood that students will benefit from peer-mediated activities.

1. Discuss with students what it means to be a good helper, and discuss the concept of cooperation. Explore ways in which students already help each other. On the basis of this class discussion, have the students generate a set of guidelines to follow when tutoring.
2. Ask students to interview their parents or an older student in order to find out what distinguishes a good helper from a poor helper. Have students share a list of characteristics of good helpers.
3. Explain to students why you will use peer teaching in your classroom. Emphasize that helping others can result in helping oneself.
4. Discuss the type of peer helping you will use in your class, when you will use it, and why.
5. Discuss and have students formulate rules for teamwork. For example, students should move quickly and quietly to their groups, use an "inside" (relatively quiet) voice, stay with their partners or groups (no wandering about), and encourage everyone to participate. The teacher can post these rules and have students review them.

6. Have students arrange the classroom to permit them to sit with their desks clustered.

7. Discuss, model, delegate, and have students select group responsibilities. For example, students may be asked to play different roles (e.g., reader, recorder, timer, checker, summarizer, and encourager). Write out the duties of each role and rotate students through the roles. Have the group of helpers meet before and after their helping experience to discuss how their goals were or were not met.

8. Choose the type of peer-teaching activity carefully, ensuring that the participants have the necessary prerequisite skills. In the case of cross-age tutoring, ensure that the tutors have mastered the required teaching skills. In Jigsaw Instruction, ensure that each student has the prerequisite skills needed to master the material for which he or she is designated to become an "expert." Also ensure that the students have engaged in goal setting in order to preestablish appropriate levels of improvement. Give students group objectives.

9. Train students how to be good helpers. Among other skills, they need to learn: how to listen, how to give good hints without giving answers, how to ask questions, how to give and elicit feedback, and how to provide praise for effort (see Highlight Box 9.1).

10. Provide reminders or procedural prompts on how to be a good helper. Post reminders such as: *Look and listen; Give directions clearly; Keep it simple; Ask questions; Give hints, not solutions; Ask if your partner understands; Give pats on the back, be an encourager; Check it out;* and *What I learned today.*

11. Model with small groups of students how to be a good helper. Demonstrate how to scaffold instruction as you monitor students' performance and understanding, fade supports, relinquish ownership, use the "art of questioning," demonstrate cognitive empathy, and praise efforts.

12. Provide students with examples of specific questions and lists of supportive statements they can use (e.g., *Try it again; Try it this way; Do you understand X?; Show it to me again; Explain it back to me*).

13. Choose the size and composition of the groups carefully. Keep groups to two or three members in the primary grades and four to six at higher grades. The group size constrains the amount of verbal exchange. In cross-age peer tutoring, we have found that a 2-year spread or a 2-grade-level spread between the tutor and the tutee is optimal.

14. Carefully choose peer groupings. Invite students to participate in the selection process, especially when using cross-age peer tutoring. Ensure that groups are heterogeneous in ability levels. Rotate partners and make

sure that low-achieving students are not regularly paired up.

15. Invite students to select names for their groups, or even design logos, in order to develop a sense of belonging to the group.

16. Ensure that there are ample materials available for all members of each group. Initially, use well-structured tasks. Use tasks that nurture interdependence (e.g., one group story, one workbook, one report). Include tasks that cannot be completed by an individual alone (tasks that require multiple skills and knowledge bases). Use group projects in which students create displays that can be shared with other groups.

17. Convey your availability to help group members. Tell students to let you know if they have any questions or if their group needs help. Also convey your availability when group work is not being conducted. Review with students how they can tell when they need help and how they can help each other.

18. Circulate during peer teaching and monitor student participation, student progress, and student dialogue. Record observations that can be used for individual, group, and class feedback. Ensure that all students are participating—that none are "social loafers" or "gofers," and that the student who is strongest academically does not assume control of the group or activity. Listen to see if students are working toward a common goal, questioning each other, checking each other's work, using "thinking language" terms, justifying their positions, admitting that they were wrong or that they do not understand, and asking others for help. See if students are following group rules and using the questions, statements, and guidelines that have been provided.

19. Work collaboratively with students to generate behavioral checklists that they can use to evaluate how well the group works or how well the tutoring session went (e.g., listen, encourage, give good hints, provide feedback, give praise, etc.).

20. After tutoring sessions ask both the tutor and tutee to fill out a Journal Sheet that summarizes their experiences. Interview group members about their reactions to the group work. Ask students questions like the following:
    - How did it go?
    - Did your group have any problems? How did your group handle these problems?
    - What did you like best about working in the group?
    - How can the group work be improved for next time?
    - Are there ways you can ask for help that make helping easier to give?

- Think of the last time you needed help. How did you ask for help? How did the helper help you? What did he or she do? How can you remember to do these things?

21. Have students write out their observations and add them to their journals. Ask them to write a mini-essay on the pros and cons of group learning. Ask them to indicate what they learned about how to be a good helper and how to cooperate.

22. Include group goals and individual accountability. Help groups monitor their goals and their progress toward their goals. Evaluate and praise and/or reward group work, as well as students' attainment of preestablished goals. Reinforce students' efforts, not just their products.

23. Have small-group discussions and feedback sessions that can lead to whole-class discussion. Share with the whole group (using an overhead projector) the problems, difficulties, strategies and helping behaviors that you observed. Have a participant (an assigned summarizer) from each group present to the whole class. Discuss the effectiveness of teamwork and cooperation, and of viewing each other as resources.

24. Once group work operates smoothly and efficiently, arrange for visitors (e.g., the principal, parents, students and teachers from other classes) to observe the class.

25. Praise and reinforce students for group work. Acknowledge the students' helping behaviors.

26. Put students into a consulting role where they have to describe and explain their group activities. For example, you can have students make a class videotape on how to be a good helper, give presentations to parents or other students on how to be a good helper, give assembly presentations on how group work is being used to learn a subject area, write a column in the school or class newspaper detailing tips on how to help, and/or include in their portfolios examples of group work activities.

27. Value and evaluate group work so students' group work contributes to their grades in class. Have students self-evaluate their performance, writing an essay on "Me as a helper," and providing examples of peer activities. They can document examples by including journal pages, testimonials from fellow students or tutees, evidence of expertise in Jigsaw Instruction, videotapes or audiotapes of reciprocal teaching, and so forth. These are markers of success. Consider how students can tell whether their helping behavior and peer tutoring helped others.

28. The discussion of peer helping should contribute to a consideration of

altruistic behaviors. Have the class "adopt" a child from an organization like the Foster Parents Plan or Save the Children. The teacher can post the child's picture and correspondence. The students can conduct fund-raising activities to support and then correspond with this child. The school can help coordinate these efforts.

29. Review how helping skills developed in class or outside class (e.g., doing chores at home that help others) can be applied to helping oneself. Have students give examples of this helping process.

30. Encourage groups to undertake new responsibilities and to explore new areas of study, engaging in collaborative discovery learning.

Appendix 9-B: Guidelines for Using Writing to Foster Reflection

A number of pedagogical suggestions have been offered on how teachers can incorporate writing into their curricula.

1. Discuss with students why writing is an important activity (e.g., why they should use writing in math class). Teachers can highlight the role writing plays in providing the teacher with feedback and in helping students plan, organize, assess understanding, and figure out what they know and don't know, what they still need help with, and ways to measure progress.

2. Establish an "authentic" reason for writing, so it becomes a purposeful act. Have students produce real products that will be of use to others beyond the classroom.

3. Ensure that there is an audience beyond the teacher and students in the class. Vary the audience (e.g., writing for oneself, parents, an absent student, next year's class, a substitute teacher, younger students, etc.)

4. Provide time in class for students to write (e.g., 5 minutes at end of class to complete a Ticket Out The Door or make diary entries), or ask them to write at home (e.g., rewrite notes, write mini-essays). The best way to teach writing is to let students write as much as possible and to provide opportunities for them to edit others' and their own writing.

5. Model writing. For example, you can fill out your own Ticket Out The Door, keep a diary of a lesson, or maintain a portfolio, and then share these with students, offering an explanation (think-aloud) of your decision making.

6. Demonstrate for students good and poor examples of writing, note-tak-

ing, diary entries, letters to absent students, Mind Maps, and the like.

7. Provide opportunities for students to discuss writing activities with peers (e.g., discussing how they put together cheat sheets, Mind Maps, or study guides, rewrite notes, write up parent interviews, etc.).

8. Post written work on the bulletin board and include examples in the class portfolio.

9. Collect students' writing (journals, logs) on Fridays and provide constructive comments over the weekend. The comments should focus on the students' accounts of the strategies they employed to solve a problem or on how they performed a task, not on spelling or grammar. All comments should be respectful. Afterward, share general comments with the class. The students' log entries should not have a specified length. Rather, students should be told to make their entries long enough to tell someone how they did the task and what they learned as a result. They should be encouraged to represent their knowledge and procedures diagrammatically, as well as providing a written narrative.

10. Have students write before class begins by asking them to make predictions: What will happen if …? How will what students learn relate to what they have learned in the past? What difficulties do they anticipate encountering, and how these will be handled, or possibly even avoided? At the end of class, students can be asked to reread their previous entries and comment on which plans were fulfilled and what surprised them about doing the task. Writing can be used as part of the planning activity, as students are called upon to state clear goals (short-term, specific, small, attainable objectives), lay out a plan or strategy for achieving their goals, anticipate potential roadblocks to the successful execution of their plans, and determine how these problems will be addressed.

11. When using portfolios, describe the different types of portfolios and explain why they are important. Have a visitor (e.g., an artist, architect, or investor) present his or her portfolio to the class. Have students present their portfolios to parents and others (i.e., create an authentic purpose for portfolios). Invite parents to write their reactions in their son or daughter's portfolio. Before students present to their parents, have them practice (orally and in writing) answers to questions that they are likely to encounter. Encourage students to include written reflections (diary comments) in their portfolio. And have students create a class or team portfolio. Portfolios can be evaluated (e.g., by a teacher, classmate, older student, family member, etc.) on a regular basis.

Endnotes

1. Another example of planning and application activities involves asking students to solve a "lost field notebook problem" (Roth, 1996). This problem provides students with a notebook of various facts and data, and it is the task of the students, usually working in small groups, to come up with a description of the research questions that the authors of the lost field notebook were working on. Such detective-like tasks require students to work together on a task to access and employ various forms of knowledge and strategies.

2. Besides Johnson and Johnson (1986), a number of other researchers have recommended training for peer helpers and cross-age tutors (Devin-Sheehan, Feldman, & Allen, 1976; Fuchs, Fuchs, Bentz, Phillips, & Hamlett, 1994; Fuchs, Fuchs, Mathes, & Simmons, 1997; Giesecke, Cartledge, & Gardner, 1993; Goodlad & Hirst, 1989, 1990; Mayrogenes & Galen, 1978; Myrick & Bowman, 1991; Rekrut, 1994).

3. Slavin (1978, 1995) has proposed a different form of peer instruction called Student Teams Achievement Division (STAD). STAD is a mixed-ability peer group procedure that combines group goals with individual accountability. Students' performances are monitored and evaluated on a point basis. Each group member earns points (0 to 30) for his or her group by demonstrating improvement on a quiz that exceeds his or her preestablished criteria. The degree to which individuals improve contributes to the group achieving its goal. Since the success of the group is dependent upon individual improvement, group members encourage and help each other to put forth maximum effort. The group rewards are based on the individual learning by all group members and result in increased efforts at peer tutoring. The STAD procedure has been used effectively in grades 2 to 12. The teams usually consist of 2 to 3 members in the primary grades and up to 4 or 5 members in later grades. The STAD procedure is designed to create an incentive structure that increases the likelihood that students will support and tutor each other.

Chapter Ten

Creating Authentic Settings: Fostering Task Planning and the Application of Skills

We have proposed that the goals of education should entail teaching students:

1. to perform more and more complex skills and strategies;
2. to do so on their own, as they move from acquiring skills to performing them in an efficient, "automatic" manner, even to the point where they can teach the skills and strategies to others; and moreover, where they can self-regulate and mindfully reflect on their performance while doing so; and
3. to transfer their knowledge, skills and strategies to new tasks and settings, even to the point where they can invent new applications for what they have learned.

In Chapter 7, we examined how teachers can help students acquire skills and strategies. In Chapter 8, we described consolidating skills and planning strategies. In Chapter 9, we considered how teachers can help students assume consulting roles both with others, as in the case of peer tutoring, and with themselves, by engaging in self-reflective writing and other forms of mental representation.

In this chapter, we will consider what teachers can do to enhance the likelihood that their students will be able to flexibly apply the strategies they have learned to new tasks in novel settings. As students move from being novices to being experts, they differ not only in their skills, but also in their understanding and in their ability to apply what they have learned to new tasks in new situations. What can teachers do to promote their students' mindfulness and help them transfer and generalize their skills and strategies? How can they increase the likelihood that their students construct knowledge (not just consume knowledge), and that they develop conceptual understanding of what they are learning (not just apply what they have learned in an unthinking rote fashion)?

Educators have learned a great deal about how to teach skills, how to conduct practice sessions, how to engage students in peer teaching, and how to use writing activities. Educators have also learned a great deal about how to explicitly teach for generalization. Transfer does not occur spontaneously; it requires guidance and modeling, nurturing and reinforcement. Teachers cannot simply "train and hope" for generalization to occur. They need to incorporate the explicit set of training guidelines that have emerged from the research literature on what educators should do to foster transfer before, during, and after a lesson or a unit.

The Nature of the Challenge

The need to follow generalization guidelines was highlighted by the philosopher Alfred North Whitehead, who observed that the knowledge individuals acquire and employ in one arena often remains "inert," and not readily applied in other areas (Whitehead, 1929). The fact that students possess knowledge and strategies does not guarantee that they will use them in contexts different from those in which they were initially acquired.

Whitehead's informal impressions have been confirmed repeatedly by empirical research (Cognition & Technology Group at Vanderbilt, 1991a, 1991b, 1994a, 1994b; Sherwood, Kinzer, Hasselbring, & Bransford, 1987; Stokes & Baer, 1979; Nickerson, Perkins, & Smith, 1985). For example, Bransford and his colleagues concluded that:

> There is not strong evidence that students in any thinking skills program improve on tasks that are dissimilar to those already explicitly practiced. Typically, children will use strategies immediately after instruction, but will not use these strategies on a later occasion, unless explicitly told to do so (1990, p. 150).

The absence of transfer by students of what they have learned is evident even on seemingly similar academic tasks. A few examples illustrate this well-known phenomenon. For instance, elementary school children were taught how to use letter substitution skills (e.g., replace the first letter in words like *hot*, *pot*, and *lot*), but did not transfer those skills to a new set of words (*bed*, *led*, *red*). The students failed to flexibly apply what they had learned to new word combinations (Cochran-Smith, 1991; Cunningham, 1990). In the area of math, students who were taught how to solve certain mathematics word problems did not transfer their knowledge to word problems that were slightly different (Reed, Dempster, & Ettinger, 1985). High-school graduates in a community college were unable to apply eighth-grade math to solve a simple volume problem that was presented in an applied context (Biemiller, 1993). Conversely, students who failed math in school were found to be capable of doing business mathematics required to survive on the streets (Saxe, 1988). Results such as these raise important questions about *what* and *how* we teach and about *what* and *how* our students learn.

In this regard, Carl Bereiter points to the "well documented finding that most subject-matter instruction in school does *not* produce conceptual understanding, but only a restricted ability to answer certain kinds of content-related questions" (Bereiter, 1995, p. 28).[1] Unless students are prompted, they generally do not use what they have learned. Students may be able to define and explain concepts at a verbal level—especially when answers are elicited by the teacher, as on an exam—but the concepts and strategies remain abstract and not fully understood, unless and until this knowledge is applied to specific, meaningful tasks. Without instruction that focuses on application, students do not readily transfer what they have learned to new tasks and new settings. This is especially true of low-performing students, who require the most explicit transfer instruction.

Put simply, educational research repeatedly demonstrates limited transfer across tasks and settings, and over time, unless generalization guidelines are explicitly built into the teaching program. Teachers must teach generic skills and then provide numerous opportunities and facilitating situations for transfer to take place. Teachers also need to systematically evaluate, value, and reinforce transfer activities. Some 60 years ago, John Dewey offered similar educational suggestions when he proposed that students should be taught general inquiry skills and scientific/technical knowledge in order to work on practical problems of life (Dewey, 1933). We will see below how much Dewey anticipated modern concerns with generalization and authentic pedagogy. A modern-day version of this call to action was captured by Von Glaserfeld (1995), who proposed that teachers should view themselves as "midwives" who facilitate the birth of understanding, and not as mere engineers of knowledge transfer.

Some Hope For Achieving Generalization

The promise that such generalization can indeed be achieved comes from several sources. The first sign of hope comes from several laboratory-based training studies that successfully taught tutees how to intentionally and deliberately transfer what they had learned to new tasks and settings (Pressley & Woloshyn, 1995). These training studies highlighted that there are two types of transfer or generalization, (1) *low-road transfer* and (2) *high-road transfer* (Salomon & Perkins, 1988). *Low-road transfer training* occurs when a skill that has been practiced to the point of automaticity in one context is spontaneously elicited by a new context. The student repeats a routine procedure or a set of skills in a situation that is similar to that in which it was originally learned. Little or no modification of the transfer task is necessary. Typically, the new situation is not much different from the context in which the task was initially performed or learned. The degree of transfer is influenced by the amount of practice the tutee received, by the variability of tasks and contexts in which the initial practice occurred, and by the degree of overlap or identical elements in the training and the transfer settings. For example, if a student is taught to drive a car, she may be able to drive a car of a different make, but not able to drive a truck.

In contrast, *high-road transfer training* involves deliberate, intentional, mindful abstraction from one context to another. It also entails mindful self-management and application of principles and rules to new tasks, often in a new setting or context. In high-road transfer, the student searches for and applies analogies that link specific situations to each other. Students must plan and construct a new task using automated skills. Sometimes new skills must be created or invented. For example, if a student driver obtains a license and visits England, where she is called upon to drive on the opposite side of the road and negotiate many roundabouts (traffic circles), her success will depend upon her ability to intentionally and deliberately self-regulate her cognitive, behavioral, and affective states. Insofar as her initial training prepared her to transfer her skills and strategies to novel tasks and settings, she will succeed.

In low-road transfer, an entire task is moved from one context to another with little modification or accommodation. In contrast, in high-road transfer, component skills and strategies learned in one setting are incorporated and integrated (sometimes in new combinations) into other tasks in novel settings. If the initial instruction is problem-focused and requires students to assume a leadership role in creatively constructing knowledge, there is a greater likelihood that generalization will occur. Students need to receive explicit instruction on transfer skills. This may appear self-evident, but surprisingly, such instruction is very rarely implemented in classrooms (Anderson et al., 1996).

Authentic Pedagogy

A series of studies of "authentic pedagogy" (Newman et al., 1996a, 1996b) underscores the importance of creating learning opportunities in which students can bridge between the skills, concepts, and strategies they are learning and their real-life experiences. By the term *authentic pedagogy*, Newman and his colleagues mean education that offers school experiences that are connected with the students' real lives. Advocates of authenticity call for students to work on problems and tasks that they are likely to encounter and that have relevance and value beyond the classroom. A classroom task is considered to be authentic when it is judged to be part of the students' world outside school and/or part of the culture of a particular discipline (e.g., what mathematicians, writers, or scientists do to perform their job). Usually, authentic tasks are complex, ill-defined, problem-based activities that require the integration of varied hands-on skills. They usually require judgment and self-regulatory skills, since they are amenable to multiple solutions (Cronin, 1993; Newman et al., 1989).

While many of these activities require prolonged investment and effort, usually with group collaboration, some authentic tasks can also be performed within a few classroom sessions. The key feature is whether the activity helps students appreciate the connection between ideas in different areas. Not every authentic task has to duplicate real-life experiences. The pedagogical goal is to challenge students with tasks that require reflective, critical thinking, deep understanding, multiple perspectives, and inquiry skills.

There also needs to be a genuine purpose for learning (e.g., to publish a school newspaper, write a letter to the local paper, design multimedia projects on a controversial topic, participate in a science fair, solve meaningful math problems, conduct ecological projects). Other activities that teachers have used to foster authentic pedagogy include theme-based activities that cut across subject areas—e.g., creating a city of the future or a species that could live in a different environment; designing a ride for an amusement park, considering such factors as the materials, design, size, location, and advertising; improving a playground; putting together a time capsule; creating a weather station; engaging in historical reenactments; developing a museum exhibit on a city covering the geology, history, culture, economics, etc.; writing up an interview with an expert; or making up a set of lessons for younger students. Each of these activities could be addressed across subject domains including math, science, language arts, music, art, etc. Authentic tasks may also include social action projects such as performing community volunteer service, conducting an oral history of senior citizens, participating in neighborhood fairs and field trips, and developing computer projects (e.g., a Web site). Many other projects could be added. These projects are designed to combat students' feelings that what they learn in school has little meaning or significance for their lives outside school.

Authentic learning tasks require students to integrate various skills and strategies, to construct knowledge (i.e., gather, organize, synthesize, interpret, problem-solve, elaborate, explain, and evaluate), on both an individual and a group basis. The students must learn to formulate and refine the questions they will study, locate resources, and make collaborative decisions and joint presentations (Bergeron & Rudenga, 1996; Brown, 1997).

Authentic pedagogy usually requires students to display their work, create exhibits, and provide accompanying presentations to an audience other than their teacher and classmates. Thus, students not only have to perform tasks or create products, but also have to describe and explain to others the processes they used. Students are encouraged to see themselves as part of a community of learners, performing tasks that are similar to what professionals in the field do.

The benefits of authentic instruction were documented by Newman and Wehlage (1995), who analyzed the achievement results of 800 high schools in the U.S. They developed a rating system that determined the amount of authentic instruction that each school provided its students. The increment in performance improvement between low- and high-authenticity schools ranged from 50% to 100%. For example, in the area of math instruction,

> An average student who attended a "high authentic instruction
> school" would learn about 78% more mathematics between grades 8
> and 10 than comparable students in a "low authentic instruction
> school" (Newman & Wehlage, 1995, p. 25).

What is most important for the present discussion is that authentic pedagogy boosted overall achievement for students of *all social classes and achievement levels.* The researchers also found that the school principal played a critical role in nurturing both authentic pedagogy and the accompanying sense of collective responsibility and shared ownership for both students and teachers. And as Newman and Wehlage observe, "students in a high collectively responsible school learned more than twice as much science between grades 10 and 12. The gain would be 116% of comparable students in a low collectively responsible school" (1995, pp. 37).

The results reported by Newman et al. are consistent with the findings of Knapp and her associates, who reported on 140 elementary schools (Knapp & Shields, 1991; Knapp et al., 1995). When teachers employed instructional approaches that emphasized meaning and understanding, created linkages between the subject area and the students' outside life, and created opportunities for students to discuss and interact, they produced greater gains over the school year in math understanding, problem-solving proficiency, reading comprehension, and writing competence than did conventional approaches that emphasized memorization. These results persisted at the fall follow-up assessment.

At the middle school level, Lehrer and his colleagues and Carver and her colleagues have demonstrated the benefits of performance-based, multimedia-designed, authentic pedagogy in improving students' involvement, effort, participation, persistence, collaboration, utilization of background knowledge, and use of learning strategies, with an accompanying decrease in disruptive classroom behaviors (Lehrer et al., in press; Carver, in press; Blumenfeld et al., 1981). Ferretti and Okolo (1996) have reported similar benefits of multimedia-designed performance-based projects in social studies for students with learning disabilities.

School and Class Size. The size of both the school and the class can influence the degree to which teachers are able to effectively introduce and implement authentic performance-based instruction. For example, Newman and Wehlage found that smaller high schools (385 to 1000), as compared to larger high schools (larger than 1200), were more effective in fostering student achievement. This achievement differential was especially evident when schools provided lengthier class periods so that students could study topics in greater depth, and when students received more practice with corrective feedback. Students in schools with a "higher sense of teacher community" scored about 27% higher on achievement measures than students in schools with a "low sense of teacher community" (Newman & Wehlage, 1995). The smaller schools provided an atmosphere more conducive to authentic pedagogy. Barker and Gump (1964) reported very similar results in the 1960s.

A recent study reviewed by Frederick Mosteller and his colleagues found that a smaller class size speeds students' learning, especially in the earliest grades (kindergarten through grade 3; Mosteller, Light, & Sachs, 1996; Ward et al., 1994). As part of a statewide comparative experiment in Tennessee, class size was systematically manipulated to consist of about 15 students (ranging from 13 to 17), about 23 students (22–25), or 25+ students. The smaller classrooms provided more opportunities for individualized instruction and cooperative learning tasks. What is most impressive about the Tennessee results is that these gains were maintained even when students were later integrated into larger classes in grade 4.

Whether one looks at research from laboratory studies that were designed to train explicitly for transfer, or data from natural experiments in which classrooms were rated for the degree of their authentic instruction, or the results of demonstration classroom projects that manipulated size or used collaborative, performance-based instruction, the evidence for transfer is encouraging. One goal of the remainder of this chapter is to examine exactly what these successful programs do that contributes to student transfer, and how all teachers can incorporate and benefit from their suggestions. Instructional programs that emphasize authentic pedagogy and that highlight transfer are strikingly different from the classroom routines (as described in Chapter 4) that emphasized the teaching and memorization of isolated facts, the rote execution of skills, and the use of recitation scripts. In these more traditional classrooms, the teacher initiates interaction by asking a question, the students respond, and the teacher then evaluates the students' performance (Tharp & Gallimore, 1991).

A caveat about authentic instruction. Before we consider instructional guidelines for fostering transfer, it is important to highlight a warning about authentic instruction. What is most important about authentic tasks is not the surface features of their apparent relevance or their real-world trappings, but rather the nature of the cognitive processes that the tasks or problems evoke. John Anderson and his colleagues note that real-world problems often involve a great deal of busy clerical work and offer little opportunity for students to exercise planning strategies (Anderson et al., 1996). The critical factor is whether the authentic instructional setting provides opportunities for high-road transfer training and nurtures conceptual understanding. For example, Anderson et al. describe a high school class that performed a "real-life" algebra problem. Upon closer inspection, it was clear that the students were spending most of their time on tasks such as making tables and graphs, which rapidly became clerical in nature. This clerical work got in the way of students' relating their algebraic knowledge to real-world tasks. It is not the academic task *per se* that determines the potential instructional value; rather, it is how the teacher and students use the task to foster transfer skills that is critical to obtaining generalization.

Ways to Determine Whether Students Are Acquiring and Applying Transfer Skills

What evidence would Anderson and his colleagues look for to determine if students were indeed learning, implementing, and applying transfer skills? How can a teacher tell if his or her students are picking up skills and strategies, knowledge, and understanding that they can apply across tasks and settings, and over time?

Clearly, the best evidence that such generalization of skills is occurring is to observe (and have students observe and record) the direct transfer of what they have learned to novel tasks in new settings. Do students actually apply and adapt what they have learned to new and more demanding tasks and situations? Do they alter or invent strategies to solve old problems in new ways or to address new tasks?

If transfer is a mindful and a deliberate self-management process, as Salomon and Perkins propose, then a second indicator that students can apply what they have learned should be evident in their social discourse. Since learning is fundamentally a social activity, the way students talk to each other about the learning process and about a particular subject reflects the degree to which they have internalized or appropriated the lesson objectives. Teachers should listen to students' conversations to determine whether they:

1. explain concepts, procedures, and strategies in their own words (e.g., providing self-generated examples and elaborations);
2. draw connections and analogies ("like" statements) between past learning and novel situations and tasks (e.g., recognizing the need to draw on past experience to solve current problems);[2]
3. self-initiate questions (e.g., "How come ...?"; "What if ...?"; "Do we need ...?"; "Can we ...?"), and undertake the gathering of additional information and resources;
4. give and receive elaborated help, focusing on the conceptual understanding of the task, not just on procedural steps;
5. work with peers to resolve disagreements or conflicts over academic issues (e.g., giving and receiving explanations—the most critical aspects of peer interactions);
6. justify their answers, offering rules and principles to explain their performance (e.g., voluntarily citing evidence, patterns, and reasons for their answers) and taking others' perspectives (saying, e.g., "I would like to see evidence that ..."; "You think that because ...");
7. attend to contradictory information and attempt to understand alternative thinking approaches (e.g., working on creating agreement and mutual understanding);
8. reflect on their own and each other's problem solutions and performance (e.g., engaging in mindful self-appraisal) and self-evaluate their understanding;

9. identify opportunities for using skills and strategies and initiate opportunities to apply and extend their skills (e.g., not only knowing what they know, but also considering what is implied by what they know).

When students talk to each other and to themselves in this fashion, they fit the definition of being intrinsically motivated, self-regulated, engaged, critical thinkers—budding experts in the midst of transferring what they know and creating new knowledge. (See Perkins, 1991; Perkins & Salomon, 1989.)

Guidelines for Nurturing Generalization

The remainder of this chapter provides a set of instructional guidelines, based on educational research, that is designed to help more students become self-directed learners. We will consider, in turn, what teachers can do to nurture transfer:

- *before* teaching students,
- *at the outset* of a class or a lesson;
- *during* the course of conducting a lesson or unit;
- *after* the class lesson or instructional unit is completed.

While these guidelines are offered sequentially, teachers will note their overlap and can sample accordingly, given the dynamic nature of a class or lesson. The guidelines are offered as a kind of cookbook that teachers can refer to, and alter, as the need arises. If the teacher's goal is to increase the likelihood that their students will transfer what they have learned and engage in accompanying self-reflective, social discourse, then teachers should compare how they explicitly instruct for transfer against this procedural checklist. What else do you do to enhance the likelihood of generalization that we have not included? Please feel free to share this information with us.[3]

Planning and Preparation

Since teachers cannot merely "train and hope" for transfer to occur, they must strategically plan and prepare transfer-engendering tasks and activities. First, they need to decide what types of transfer tasks to employ. This selection process must take into consideration the *developmental appropriateness* and *interest level* of the transfer tasks for the students.

If the transfer task is too similar to the training task, it will not challenge the students. If it is too dissimilar to the training task, it will be judged as too diffi-cult, and will not engage students or trigger them to apply what they already know. Judgments about the degree of similarity should be made not on the basis of surface features, but on the basis of the cognitive demands and the number and complexity of the decision-making steps students are required to perform. Teachers should select instructional tasks that are similar (but not identical) to the desired generalization tasks, and situations that are likely to be valued and rewarded by others in the transfer setting. Thus, in selecting transfer tasks, the teacher needs to have a theory of the task, skills, and strategies that are being taught (e.g., what expert readers, writers, math problem solvers do), what pre-requisite skills students need to bring to the transfer tasks, and what variables exist in the generalization setting that need to be included in the instructional setting (e.g., possible distractions, time pressures, etc.). The teacher attempts to provide students with the best fit between their abilities and the cognitive de-mands of transfer tasks. Since the process of choosing transfer tasks is complex, teachers should actively collaborate with students in the selection and develop-ment of instructional goals and procedures and in the selection of transfer tasks.

If teachers are going to have students practice their skills on authentic tasks, they need to invite the students to choose from an array of options that may be of interest to them and that match and extend their abilities. As with training tasks, transfer tasks can be dimensionalized for their level of difficulty, in terms of the cognitive skills, planning requirements, and level of self-direction required to accomplish the task. Some students lack prerequisite skills and/or planning and self-direction skills; they lack the ability to see patterns and draw analogies, or the memory capacity and speed of information processing to see or generate the connections between what they have learned in the past and what is re-quired by the transfer tasks. As we will consider below, teachers need to pre-pare students for such transfer activities and systematically evaluate for transfer.

As we will consider in the next chapter, the selection process also involves choosing transfer and training tasks that capture the core or "central conceptual structure" of the skill that is being taught (Case, 1992). There are many tasks (both training and transfer) that students can be asked to work on, but skillful teachers select training tasks that will yield benefits with "ripple effects" in mul-tiple areas, well beyond the initial training tasks.

Sometimes, these "central conceptual structures" are domain-specific (e.g., order of operations in math, or story structure in writing). Alternatively, they may entail more generic, metacognitive, self-regulatory skills that can be used across tasks, such as goal setting, planning, monitoring, self-questioning, time management, note-taking, summarizing, visualization, and clarification. These executive skills should be taught in context and blended into ongoing school activities. Study skills taught in isolation (e.g., as a separate class) do not generalize to various academic subjects unless they are used by teachers and students in each academic area (Pressley et al., 1987). Students must see strategies in action and experience the benefits that accrue from strategy use in each subject area.

Students learn by doing and by combining abstract instruction with concrete examples. They need to employ the strategies they are learning in natural settings with their fellow students. One strategy that educators have used is to engage groups of students in enjoyable games and activities (e.g., playing Parcheesi, Rightstart, Bridge, Monopoly) that are designed to provide opportunities to practice and integrate their skills and task-planning strategies. When these games are well structured and monitored by teachers, they represent yet another vehicle for nurturing transfer skills.

In summary, teachers need to thoughtfully plan:

- what transfer tasks will be used;
- what transfer strategies will be explicitly taught;
- what student collaboration will take place;
- what will be said to students at the outset of, during, and after transfer activities in order to increase the likelihood of generalization;
- how transfer skills will be assessed on performance-based measures.

At the Outset of Transfer Activities

Students need to plan and prepare for transfer activities in the same way that teachers do. Thus, there is value in having the class discuss and understand the nature of transfer. The following guidelines provide some suggestions for how teachers can prepare students to transfer what they are learning.

1. *Discuss with students the nature of generalization and task construction strategies.* For example, discuss the differences between low- and high-road transfer tasks, which call for automatic and mindful transfer, respectively. You can share personal examples of when you were called upon to transfer knowledge and skills (e.g., stories of travel experiences, or transfer from one motor skill to another), and ask students to provide similar examples, sharing both in-school and out-of-school experiences. The class can generate a bulletin board or Mind Maps of examples of transfer activities. Students can interview family members about when

they employ skills that they learned in school, either on the job or at home. Invited guests can share with the class how they employ transferable skills on the job. The object of these activities is to convey to students that generalizing and applying what they have learned is as much a creative attitude or mindful disposition, as it is a set of specific skills. Students must learn to be on the lookout for occasions to apply what they have learned.

2. *Give students the opportunity to discover a transfer strategy before it is explicitly taught.* If possible, arrange for students to encounter the need for the transfer skills before they are taught. Students are more likely to use instruction when they see the need for a specific skill or strategy and seek assistance than when such instruction is unsolicited. Moreover, students are more likely to use strategies if they come up with them themselves, than if the ideas are offered by others (Blumenfeld, 1992; Meichenbaum, 1977). Students are more likely to apply what they have a stake in—skills for which they have some interest and sense of ownership. You should present authentic, performance-based tasks in a familiar context that students can relate to their personal experience.

3. *Raise a concern for transfer from the outset, even when basic skills are being taught.* The likelihood of generalization is enhanced when teachers highlight why specific skills and strategies are being taught, the conditions under which they will be useful, the reasons why they work, and how using them will help students achieve both short-term and long-term goals.

4. *Tell students explicitly that you expect them to apply what they have learned and that their ability to transfer will be systematically assessed.* Indicate that you are interested not only in their answers, but also in how they come to their answers (i.e., the strategies they employ).

5. *Remind students to generalize by applying what they have learned, and help them generate reminders* (e.g., mnemonics, procedural checklists, visual displays, cue card questions, posters such as "Goal, Plan, Do, Check") that they can use with peers, as well as with themselves. Make repeated reference to these reminders, labeling the strategies by name and highlighting how what students are now doing is like what they have done in the past and will be doing in the future (McTighe & Lyman, 1988).

6. *Discuss possible patterns or cues that students can use as reminders to apply their skills and strategies.* Students can be given practice sorting problems and tasks into those requiring different strategies (e.g., differ-

ent types of math problems or different types of essays). In order to assess their understanding, you can ask students to generate problems of different types that illustrate abstract rules or principles. For example, students can be asked to rewrite math problems, incorporating their everyday experience.

7. *Examine with the students any possible barriers to employing their knowledge, skills, and strategies on new tasks.* These barriers may be in the form of students' stubborn misconceptions and procedural bugs. Some students may hold the false belief that if they can't solve a problem right away, there is little sense in continuing to put out additional effort. These and other such beliefs need to be addressed directly. Similarly, some students may habitually respond to surface features of a transfer task and fail to notice the deep-structure features. Students may mindlessly apply an algorithmic solution in a rote mechanical fashion, whether it applies or not. You need to anticipate such possible barriers and incorporate them into the training.

8. *Contextualize what you teach, and put it into some historical perspective.* For example, students can be encouraged to read biographical accounts of how others have overcome barriers to solve problems.[4] All too often, information taught in school is presented in an ahistorical fashion, and students view what they are asked to learn as arbitrary and of little relevance to their lives. Students need to be challenged to wonder where this material came from, who discovered the information, how they discovered it, and what practical or theoretical problems they were trying to solve. Unless teachers can infuse instruction with passion and with the fascination of inquiry, there will be little incentive for students to learn, let alone generalize.

9. *Highlight relevance by choosing authentic tasks that are thematic and that lend themselves to cross-disciplinary study.* For example, educators have used ecological and social science topics such as studying survival, conservation, and control. Working on such topics can help students feel they are part of a community of learners, especially if they use computers to communicate with others about their solutions to such problems. Once again, it is important to have *all* students, no matter what their ability levels, engage in such consulting or expert roles.

10. *Present the ability to transfer learning as a challenge for individuals and for the class.* Discuss future situations in which students will be called upon to demonstrate transfer. Actively involve students in identifying opportunities for the generalized use of skills and strategies, and

discuss how they can personally modify strategies for transfer purposes.

11. *Select transfer tasks carefully* in terms of developmental appropriateness, difficulty level, and the degree to which they are valued and reinforced by the natural environment (in other classrooms, in work settings, and at home).

Fostering Generalization During Transfer Activities

An array of instructional strategies can be used to foster transfer, including direct instruction, modeling, Socratic questioning, conferencing, scaffolding, individualized assessment and feedback, peer teaching, labeling, reinforcement, and relapse prevention. Below are more specific guidelines for fostering generalization.

12. *Provide students with in-depth, extensive training on skills and strategies to the point of proficiency.* Students are more likely to transfer what they can do well. They are more likely to transfer skills and task-planning strategies that they have consolidated and have been able to consult on than those skills and strategies that they are still in the midst of acquiring and mastering. Prolonged training is required in order to allow students ample time for conceptual understanding to develop. Brief, short-term instruction should not be expected to produce long-term generalization.

13. *Promote student awareness of skills and strategies in context.* Try to embed skills and strategies in valued tasks. When they arise in context, you and your students should label and categorize them and recognize their usefulness on new tasks and in novel settings.

14. As in the case of teaching skills, *access students' knowledge* about how to transfer, *provide an advance organizer* relating to what the transfer instruction will be and why it is important to learn it, and *provide informed instruction* about how this specific transfer lesson will be conducted. You can use artful questioning to access students' knowledge about transfer strategies. For example, you may ask:
    - "Have you seen this type of problem before?"
    - "In what way is this problem the same as (or different from) the ones you have solved before?"
    - "What have you learned in the past on problems like this that you can use here?"
    - "What are all the different ways we can go about solving this problem?" (Use brainstorming.)

15. ***Explicitly instruct how to transfer.*** When you want students to engage in a specific transfer activity, you should explicitly ask them to do so, and teach them the skills and strategies required to achieve generalization. Provide *direct instruction.* For example, students should be taught how to identify and specify various types of problems, plans, and strategies, and how to evaluate their effectiveness. This approach is illustrated in the explicit teaching of a "story grammar" strategy to generate and evaluate writing. With this strategy, students are taught that their story should have a person with a problem, some plan for addressing that problem, and an outcome (McKeough, 1992). Teachers have modeled how to use this structure to generate various types of stories, have provided students with practice in identifying and producing stories that fit this structure, and have had students rehearse this strategy across academic domains (including writing a history paper, generating math problems, and demonstrating reading comprehension). As students develop competence, teachers can gradually fade (scaffold) their assistance, supportive cues, and prompts, and thus transfer strategy control to students.

Note that you can also incorporate *discovery-oriented instruction,* in which students must discover the story grammar or other strategies that authors use to tell their stories. Instead of giving students the strategy, you can challenge them to discover it for themselves. Students can be supported, praised, and reinforced for identifying and employing transfer strategies.

16. ***Conduct instruction across tasks and settings.*** The wider the range of training activities and the more exemplars that are used, the greater the likelihood of generalization.

17. ***Model the use of task-construction strategies by thinking aloud while doing transfer tasks.*** Pose questions to yourself and invite students to interrupt you and offer answers. As noted, this modeling should not be a monologue, but rather an interactive student-teacher dialogue. For example, while doing tasks, teachers can model the use of:

- self-interrogative questions;
- "like" statements;
- rules and retrieval cues;
- use of strategies that they refer to by name; and
- coping strategies for handling plans that falter or performance setbacks.[4]

This modeled self-dialogue may include such probes as:

- "Where have I used this before?"
- "Is there anything I have learned before that is like this?"
- "What plan (strategy) should I use?"
- "What should I do next?"
- "What steps have I missed?"
- "What might get in the way of …?"

18. *In order to determine that students are indeed internalizing the transfer strategies, ask students to think aloud while performing transfer tasks.* Such think-aloud samples may be elicited by asking students to describe, defend, and elaborate on their strategies. For example, you may ask students *what* and *how* questions:

- "What did you do to achieve X?"
- "How did you figure out how to do X?"
- "How did you remember to …?"
- "What (clues, rules, strategy) did you use to …?"
- "What questions did you ask yourself in order to check …?"
- "What back-up strategies did you have in place in case …?"
- "In spite of the fact that you (got the first part of the problem wrong, were stuck, gave up), you were able to … How did you do that?"

A second way to solicit thinking aloud is to do so directly by asking students to share with a peer the task-construction strategies they used to perform a task or achieve a goal. They can ask each other, "What was your plan? What problems did you encounter, and how did you handle them? What did you learn as a result of doing this task?" In turn, peers can share their think-alouds with other small groups of students, and eventually, with the whole class. Students can be invited to record evidence of transfer activities and generalization strategies in their daily diaries and in their portfolios.

Peers can be explicitly trained in how to ask questions and how to answer them with explanations and reasons. For example, King and his colleagues trained fourth- and fifth-graders to use guided, cooperative questioning to help them focus on the integrative connections between different aspects of a topic and between the topic and out-of-school experience. The students were initially given prompt cards with items to guide their questioning and guidance on how to provide answers. The training produced improvements in students' comprehension of the topics and in their ability to draw inferences and make connections to other knowledge (King, 1991, 1994).

19. *Use questions to lead students to verbally and diagrammatically (re)-formulate their task plans, access relevant information, and use their knowledge, skills, and strategies in new ways to accomplish tasks.* In turn, students can learn to ask themselves these same questions, as they become their own teachers. Teacher questions such as "How could you teach someone else to do this task?" can foster transfer. Some questions—such as, "What would happen if ...?"; "How does that (contradictory information) fit in with your explanation of ...?"; "Can you think of anything this does not explain?"—can also encourage students to reorganize their existing knowledge.

20. *Have students who disagree on specific positions work together to resolve their differences.* Such exchanges can provide another way for students to generate arguments (questions and explanations) that will expand their abilities to apply what they have learned. Out of such peer disagreements can come cognitive growth, and in turn, generalized skills and strategies. Students need to learn to use artful questioning with peers with whom they disagree.

21. *When you witness transfer activities, label and reinforce students' efforts at transfer.* Comments that reinforce transfer include the following:

   - "I can see that you are becoming your own teacher (coach)."
   - "Well done, you are taking charge of your own learning."
   - "You used your checking (planning, revising, etc.) strategy on this new problem. Good job!"
   - "You figured out how to link together what we did before and what you are working on now. Excellent!"
   - Do I have your permission to share your transfer strategy with the other students? I am sure they can use it. Thanks."
   - You went beyond the information given in the problem to solve this. How did you figure that out? ... Well done!"

22. *Engage students in relapse prevention training.* Failure and setbacks are inherent in learning any skill, including learning how to transfer skills and strategies. Thus, it is important to anticipate and share with students ways to cope with and ways to benefit from such failures. For example, teachers can remind students that scientists often learn the most when their experiments don't work. Such failures should be the occasion for students to become "detectives" or "Monday-morning quar-

terbacks," analyzing the variety of factors that may have interfered with transfer:

- Is it possible that the transfer task was too difficult or too dissimilar from previous tasks?
- Was the absence of transfer due to a lack of adequate training (the length, speed, and content of training), an absence of multiple examples, or a failure to include training tasks that incorporated the core conceptual structure required to perform the transfer tasks?
- Was it the instruction (a failure to prepare students adequately, or a lack of ongoing prompts, or a failure to consider stubborn misconceptions and procedural bugs) that led to transfer failure?
- Is it possible that students have inadequate prerequisite skills (e.g., the teacher mistakenly expected transfer on skills and strategies that students are still in the process of acquiring)?
- Is it possible that students may not have been adequately engaged and challenged with authentic tasks that interest them?

When both students and teachers learn to analyze transfer failures together in an analytically constructive fashion, a truly self-regulatory learning environment is established.

Fostering Generalization at the Conclusion of Transfer Activities

In order to help students consolidate and generalize the transfer skills and strategies they are learning, they need to be placed in a consulting role where they can describe to others, and to themselves, the transfer strategies they use to perform authentic tasks. The teaching strategies described in Chapter 9 (e.g., peer work such as cross-age tutoring, writing, diagramming) can be used in nurturing students transfer skills. Moreover, students need to take credit and make self-attributions for the transfer skills they evidence. Continuing with our list of transfer guidelines, teachers can:

23. *Have students present their projects to others.* Such public displays put students into a consulting role where they have to describe, elaborate, and defend the transfer strategies they used. They provide an occasion for both acknowledgment and praise, as well as an opportunity for students to engage in social discourse reflecting their task ownership.

    In preparation for public displays, students can rehearse—orally or in writing—the procedural steps they employed to perform transfer activities and to produce products. Students can even be asked to teach (demonstrate for) others their transfer strategies.

24. *Ensure that students take credit for their improvement and achievements so they come to see the connections between their efforts and strategy usage and the positive consequences that follow.* Teachers cannot leave this important attribution process to chance. Instead, they must ensure that students take the data from their projects and performance improvements as evidence to confirm the personal view that they can become good readers (relative to where they began, not compared to others), more effective math problem-solvers, members of a community of learners, and budding experts.

    Teachers can use praise, "overheard compliments" (praising a student to others in earshot of the child), solicited praise from others, and students' self-evaluations to foster this self-attribution process. Teachers can ask students to compare their present performance with their performance in the past. What is different? What did they do to bring about such changes? After listening, the teacher can reflect, "Are you saying to me (to the class, to yourself) that you can now *notice* when you are having a problem? You have a *plan* you can call upon? You have *choices* and can *catch yourself*?" (Use of metacognitive verbs highlights the students' self-regulatory skills.) "Where else could you use these skills? What, if anything, might get in the way of your using these skills and strategies? What can be done about this?"

25. Once students have mastered a strategy, *encourage them to analyze novel tasks and situations and to personally adapt previously learned transfer strategies or design their own transfer strategies.*

26. *Provide students with "booster sessions" on transfer strategies,* and engage them in discussions of the improvements that result from using their strategies effectively.

27. *Regularly assess students' use of transfer strategies.* Performance-based authentic assessments provide a useful means by which you can offer students constructive feedback and teach them how to become "detectives" who can figure out the basis for both their transfer failures and their transfer successes. Also, students come to value that which is evaluated in class.

28. *Involve significant others in the learning and transfer process.* For example, if the students spend time with other instructors, collaborate on strategy use with these teachers or with peer tutors. As discussed below, involving the students' parents is critical to ensuring generalization.

We will now consider two of these transfer activities in more detail. First, since what students are tested on often determines what they learn, we will consider how teachers can conduct *authentic assessments* as a means to foster generalization. Second, since one of the most important factors determining student success is *parent involvement*, we will consider how teachers and schools can involve parents as collaborators in meeting the challenge of generalization.

The Role of Assessment in Nurturing Student Generalization

One goal of instruction is to teach students how to self-monitor and self-evaluate their understanding and performance and to take remedial steps when appropriate. In most instances, students look to a teacher-generated or text-generated source to perform this evaluation. For example, Nuthall (1995) reported on studies of fifth-graders who were asked how they knew when they understand the math they were learning in class. The students reported that they knew they understood a math procedure when they got it "right," and they knew it was right when the teacher *said* it was right. Mathematical understanding in these classrooms had become equated with getting the same answer as the teacher (or sometimes, the textbook or the calculator). As Nuthall observes:

> For the students, the classroom tasks had become matters of doing what the teacher wanted, and "understanding mathematics" meant nothing more than getting the answers right. Managing test requirements had replaced genuine engagement with mathematics (p. 7).

Since evaluation is so critical in determining what and how students learn, any efforts to foster generalization skills must carefully consider the assessment process. How do students in your classroom view assessment? How do you think they would answer the following questions:

- How does your teacher know what you have learned?
- What kind of tests do you receive?
- What are all the different ways you can show what you learned?
- Can you tell your teacher what she should ask you in order to show what you know and how you know it?
- Of the different assessment procedures that your teacher uses, which one would you choose in order to show what you have learned and how you learned it?

The way students answer such questions indicates the degree to which they perceive that they have assessment options and can assume responsibility in self-evaluating their understanding and performance.

Students' tendency to look to the teacher as the standard bearer of performance is further reinforced when teachers use exams that require students to "recognize" (and regurgitate) what has been conveyed by the teacher or by the textbook. Research indicates that fewer than 10% of most teacher-made classroom tests measure performance above the level of simple recall (Brophy & Good, 1986; Cai et al., 1996; Linn, 1993; Linn et al., 1991; Newman, 1990).

While there may be an appropriate role and function for tests that assess for specific declarative knowledge (knowledge of facts) and for procedural/conditional knowledge (application of specific procedures), especially when students are acquiring and consolidating skills, there is also a clear need for exams to help students monitor and evaluate their higher-level processes. These latter modes of evaluation have been called *authentic assessments*. Authentic assessments are designed to provide performance-based measures that have a purpose beyond demonstrating to the teacher what students know. Authentic assessments are as much concerned with the processes that students use in solving problems as with the answers they obtain. They are designed to assess students' conceptual understanding and analytic thinking processes. While many students can select the correct answer on a test, far fewer are able to successfully explain how they arrived at the answer.

Consider an assessment approach offered by Lane and her colleagues to promote students' mathematical thinking and reasoning skills (Lane, 1993; Lane et al., 1996). The purpose of their assessment approach was not only to evaluate, but also to help promote higher-level conceptual, procedural, and strategic mathematics knowledge, as well as math communication skills. For example, on a multiple-choice math question, they required students not only to select the correct answer, but to also explain their answers. They also presented students with a math word problem and asked them to generate three different mathematical questions that could be answered using this information. Younger children were presented with two pictures, each containing different numbers of objects (boys and girls, cars and airplanes, or balls and bicycles). The students were asked to generate as many questions (problems) as they could using these two pictures (e.g., "Are there more boys than girls?" or "Are there more people than things you can ride on or play with?") Another question that called for students to use higher-level mathematical thinking presented them with a graph entitled "Tony's Walk," and asked them to write a "story" about Tony's walk, based on the graphic time-by-distance presentation. On other test items, students were asked to explain why a particular answer was correct or how they went about finding an estimate to their answer. (See also Kammen, 1996; Katz & Chard, 1989.)

Students' answers to these open-ended assessments can be reliably scored for mathematical and strategic knowledge and for mathematical communication skills. Such authentic assessment procedures link evaluation and teaching practices, as teachers can provide students with model answers and then teach them strategies for thinking and communicating mathematically. This careful and sensitive ongoing assessment will also help teachers determine the developmental appropriateness of what students are learning and possible barriers to transfer. Teachers can keep a running record of students' progress. Students can also be encouraged to keep running records of when they use strategies and how they modify them.

Table 10.1 provides a comparison of standardized testing and authentic assessment approaches. We propose that there is a place for both types of assessment approaches, but there needs to be more of a balance. Right now too little attention is paid to authentic assessments. Since students and parents learn to value whatever is evaluated and included on report cards, educators need to place greater importance on evaluating students' consulting and application skills. Teachers' grading systems also need to convey the importance of producing authentic products. Table 10.2 provides a list of possible alternative ways to conduct student assessments. If you are a teacher, how many of the procedures enumerated in Table 10.2 do you use?

TABLE 10.1: Comparison of Standardized Testing and Authentic Assessment

Standardized Testing	Authentic Assessment
Primarily designed to measure students' knowledge and recall and their ability to solve routine problems.	Performance-based assessment connects students' learning with real-world experience.
Format calls for brief responses—multiple-choice, true-or-false, fill-in-the-blank, and short-sentence answers.	Assesses higher-level problem-solving inquiry skills, application and interpretive analysis of prior knowledge.
Students reproduce specific bits of information that the teacher or the text previously supplied. Assesses a limited range of skills, little beyond retrieval.	Demonstrates knowledge, conceptual understanding, and application.

TABLE 10.2: Ways to Conduct Assessment

Social Discourse Indicators (as time permits)

- Interview students individually, in pairs, or as a group, to determine how things are working and to tap their knowledge and understanding of transfer strategies. (See the metacognitive interview in Chapter 3.)
- Ask students to think aloud as they solve problems.
- Listen to students' social discourse. Listen for spontaneous statements when they are involved in collaborative learning (e.g., do they initiate questions, deliberately seek out information, provide elaborated help?).
- Ask students specific questions about how they arrived at their answers or how they would teach a skill or strategy to someone else.
- Survey the class explicitly about their level of comprehension (e.g., ask how many students feel lost, hazy, clear, or able to teach others).
- Ask students about their confidence (self-efficacy) and enjoyment in performing various academic tests.
- Ask students about the amount of non-class time and effort they spend on a particular academic task (e.g., reading, writing).

Writing Indicators

- Ask students to fill out a history-taking questionnaire at the outset of the term. Solicit students' self-appraisals of their strengths and weaknesses, level of interest, goals, etc.
- Have students keep daily logs, graphs, Tickets Out The Door, portfolios, and scrapbooks.
- Have students provide written rationales or explanations for their answers.
- Have students create concept maps, semantic webs, and essays.
- Have students self-monitor using graphs and fill out a procedural checklist of how they performed a task.
- Examine students' notes, and have them self-evaluate their note-taking abilities).

Performance-Based Indicators

- Observe students while they perform academic tasks.
- Conduct an ongoing running record and miscue analysis in order to infer the students' level of understanding and to identify procedural bugs.
- Ask students to show you how they performed a specific activity.
- Ask students to sort problems into different types.
- Ask students to generate problems based on answers (e.g., present students with multiple examples and have them generate problem representations).
- Have students create exhibits and projects.
- Have students do videotape demonstrations.
- Have students give presentations (e.g., put together a class diorama).
- Have students create a performance skit or drama.

A major objective of assessment is to teach students to conduct self-assessment and assessment of peers. Students cannot become experts in any area unless they can evaluate themselves as learners. Self-assessment is a teachable skill that facilitates generalization. For example, students can be invited periodically to explain the purpose of a strategy and to repeat or demonstrate the basic steps. The class can hold discussions of specific examples of where and how they have been able to use what they have learned in different situations, even those that were not anticipated.[5]

Our present three-dimensional model of mastery suggests that teachers should be able to provide students and parents with feedback not only on how well students have acquired skills (as they move along the X-axis), but also on how well students can describe what they have learned (both orally and in writing), how well they can teach it to others (as they move along the Y-axis), and how readily they use strategies to apply these skills to new tasks in novel situations (as they move along the Z-axis). The model of mastery provides a useful way to communicate to parents and involve them in the generalization process.

The Role of Parent Involvement In Fostering Student Generalization and Mastery

The importance of involving parents in the education of their children was highlighted by two U.S. Department of Education reports. The first concluded that:

> One of the most significant factors in creating a good school is always going to be parental involvement in its life and progress (1992, p. 7).

When the U.S. government established its Education Goals for the Year 2000, one of the eight goals was:

> By the year 2000, every school will promote partnerships that will increase parental involvement and participation in promoting the social, emotional, and academic growth of children (1994, p. 10).

Since children are better served when their parents and their school personnel are working together on their behalf, schools should actively promote such collaboration and actively encourage greater parent involvement. There are many ways that schools can communicate more regularly and effectively with parents, make school environments more inviting for parents, and involve parents in their students' learning processes and in the decision-making processes of the school. When schools see parents as partners, what the children learn in school has a greater likelihood of being extended into their real-world experience. Similarly, what children experience outside of school is more likely to be brought into school.

Appendix 10-A provides a Parent Involvement Questionnaire designed to evaluate how parent-friendly schools are in creating this partnership. Parents are untapped resources who have to be mobilized, especially for those students who are struggling academically. This represents a particular challenge with those parents of struggling students who are least able or willing to partner with schools.

It is obvious that many demands and responsibilities outside the school influence the degree of parents' involvement in their children's learning. The educational goal is to develop a fit between the degree of potential parent involvement and the school's expectations. The objective is to create an inviting learning environment for parents and to provide them with multiple options of ways to become involved in their child's education. The data is convincing that getting parents involved in their children's education enhances the children's academic performance (Eccles, 1993; Eccles & Harold, 1993; Epstein, 1992; Griffith, 1996; Hoover-Dempsey & Sandler, 1995; Mertens & Voss, 1993; White, Taylor, & Moss, 1992). For example, recall the project described in Chapter 9 in which Mertens taught elementary school children how to interact with their parents on math-related activities. Such proactive parent-directed activities are needed to provide students with opportunities for social discourse with significant others in their lives about the *how* and *why* of what they are learning in school. Teachers cannot leave such social exchanges to chance. The research reviewed in Chapter 3 indicates that those students who succeed academically receive multiple opportunities for nurturing social exchanges with parents. The Parent Involvement Questionnaire provides a list of additional ways schools can engage parents in their children's learning processes. It can be viewed as a kind of report card on how well teachers and principals are doing in creating a collaborative partnership between the school and the home.

Summary

We have enumerated a list of instructional activities that teachers can use to nurture transfer in their students. They include what teachers can do before, during, and at the conclusion of instruction in order to foster generalization. (The guidelines explored in depth above are briefly summarized here.)

Teaching Techniques to PREPARE Students for Transfer

1. Discuss with students the different types of transfer. Lead them to view generalization as an attitude or mental disposition.
2. Give students an opportunity to discover the need for transfer strategies, and encourage them to come up with requests to learn transfer strategies.
3. Raise concerns for transfer from the outset of teaching skills. Comment on the why, when, and how of learning skills and strategies. Label and refer to transfer strategies whenever they are used.
4. Tell students explicitly that transfer is expected and that it will be evaluated routinely.
5. Use reminders that you and the students have generated. Use "like" statements.
6. Have students attend to patterns in problems. Have them sort and generate problem types as a way to learn pattern recognition.
7. Anticipate and discuss with students possible barriers (stubborn misconceptions and procedural bugs).
8. Contextualize instruction (relate it to the students' personal experiences, provide historical accounts). Convey enthusiasm and passion for the subject area and fascination with the inquiry process.
9. Use authentic, performance-based learning tasks that are thematic and interdisciplinary. Create a community of learners.
10. Present the task of transferring knowledge, skills, and strategies as a challenge to find opportunities to apply what students have learned.
11. Select transfer tasks carefully (evaluating for their difficulty level and value beyond the training setting).

Teaching Techniques to Use DURING Transfer Activities

12. Provide prolonged, in-depth training to the point of proficiency in order to ensure the students conceptual understanding.
13. Promote awareness of skills and strategies in context. Point out and label skills and strategies as they occur in ongoing tasks and discuss their usefulness.
14. Begin by accessing students' knowledge of transfer strategies and by providing both advance organizers and informed instruction regarding transfer training sessions.
15. Explicitly instruct how to transfer. Use direct instruction, discovery-oriented instruction, and scaffolded assistance.

16. Conduct instruction across tasks and settings. Use multiple examplars.
17. Use think-alouds and model the use of task-construction transfer strategies.
18. Ask students to think aloud and to record how they used their transfer strategies in their diaries, journals, and portfolios. Have peers share their transfer strategies with each other.
19. Use artful questioning to engage and challenge students to transfer skills and strategies.
20. Have students engage peers with whom they disagree so they have to defend and elaborate their positions.
21. Label and reinforce students' transfer activities.
22. Use relapse prevention training procedures. Teach students how to analyze transfer failures and successes.

Teaching Techniques to Use at the CONCLUSION of Transfer Activities

23. Put students in consulting roles. Have public display of students' projects, with accompanying prior rehearsal (oral and written) of explanations of transfer strategies. Have students teach (demonstrate) transfer skills to others.
24. Ensure that students take credit and make self-attributions (to effort and strategy usage) for performance gains and transfer activities.
25. Provide students with opportunities to design and personalize transfer strategies.
26. Provide booster sessions.
27. Use performance-based authentic assessments and provide constructive, ongoing feedback.
28. Involve significant others, including other teachers, peer tutors, and parents.

Appendix 10-A: Parent Involvement Questionnaire

Donald Meichenbaum, Univ. of Waterloo, & Andrew Biemiller, Univ. of Toronto

This questionnaire is designed to determine how you and your school involve parents in the education of their children. It provides a list of possible ways to involve parents in terms of:

(a) communication (both written and oral) about school activities and about specific topics such as homework;

(b) possible collaborative activities with parents; and

(c) administrative support for parent involvement.

There are no right or wrong answers to these questions. The intent of this questionnaire is to have educators consider and reflect upon the many ways to involve parents in the education of their children. Certainly, the feasibility of some of these suggestions will vary depending upon the grade level, subject area, and school setting. **Please duplicate this Questionnaire if you wish to use it.** We have provided space for you to indicate other ways you and your school have involved parents. Please feel free to send these suggestions to us so that we can revise the questionnaire.

COMMUNICATION WITH PARENTS

Please answer each of the following questions by circling YES or NO.

A. Written communication with parents

YES NO 1. At the beginning of the school year, I send a letter home to each parent.

2. In my written correspondence with parents, I:

YES NO (a) mention how much I look forward to working with their son/daughter and with them.

YES NO (b) comment on the need for parents and teachers to act as collaborators and partners and have a continuing exchange, and I encourage them to be an advocate for their child.

YES NO (c) indicate that I will call them when I need their help, as well as when their son/daughter does well.

YES NO (d) extend an invitation to parents to call me to arrange a visit to meet (highlight the importance of two-way communication).

YES NO 3. I provide parents with a written general description of what we will be working on during the term and why these activities are important.

YES   NO   4. Later in the school year, I provide parents with an ongoing assignment calendar of the work we will be covering in class over the next few weeks and why this work is important (e.g., description of unit objectives, types of problems and assignments, and ways in which students will be assessed; lists of books to be used, recommended children's books, and upcoming school events).

YES   NO   5. I provide parents with ongoing written communication in the form of a class newsletter about what the class has been doing and learning, and some of the things students will be learning in the near future. (Students can participate in the production of this newsletter.)

YES   NO   6. I indicate to parents that over the course of the school year, their son/daughter will be asked to interview them (or other family members, relatives, neighbors) about learning and helping strategies, and about when they use math and written language in their day-to-day activities.

YES   NO   7. I indicate that students will be bringing home a folder of their schoolwork labeled TAKE HOME/BRING BACK. There will be space for parents to initial and comment on this work.

YES   NO   8. I provide parents with a survey/questionnaire to provide information about their child's reading behavior (e.g., average amount of reading time per week, leisure reading habits, favorite books, reading strengths and weaknesses).

YES   NO   9. I occasionally send parents a Teacher-Gram and invite them to send back a Parent-Gram about their child's progress.

B. Oral communication (phone calls/meetings) with parents

YES   NO   10. I call each parent (at least once per year, preferably once per term) to give positive feedback (i.e., convey something their child did well).

YES   NO   11. The ratio of positive to negative phone calls that I make to parents per month is 3 or 4 to 1.

YES   NO   12. I keep track (in a running log) of each parent telephone call, recording the date, the name of the student, whom I spoke to, the topic, the parent's reactions, and any follow-up plan.

YES   NO   13. I schedule meetings with parents to review their children's progress.

YES   NO   14. At these meetings, I usually indicate what their child has studied in class, and discuss their child's study habits (finishing assignments, studying, helping others), academic achievement, and classroom behavior.

YES   NO   15. At parent-teacher conferences, I have students attend so they can actively participate (e.g., show work from their portfolios, become self-advocates). Students are advised beforehand on how to contribute to these sessions.

YES   NO   16. I encourage students to share with their parents what they do in class, in their homework, and in their other school activities.

C. Communication with parents about homework

YES   NO   17. I inform parents about my expectations concerning homework (e.g., amount, time schedule) and comment on the benefits of students' doing homework.

YES   NO   18. I provide parents with a list of suggestions on how they can help their son/daughter with homework (e.g., ways parents and students can work out rules related to the setting, times, and routine, ways to motivate students to do homework, ways to provide help contingent on their child's request and need, ways to monitor homework loosely, ways to balance homework with other activities).

YES   NO   19. I ask parents for their observations on their child's homework activities (e.g., difficulties, limitations, what went well). I ask parents to initial the homework assignments.

YES   NO   20. I provide parents with specific suggestions for working with their children (e.g., read for 15 minutes with their children most nights; ask their children about their school activities and what they have learned each day in school).

YES   NO   21. I provide parents with books and other learning materials to use at home with their children.

YES   NO   22. I encourage parents to give their children home roles and responsibilities, especially those that involve serving others and that occur on a routine basis (setting the table, doing shopping, etc.).

D. Involvement of parents

YES   NO   23. I invite parents into my classroom to observe teacher-led and student-led activities (e.g., how I read stories aloud to students, how students do cross-age tutoring, etc.).

YES   NO   24. I review with parents how they can make their home more literacy-friendly (encourage their children's leisure reading behavior).

YES   NO   25. I invite parents to assist in my class.

YES   NO   26. I make parents feel welcome when they visit my class (e.g., have students give tours, have a display center with sample work available, have a list of things parents can do to help).

YES   NO   27. I encourage parents to keep a running diary or journal of their children's progress and difficulties and to share this with me.

YES   NO   28. I review with parents biographical information about their son/daughter and journal entries they have provided.

YES   NO   29. I welcome parent evaluation of my teaching practices, students' progress, and class and school programs.

YES   NO   30. I solicit information from parents about their interests, talents, and hobbies so I can request their involvement and help.

YES   NO   31. I provide students with tasks or games in which they can involve their parents (e.g., see the math project by Mertens described in Chapter 9).

YES NO 32. I provide parents with a list of choices of how they might become involved at school and/or at home with their child's education.

E. Administrative support for parent involvement

YES NO 33. My school views parents as partners in the students' education.

YES NO 34. My principal and/or department head encourages parental involvement and the maintenance of ongoing parental contact (in writing, phone calls, meetings).

YES NO 35. My school holds workshops for teachers on how to work collaboratively with parents.

YES NO 36. My school has created an environment that is inviting to parents (e.g., signs welcome parents into the school; office staff welcome them; teachers greet parents when they pass them in the hall; there is a parent reception area with relevant written material and newsletters).

YES NO 37. My school has a parent-teacher association that meets regularly.

YES NO 38. My school solicits parent input on important decisions concerning their children (parents are members of the governing council of the school).

YES NO 39. My school has a parents' night (or family night, or grandparents' gala) when parents can participate in tours and activities and discuss their child's progress with the teacher (e.g., a portfolio night when students can show their work).

YES NO 40. My school invites parents to participate in school activities (e.g., staff the library, chaperone school trips, share ethnic activities, help with fund-raising).

YES NO 41. My school has special events for parents to discuss particular topics (e.g., parent involvement, report cards, transitions to new grades such as middle to high school, selection of courses, drug abuse, etc.).

YES NO 42. My school holds special evening sessions for parents on learning-related activities (e.g., how to help with homework, how to read to students, how to bolster students' self-esteem, why some students succeed in school).

YES NO 43. My school has a parents' night on a specific subject (e.g., math night) so parents can understand what and how the students are being taught.

YES NO 44. My school has a back-to-school night during which parents are invited to experience the kinds of activities and tasks their children are asked to perform in class.

YES NO 45. My school involves students, teachers, and parents in cooperative learning activities in which they assist each other in achieving learning tasks and goals.

YES NO 46. Parents attend an "open house" where students have opportunities to showcase their work. Students rehearse for this event.

YES NO 47. My school has encouraged parents to identify with its mission statement.

YES NO 48. My school provides both before-school and after-school programs for students to help accommodate parents' work schedules.

YES   NO   49. My school is located in a high-poverty area, and we have undertaken such activities as having parent night in a local church or laundromat (e.g., offering free use of the laundromat with a parent visit).

YES   NO   50. My school provides or helps to coordinate with other agencies a home-visiting outreach program.

YES   NO   51. My school provides specific skill programs for parents (e.g., helping parents improve their literary skills) or referrals to other services.

YES   NO   52. My school provides support to parents in obtaining their GED.

YES   NO   53. My school is involved in a parent literacy program (i.e., after-school educational assistance to children in the presence of their parents).

YES   NO   54. My school provides transportation and day-care services when parents are visiting the school.

YES   NO   55. Parents are notified immediately about any unexplained student absences.

YES   NO   56. My school has an active truancy prevention program that involves parents.

YES   NO   57. My school has established involvement and activities with local business and community leaders (e.g., an apprenticeship program).

YES   NO   58. Parents in my school view their involvement as a responsibility to their children.

YES   NO   59. Parents are asked to sign a contract indicating their responsibilities to the education of their children.

YES   NO   60. We monitor parent involvement and try to understand the factors that contribute to their noninvolvement (e.g., failure to attend meetings, volunteer, call or meet with the teacher, review students homework, portfolio, etc.).

Please indicate any additional activities and procedures you use to involve parents, or ideas about what you would like to see your school employ.

Endnotes

1. The following example, offered by Silber (1986), illustrates what Bereiter had in mind when describing the lack of conceptual understanding. Often students view what is taught in class as "rules of the game" that are arbitrary and have little or nothing to do with the real world. To illustrate this point, consider how students answered the following math problem:

    The 130 students and teachers from Marie Curie School are going on a picnic. Each school bus holds 50 passengers. How many buses will they need?

    (a) 2; (b) 2R30; (c) 2⅗; (d) 3

    Silber reported that only 35% of sixth-graders chose the correct answer, (d). Most students failed to recognize that you cannot have fractions of buses. Obviously, the students did not connect their mathematical knowledge with their real-world knowledge.

2. In discussing the ways students use analogies, Brown (1997) draws a useful distinction between "surface" and "deep" structural analogies. For example, when students note the similarities between an automobile and the human body by comparing headlights to eyes, they are responding to the surface features of these two objects. A deep structure analogy could involve comparing the automobile engine to the human heart in terms of their central functional significance. Other examples of surface and deep structural analogies are, respectively, comparing plants to straws, and comparing plants to food factories. The latter analogy conveys a deeper understanding and greater transfer, as students apply their knowledge in new ways. Teachers should be attentive to how students use analogies (surface or deep structures).

3. Donald Meichenbaum: University of Waterloo, Psychology Department, Waterloo, ON N2L 3G1, Canada (e-mail dmeich@watarts.uwaterloo.ca). Andrew Biemiller: University of Toronto, Institute of Child Study, 45 Walmer Rd., Toronto, ON M4T 1T3, Canada (e-mail a.biemiller@utoronto.ca).

4. Another means of modeling is to have students read biographical accounts of how famous people developed coping strategies. For example, have students study how Benjamin Franklin taught himself to become a good writer (Benjamin Franklin Writings, 1987), or how famous contributors learned to handle rejection.

5. An example of this interview strategy was offered by Harris and Graham (1996, p. 212). They suggest that when teaching students writing, teachers should ask them the following types of questions before and after strategy instruction:

    "What is good writing?"

    "When skilled writers write, what kinds of things do they do?"

    "Why do you think some kids have trouble writing?"

    "What kinds of things do you do to help you plan a paper?"

    "If you were having trouble with a writing assignment, what kinds of things would you do?"

    "What kinds of changes would you make to improve your paper?"

    "What things do you like to say to yourself while you write? Why?"

    "Has strategy instruction helped you with anything besides writing? (If so, how?)"

"Have you changed the strategies or procedures since learning them?"

"What do you see as the limitations (or strengths) of this strategy?"

"Since you are a collaborator in this instruction, help me think about teaching this to the next group of students. What would you do the same? What would you do differently?"

Chapter Eleven

Applying the Three-Dimensional Model of Mastery to Analyze Selected Educational Programs

Our three-dimensional model of mastery proposes that the most effective educational programs will include the following:

1. academic tasks that students find engaging, challenging, and relevant to their life experiences;
2. settings and roles that require students to *acquire* (learn), *consolidate* (practice), *consult* (help and teach others; engage in reflective writing and self-monitoring), and *apply* (transfer) what they have learned to new tasks in novel settings;
3. complementary teacher roles of instructing, scaffolding, and mentoring;
4. high-level consultative and self-directive experiences such as able students now receive;
5. applied, authentic learning tasks that have been demonstrated to support task construction—use of learned skills and strategies in a variety of meaningful contexts and on tasks that can be varied for level of difficulty; and
6. opportunities for students to present their products and activities to others and to describe how they were able to achieve these objectives.

In this chapter, we describe five educational projects that meet these criteria, or approximate them. Each program has proven "successful" in fostering students' academic performance. The programs cover the full range of educational challenges, ranging from elementary-school math instruction, to middle-school reading and writing instruction, to computer-based high-school instruction. An examination of each program illustrates how educators can:

a. move students along the X-axis, teaching them skills and strategies to the point of proficiency;
b. put students in a consultative role by employing peer and self-reflective activities, as the students move along the Y-axis of self-direction;
c. challenge students with "authentic" tasks that require them to transfer and construct knowledge along the Z-axis, the planning/application dimension.

Our central themes are illustrated in each of the five programs we have chosen to review:

- *Rightstart*—an elementary-school program for developing "number sense," which leads to effective learning in a variety of math-related contexts (developed by Griffin, Case, and Siegler);
- *Transactional Strategies Instruction*—a program for developing reading comprehension in the primary grades (developed by Pressley and his colleagues);
- *Jasper Project*—a program for developing applied mathematical problem-solving skills (and related computer-based skills) for elementary- and middle-school students (developed by the Cognition and Technology Group at Vanderbilt);
- *Computer-Supported Intentional Learning Environment (CSILE)*—a program for supporting middle and intermediate students' intentional learning and knowledge building (developed by Scardamalia, Bereiter, and Lamon); and
- *Fostering Communities of Learners (FCL)*—a program designed to teach research and inquiry skills to elementary- and middle-school students by incorporating Reciprocal Teaching, Jigsaw Instruction, and other settings with deliberately planned consultation roles (developed by Brown and Campione).

In summarizing and reviewing each of these programs, we will address the following points:

1. *Areas of student growth sought* (what success/mastery looks like). In this section, we will be concerned with the degree to which intended out-

comes have a skill versus a planning or application focus, and the degree to which high levels of self-direction are sought.

2. *A brief description of the methods and materials used and the program time required.* In particular, we will note the amount of time per week required during trial implementations, and the overall time period during which tests of the program were implemented. (Note that in general, each of these programs is seen as involving one or more learning settings that ought to be part of an ongoing school program, rather than a unique add-on experience that might be introduced once in awhile or only during one year.)

3. *Learning tasks, roles, and settings used.* As reviewed in Chapter 6, any attempt to bring a wide range of students to consultation levels of self-direction involves creating roles in which students can legitimately direct task construction and implementation. We will review the actual roles used by students and teachers. In several of these projects, very deliberate attention has been paid to creating what we would call student consultation roles. (This is particularly true of the CSILE and the FCL programs.)

4. *Empirical evidence of the impact of the program on children* in each dimension of mastery: skills, task-planning strategies, and self-direction.

5. *Findings regarding individual differences.* We examine whether there is evidence that the program effectively increases task planning and self-direction among relatively low-achieving students.

6. *Reported problems* in implementing the programs.

7. *Reasons why we chose this program* to illustrate the three-dimensional model.

Rightstart

The Rightstart program is designed for beginning elementary students (kindergartners and first-graders). The impetus for this readiness program came from two observations:

1. that a sizeable minority of children do not succeed in acquiring math skills; and

2. that, of those children who do acquire beginning math skills, most often apply these skills in a rote, unthinking fashion, failing to understand the underlying math concepts.

For example, even though children may be able to say aloud the numbers from

1 to 10, they do not know whether 5 or 4 is a bigger number and why. In short, they lack a conceptual sense of number.

Areas of Growth Sought

Case and his colleagues (Griffin, Siegler, and Capodilupo) proposed that a "sense of number" is what they call a *central conceptual structure* that underlies children's mathematical understanding (Case, 1996; Case et al., 1991; Griffin et al., 1994, 1995). Case argues that central conceptual structures are critical to intellectual development and should provide the basis for any training program. Case defines these structures as being "central" in the following ways:

> First they are central in that they form the conceptual "center" of children's understanding of a broad array of situations, both within and across culturally defined disciplines or content areas. Second, they are central in that they form the *core* elements out of which more elaborate structures will be constructed in the future; in effect, they constitute the conceptual kernel on which children's future cognitive growth will be dependent. Third, they are central in that they are the product of children's central processing: although the content that they serve to organize is modular, the structures themselves reflect a set of principles and constraints that are system-wide in their nature and that change with age in a predictable fashion. They thus possess certain general commonalities in form that transcend the specific domain to which they apply (Case, 1996, p. 5).

In other words, Case is proposing that if educators can identify the core conceptual structures that underlie a particular domain and train students on tasks and activities that tap those processes, the result will be much better transfer effects. Such conceptually-based readiness training should have a broad "ripple effect" on students' achievement.

In the area of math readiness, Griffin, Case, and their colleagues were able to demonstrate that teaching students a conceptual system of number led to improved math performance that generalized to a wide variety of quantitative problems. Before we examine the evidence regarding the Rightstart program, let us consider how they trained children on number knowledge and skills.

Teaching Methods

The Rightstart program consists primarily of a series of sequenced kindergarten activities (games) designed to help children understand various concepts related to numbers. The games are generally played in groups of four to five children, plus a teacher. Each child would participate in 40 to 60 group training sessions, each of which lasted approximately 20 minutes. These games were designed to emphasize:

1. verbally counting up from one to ten;
2. verbally counting down from ten to one;
3. mapping numbers onto objects when counting (e.g., pointing to objects on a line while counting);
4. mapping numbers onto sets of appropriate size;
5. increments (the idea that one additional count or "number up" represents a set incremented by one);
6. increments of "number down" tasks;
7. relative numerosity or "size" tasks (e.g., understanding that XXX objects is more than XX objects, and hence 3 is more than 2);
8. use of relative magnitude judgments (e.g., A is larger than B since A contains three units, while B contains only one); and
9. mapping numbers onto written symbolic representations.

An illustrative training game involves having children count a number of chips of one color into a jar. Others in the group check each child's counting. Each child has a different number and different color. After putting chips in the jar the children are asked, "Which color has the most?" and "Are there more red chips or more blue chips?" etc. After the children answer, the chips are dumped out, sorted, and piled to see which color has the most. Various magnitudes of numbers are used. A variety of other fun games are used to cover the teaching objectives outlined above.

In order to ensure that these skills are not learned in a rote fashion, teachers pose questions such as "How did you figure that out?" that encourage group discussion. Such probes permit children to

> articulate and formalize their knowledge, and to learn from each other. This was particularly useful for children who tended to be very quiet, unless specifically called upon. It also was useful for the teacher, who could get a better idea of each child's current knowledge state (Griffin, Case, & Capodilupo, 1995, p. 144).

Case suggests that Rightstart activities provide students with an opportunity to explore the number system, much as children come to know their neighborhood through exploration. Exploration on well-designed, sequenced tasks permit students to make decisions to change numbers, quantities, or other characteristics of the number system, and then observe the consequences.

The lessons (games) of Rightstart are designed to provide students with:

1. direct instruction on a series of sequenced tasks that build on prior knowledge, so they are "doable";
2. self-directed discovery (exploration) activities that provide opportunities for students to see the consequences of their personal experiments;
3. deliberate practice activities that consolidate newly acquired skills and conceptual understanding;
4. consultation activities in which students are asked to reflect and share the processes they used to play the mathematical games.

Effectiveness of the Rightstart Program

A number of studies of the effects of the Rightstart program on kindergarten children have been completed. It is clear that the program dramatically improves children's number sense, as measured by knowledge tests at the end of kindergarten, compared to a number of different control groups (e.g., children taught other math readiness skills or children who participate in reading programs). Overall, by the end of kindergarten, roughly 70% of Rightstart children can pass number knowledge tests, compared to less that 30% of comparable children without Rightstart. These results persist, so by the end of the first grade, Rightstart graduates perform markedly better in oral arithmetic and word problems. Finally, the improvement for Rightstart students generalizes to other areas including telling time, solving balance-scale problems, sight-reading music, and dealing with concepts of distributive justice.

Effectiveness of the Rightstart Program for More vs. Less Advanced Children

What is most impressive is that these results were evident for disadvantaged kindergarten children, whose level of number knowledge after Rightstart training was comparable to that of advantaged children. Furthermore, the percentages of disadvantaged children passing all items for the 6-year-old level (level 1) was quite high—ranging from 53% to 87% of children taught. In the group followed through grade 1, 100% passed the number knowledge test at the end of grade 1 (83% of controls passed the test). However, data is not available on what happens with the less cognitively advanced children (whether from advantaged or disadvantaged populations) during lessons, nor on whether lower number knowledge at the end of kindergarten is associated with lower math progress during grade 1.

Problems in Using the Rightstart Program

No problems were discussed by the authors of the program. We note that Rightstart is a rather labor-dependent program. Additional staff may be required to implement it. (A videotape of the program suggests that small-group instruction was being successfully implemented in regular classrooms with normal staffing, rather than requiring separate space.) As effective compensatory education, the program may well justify additional staffing. However, unless it can be demonstrated to work with larger instructional groups, it is not clear to us that it is feasible in a single-teacher kindergarten class in the absence of additional support.

Why We Chose To Include Rightstart

The Rightstart program has had (and continues to have) considerable success in improving children's mathematical knowledge and achievement. In addition, it illustrates the advantage of creating educational programs with well-sequenced tasks that engage underlying conceptual structures and processes. In the case of Rightstart, the central conceptual structure focuses on number concepts, but Case has proposed that other central conceptual structures be included in training—namely, *narrative structure* (the relationships between actions and consequences) and *spatial structure* (involving figures represented on a two-dimensional surface). Case's training approach challenges educators to identify the "central conceptual structures" of whatever skill they are teaching, and to consider how the training tasks can be sequenced conceptually.

A second reason we wanted to highlight the Rightstart program is because it combines various teaching procedures that move students along the X (skills), Y (self-direction), and Z (transfer) dimensions of mastery. On the X-axis, Rightstart sequences tasks in terms of their difficulty levels, creates an inviting learning environment by using engaging game-like activities, and uses a combination of (a) direct instruction (including activating students' prior knowledge and providing an advance organizer in the form of questions), (b) discovery learning (exploration opportunities), and (c) scaffolded assistance. Students were moved along the Y-axis as they consolidated each skill to the point of proficiency. Students were also called upon to reflect in small groups on their solution approach, so that they were moved into a consulting role. Finally, movement along the Z-axis was also ensured, as students had to address the core concept of number sense on many different tasks, each of which tapped the central conceptual structure of number. As a result of this instructional approach, students evidenced generalization (mindful abstract application or high-road transfer) on tasks that were distant from the original training tasks. Moreover, this improvement was maintained at a one-year follow-up assessment.

Transactional Strategies Instruction

We now shift the focus from math skills instruction to promoting reading comprehension. The impetus for the Transactional Strategies Instruction (TSI) program was the recognition that students who are lagging in reading comprehension are at high risk for academic failure. Variations of this program have been used in both primary and intermediate reading instruction. In order to develop classroom-based interventions for reading comprehension, Pressley and his colleagues (El-Dinary, Brown, Schuder, Gaskins, and groups of teachers from the Benchmark School in Pennsylvania and from Montgomery County, Maryland) developed an instructional approach that focuses on extensive, long-term strategy instruction.

Areas of Growth Sought

The long-term goal of TSI is markedly improved reading comprehension—"internalization and consistent adaptive use of strategic processing whenever students encounter demanding text" (Brown, Pressley, Van Meter, & Schuder, 1996, p. 19). The authors use the term *strategic processing* to refer to a number of specific strategies that can be invoked to guide problem-solving when one experiences a failure of comprehension. Examples include actively relating current text to prior knowledge, predicting upcoming events in a text, generating questions and interpretations while reading, visualizing events being read, summarizing content periodically, and seeking clarification when meaning is obscure. In addition to comprehension strategies, strategies for identifying printed words—ranging from decoding to context use—were also taught and modeled. (For a detailed discussion of effective reading strategies, see Pressley & Woloshyn, 1995.) Central objectives of TSI include mastery and integration of a number of specific

comprehension strategies, and understanding of when each of several potentially effective strategies is likely to aid the reader's efforts to comprehend text.

Teaching Methods

As summarized by Rachel Brown and her colleagues (Brown et al., 1996), TSI is
seen as a continuing program (over more than one year) that involves a number
of components.

- The teachers introduce effective comprehension strategies by explaining,
  modeling, and re-explaining them. In one application of TSI with second-grade children, eight different strategies were introduced—one at a
  time, with each one taught well.
- The teachers provide students with guidance on the use of strategies
  when needed. They provide hints to students about potential strategic
  choices they might make. Teachers give many mini-lessons about when
  to use particular strategies.
- The importance of using strategies is emphasized in all lessons. Students
  are reminded that using strategies helps them comprehend what they read.
- Information about when and where to use various strategies is frequently
  discussed. Teachers consistently model the flexible use of strategies. In
  addition, students are expected to explain to one another how they use
  strategies to process text.
- The strategies are used as a basis for much of the instructional dialogue
  about text. Discussion of text content occurs as teachers interact with
  students. Teachers both respond to students' use of strategies and prompt
  additional strategy use.
- The teachers integrate subject content and strategy instruction.
- The teachers motivate students to use strategies and convey that the way
  they tackle academic tasks does matter and has practical utility (results
  in performance gains).
- The teachers encourage students to believe that they become good readers, writers, and problem-solvers by employing strategies.

Although the reading group is the primary learning setting for TSI, the developers note that TSI also occurs in other settings:

> Although the reading group is an important [TSI] component, the
> teaching of strategies extends across the school day, during whole-

class instruction, and as teachers interact individually with their students (Brown, Pressley, et al., 1996, p. 21).

We lack specific information about the time spent by children in TSI groups, in preparation for TSI (e.g., reading), and in other TSI-related activities.

TSI is "transactional" in at least two senses. It involves transactions in the psychological sense that "the activities of the group are determined jointly by teachers and students as they interact with the text" (Pressley et al., 1992, p. 515). The authors suggest that TSI is also transactional in a "literary sense," in that "teachers and students jointly construct understandings of the text as they interact with it" (Pressley et al., 1992, p. 516). Another way of putting this is that each participant in a TSI group has some authority to contribute to the group's product—understanding of a text. These transactions are a two-way street, not simply a superior (teacher) directing subordinates (students).

As is true of most of the programs described in this chapter, a basic assumption is that through providing verbal guidance and consultation to others in their working group, students become increasingly capable of guiding themselves in comprehension activity. Pressley et al. (1992) write:

> Each student is presumed to benefit from participating in the group process. Long-term participation in such a group is hypothesized to result in internalization of the "executive" activities of the group. That is, the types of decisions once made by and in the group are eventually made by the individual participant when he or she reads alone. That is, teacher- and peer-scaffolded processes eventually become the student's own text-processing behaviors. The thought processes that were once interpersonal become intrapersonal. Comprehension competence develops in part via internalization of social interactions (e.g., Vygotsky, 1978) (p. 516).

Learning Roles, Tasks, and Settings Used

Reports by Pressley, Brown, and others suggest that Transactional Strategies Instruction primarily occurs in one learning setting—the TSI group. Each student is expected to participate in this learning setting on a nearly daily basis during years of teaching. TSI instructional groups include some direct instruction of strategies (in our terms, acquisition roles for students). However, most of the time students have the cooperative task of "constructing the meaning of a text," as it is understood by the instructional group. Each student is presumed to be at least somewhat competent with respect to this task, and each (in addition to the teacher) acts in a consulting role to the rest of the group—offering suggestions, applying specific comprehension strategies, etc.

The teacher has several roles: (1) an instructing role when introducing (explaining, modeling, re-explaining) comprehension strategies and when modeling decisions on how to use particular strategies; (2) a consulting (scaffolding) role when guiding students in constructing meaning for a passage by posing questions and relating answers of different students; and (3) a participant or collaborative (mentoring) role as students assume more responsibility for passage comprehension.

Effectiveness of Transactional Strategies Instruction

R. Brown and her colleagues recently reported on a study of the effectiveness of TSI with second-grade children. Five reading groups of low-achieving second-grade children received a version of TSI (Students Achieving Independent Learning—SAIL). The SAIL groups were compared to five comparable groups of children who received "instruction typical of second grades in the district" (a suburban county outside Washington, D.C.). Children in these ten reading groups were studied over a year of instruction. There were almost no significant differences between the TSI and non-TSI children at the beginning of the year. By the end of the year, children in the five TSI groups showed substantial and statistically significant gains on standardized measures of word identification and reading comprehension. Gains of 13% on word identification items and 19% on reading comprehension items, compared to the non-TSI children, were reported. (This is impressive; other programs, including Reading Recovery and Success for All, have failed to show significant results on reading comprehension measures.[1]) Significant TSI gains were also reported for strategy use (including increased use of strategies that were not explicitly taught), and for some aspects of story retelling. Finally, in a "think-aloud" analysis, the TSI children used more than twice as many strategies as the other children. In summary, across five different classes, TSI children came to use strategies more when reading, and demonstrated improved reading comprehension.

Effectiveness of Transactional Strategies Instruction for More vs. Less Advanced Children

Unlike some other projects, the TSI research has largely been conducted with children who have relatively less advanced skills. The study just described involved such children. Earlier developmental work has emphasized the usefulness of TSI with less advanced children and its efficacy in a school for children with learning disabilities. Thus, what is missing is information on what happens when more advanced children are included.

Pressley and his colleagues suggest that Transactional Strategies Instruction can be accomplished with heterogeneous groups. For example, in a 1992 article, they wrote,

> More capable students provide support and encouragement for less capable students. In the best of this kind of practice, students seem to be equals in status within the group, in spite of real differences in skills, abilities, and relevant background knowledge. As joint participation continues, students grow ever more competent in this group setting (Pressley et al., 1992, p. 516).

In their 1996 study, more homogeneous ability groups were used. It is worth noting, however, that within these groups, children in the (higher-achieving) TSI groups became more similar—i.e., standard deviations became much smaller over the year—while the (lower-achieving) non-TSI groups' standard deviations were only slightly reduced.

We do not know if more advantaged students would benefit as much from TSI approaches. It may be that they spontaneously use strategies without instruction. If this is true, TSI instruction would reduce differences between high-achieving and low-achieving students. On the other hand, high-achieving students may also benefit from such instruction and may show additional gains.

Problems in Using Transactional Strategies Instruction

Michael Pressley and his colleagues mention two problematic issues regarding TSI. The first is teacher preparation. As with each of the other programs described here, the authors stress that teachers require considerable training and experience to successfully implement their program. As one reads the detailed transcripts provided in some of their papers, it is clear that effective TSI teachers need to be able to think in TSI terms "on their feet"—during ongoing classroom dialogue. The teachers who participated in the TSI outcome research reported here had been actively involved in the development of TSI. Whether such active involvement in program development is a necessary part of training in the program remains to be seen. (The same comment can be applied to any innovative educational program.)

The second issue involves the conditions necessary for "transactional" activity. Pressley et al. cite several such conditions derived from "communications literature." They hypothesize that students must be:

- reasonable, making accommodations between their points of view and those of others;
- committed to peaceable interaction;
- committed to ensuring that all feel free to participate;
- committed to equality within the group; and
- committed to respecting group members.

All forms of collaborative learning settings appear to require interactions constrained along these lines. A good deal of research on "consulting etiquette" is needed to determine how these conditions can be maintained, and what steps are appropriate when an individual cannot adhere to these conditions.

Why We Chose to Include TSI

TSI is an exemplary program that illustrates how good strategy instructors go about teaching skills and strategies. TSI is based on the supposition that sophisticated thinking processes are developed through long-term interactions with others that are eventually "internalized" by students. The many transactions with students reflect a dynamic interplay between explanations, modeling, re-explanations, and further modeling, as students and teachers work through important content in the curriculum. In addition, teachers use dialoguing, conferencing, sharing, and prompting. Students are also put into consultative self-directive and reflective roles that foster transfer and mastery.

The Jasper Project

Areas of Growth Sought

This project is concerned with improving the use of mathematics in realistic applied problems. The basic objective is to facilitate the use of mathematical skills and strategies in a wide variety of problem contexts. Three goals were specified:

- to develop critical mathematical problem-solving and reasoning skills;
- to develop an appreciation of mathematics as a useful, interesting, and

realistic part of the everyday world; and

- to develop an understanding of specific mathematics concepts and skills necessary to solve adventure-type problems, including, for example, time, measurement, and basic statistical sampling.

Three specific problem contexts have been used to date: travel planning; uses of statistics in planning business tasks, and uses of geometry. More generally, the project is focused on task planning/application and the transfer of mathematics skills to various problem domains. As described in McGilly's *Classroom Lessons*, the educational settings created in the Jasper Project rarely involve direct instruction of computational or other mathematical skills (Cognition and Technology Group at Vanderbilt, 1994a). Rather, "Jasper" activities involve the presentation of complex stories, which require students to identify and solve a number of computational and measurement problems. Before expert (Jasper's) solutions are shown, students may devote time over a week or more generating and comparing solutions to these problems.

Teaching Methods

Mathematical problems are presented as episodes in a televised (or videodisc) series, *The Adventures of Jasper Woodbury*. Consider the episode "Rescue at Boone's Meadow." As described in McGilly (1994):

> … Jasper finds a wounded eagle while on a camping trip. He radios for help from his friend Emily Johnson; students help Emily find the best way to rescue the eagle. The problem involves consideration of a number of means of transportation (by car, by foot, or by ultralight aircraft), routes, and pilots. Having determined that the ultralight is the best way to get to the eagle, students need to consider fuel capacity, fuel consumption, payload limitations, and other factors in order to determine the best way to use it (Cognition and Technology Group at Vanderbilt, 1994a, pp. 164-165).

The complete episode runs approximately 30 minutes and introduces relevant facts in the course of an interesting narrative. Toward the end, the story is interrupted to specify the basic problem: determining the fastest way to bring the injured eagle from Jasper's location deep in the woods to a veterinarian's office in town. (Haste is necessary for the eagle's survival.) The rescue is impeded by many factors, such as limited fuel and fuel capacity and long distances to overcome. Students are asked to come up with possible solutions. The story has been presented in a videodisc format, which facilitates quickly reviewing any particular part of the story as needed. (However, it can also be presented through conventional videotape.) As envisioned by the Jasper developers, "Under the guidance of instructors, students generate the solution plans and subgoals, search for relevant data, and work cooperatively in small groups to find solutions" (McGilly, 1994, p. 171). They note that many other individualized and group approaches have been adopted by the hundreds of teachers who have tried Jasper.

The nine available Jasper adventure stories (as of 1996) were constructed according to the following design principles (from McGilly, 1994, p. 163):

1. Videodisc format. (Note that a videotape format can also be used.)
2. Stories with realistic, open-ended problems to be solved.
3. Problem complexity (each story involves at least 15 steps). For most, multiple solutions are possible.
4. Students must generate and formulate the subproblems necessary to solve the major problem posed in each story. Students are encouraged to co-operate to solve the problems.
5. All data needed to solve the problems are in the video.
6. Teachers of other subjects are encouraged to use the Jasper skills in their classrooms, building links across the curriculum.
7. Sets of three adventures involving similar problems are used in order to allow students to experience and discuss issues of transfer from one case to the next. The three problem areas are travel and maps, geometry (spatial construction), and statistical estimation.

Use of the Jasper materials is intended to emphasize a "generative model" in which students identify relevant subproblems and generate and test solutions to these problems. Teachers are described as providing "guidance" (a procedure that is not completely spelled out). It is probably safe to say that the Cognition and Technology Group would subscribe to the principle of providing the least direct assistance necessary to allow students to make progress on their overall task. The Jasper problems also allow for comparisons of alternative solutions, and the concept of relative effectiveness rather than absolutely "right" or "wrong" solutions.

In a large 9-state trial of the program in 52 different grade 4 to 6 classes, actual classroom implementation of instruction and learning activities using the Jasper materials varied greatly. The Cognition and Technology Group writes:

> There was wide variation in how teachers implemented the instruc-
> tional model, especially regarding the use of large- and small-group
> generative activity. In some classes, problem solving was teacher-
> driven and students' activities were mostly focussed on fact finding.
> In others, problem solving was more consistent with the generative
> model we discussed above (McGilly, 1994, p. 180).

The Cognition and Technology Group reports that classes usually spent about "a week" on each Jasper problem undertaken. By "a week," they mean the time period that was normally devoted to word problems during a week in a particular class. Most classes tried at least three Jasper problems over an academic year. The use of multiple problems encouraged transfer, as students had to apply what they learned in one case to other problems.

Learning Roles, Tasks, and Settings Used

The "generative model" of the Jasper problems results in students' being placed in consulting roles concerning planning-focused tasks in a collaborative setting. The Jasper project fundamentally involves generating complex tasks around which students can interact. Within small groups, each student is apparently expected to contribute ideas for specifying subtasks and planning steps to solve these subtasks. (For example, one subtask in the Boone's Meadow problem is determining how much gasoline would be required to fly the ultralight aircraft to Boone's Meadow and back. Another involves comparing this to the amount of gasoline the ultralight could carry.) It is apparently assumed that each student also participates in judging the potential effectiveness of proposed subtasks and, of course, in actually performing the planned computational skills.

No actual research describes this group process in action. Thus, we do not know to what extent students actually participate collaboratively, nor whether degrees of participation are associated with resulting improvements in problem-solving ability. (As we will see, there is evidence that as a group, students from Jasper classes do show significant problem solving improvements relative to matched controls; Cognition and Technology Group at Vanderbilt, in press.)

The teacher's role is not clearly specified in reports of the Jasper Project. The best information on possible teacher roles comes from one of the evaluative studies of the Jasper program, in which an investigator or teacher uses three levels of questions to prompt student planning. Essentially, this is a description of a scaffolding role. At the most general level, questions restate the basic problem posed in a specific Jasper story (e.g., "What's the best way to bring the eagle to the veterinarian?"). If this is not sufficient to prompt a complete solution, a second level of questioning is used to prompt each of the main sub-problems that must be addressed to solve the basic problem. Examples might include "How much fuel will the ultralight need?" and "How much can it carry?" (The answer to this second question is not simple.) Third-level questions prompt steps for solving the major subproblems (e.g., "In order to figure out the fuel you will need, what specific information about the distance and the speed do you have?"). Note that none of these levels amounts to simply teaching or demonstrating a solution. Note also that this approach assumes that at least some of the children in each working group possess the computational skills needed for carrying out the tasks once a solution has been planned. It could be argued that the teacher's role also includes knowing whether students can actually perform the requisite skills.

Effectiveness of the Jasper Program

A number of studies have been conducted on the Jasper Project. The largest, as noted above, involved implementation of the Jasper program during one year in 52 grade 4 to 6 classrooms. On measures of "complex problem solving skills" and traditional "word problems," Jasper students showed significant gains in comparison to matched control students. No differences were seen on computational skill (as expected). Small but significant differences favoring Jasper students were found in self-reported "confidence" regarding math and in the perceived utility of and interest in math. Considering that these results were obtained across a wide range of implementations of the Jasper program, and are not adjusted for levels of student ability, they are encouraging. In essence, participating in a Jasper program enhances students' abilities to apply math skills in new contexts.

Effectiveness of the Jasper Program for More vs. Less Advanced Children

Unfortunately, no data is reported on the effects of math skill levels on Jasper outcomes. Given the general perspective presented in this book, it would be very useful to know if learning settings can be created that allow less-advanced students to successfully assume effective consulting roles while working on Jasper tasks. There is mention of modifying the tasks to make them more or less difficult, or to create alternative problems. It would be important to consider ways of modifying the tasks to make them solvable by less-advanced students (as well as by younger students).

Reported Problems in Using the Jasper Program

The Cognition and Technology Group has stressed the importance of effective professional teacher development in the use of Jasper materials. There has apparently been a wide range of different implementations. Analysis of outcomes does not report the effects of relatively generative approaches vs. more "teacher-centered" approaches.

The Cognition and Technology Group notes that the current educational environment puts programs like Jasper in competition for time with state- and province-mandated assessment processes, and with highly specific mandated learning objectives (usually defined for specific grades). Hence, activities primarily concerned with the application of learned skills, and with placing students in effective consulting roles, are often set aside because of demands that students *acquire* additional skills. Bringing skills or application strategies to high levels of self-direction remains a lower priority in educational practice, despite continuing criticism that graduates can't apply learned academic skills.

The relationship between skills (computation and measurement) instruction and effective strategic problem solving is not directly discussed in the available research report on the Jasper Project. Similarly, the question of whether such skills should be acquired or consolidated prior to undertaking Jasper problems that require these skills remains unanswered. Since there was no report of gains in math skills and concepts, we can assume that those lacking them at the beginning of Jasper work did not gain them as a result of working on Jasper problems. However, we do not know what percentage of students, if any, lacked the basic computational and measurement skills required for the problems.

Why We Chose to Include the Jasper Project

The Jasper Project illustrates part of an effective learning setting—superbly crafted application tasks. Less attention has been paid to the details of the overall learning setting in which Jasper problems are used: to the roles students and teachers should play, and to student competence with prerequisite skills.

It is interesting to imagine a Jasper task in Language Arts. One example might be script-writing for a TV show. A more traditional example would be preparing a school newspaper or public debates.

Given our enthusiasm, it is interesting to note what we don't know about Jasper.

• Who does what in collaborative Jasper groups?

- Are gains universal, or are they limited to advanced students (the "rich getting richer")?
- Would a modified Jasper program elicit more effective problem solving from less-advanced grade 6 students? Alternatively, did teachers successfully scaffold less advanced students, providing assistance with computation, etc., so that these students experienced success in solving Jasper problems?
- What roles do teachers take on during collaborative Jasper work?

Computer-Supported Intentional Learning Environments (CSILE): A Program for Supporting Intentional Learning and Knowledge-Building

Areas of Growth Sought

The fundamental objective of this educational program is the intentional "construction of knowledge" by students. For some years, Bereiter and Scardamalia have been concerned with what they call "intentional learning," engaging in tasks of which the chief goal is increased knowledge (Lamon et al., 1996). (These authors are apparently less interested in intentional *skill* learning.) They stress that "knowledge" is a fundamentally social and public phenomenon. Hence, simply storing facts and procedures internally does not amount to constructing knowledge. Arriving at a shared understanding of a topic among a group of learners does. In order to "objectify" public knowledge, Scardamalia and her colleagues developed a system for constructing a communal database, shared among a working group in a manner similar to the circulation of research papers (unpublished and published) within a community of researchers. The ultimate observable product of the collective efforts of a group of students is a complex database or hypertext (including language units and graphics) regarding their joint understanding of a topic. In short, CSILE refers to a rather generalized context for learning about things, rather than to any specific task or content. The goal is improved "comprehension," broadly defined, and improved writing or "communication of knowledge," broadly defined.

There is much to be said for the intentional learning focus of the CSILE program. As the authors note, normal schoolwork rarely has learning and understanding (of skills, strategies, or knowledge) as students' primary task goals. Typically, students' main goal is to complete the work, please the teacher, pass the test, etc. Rarely are students in the position of evaluating the success of a school task in terms of what they *learned*, rather than what they *did*. When students do make such evaluations, they typically concern skills acquired. Only rarely do students evaluate their problem-solving strategies or strategies for constructing knowledge.

Teaching Methods

The heart of the CSILE "environment" is comprised of computer *software*—a networked database and graphics program—and *hardware*, usually a set of eight linked computers combined with a printer and modem. Thus, eight children at a time can work in the CSILE environment. (The number eight represents about a third of a primary class or a quarter of a grade 4, 5, or 6 class.) Each student ("author") can create text notes on a subject (readable by all students in the classroom). Others can attach comments (also readable by all), but cannot change the author's original text—only the author can do this. Authors can also create "graphical notes" (pictures, diagrams, etc.). Again, others can append alternative graphical notes, but cannot change the original. This system allows for extended discussion between students without some of the problems that often occur in the context of spoken dialogue—dominance by one or two people, insufficient wait time to consider responses, etc. Furthermore, this "discussion" can proceed and build over a matter of days or weeks, partly because it is in print rather than in more ephemeral speech.

Scardamalia et al. (1994) describe CSILE in action:

> Teachers work CSILE activities into the curriculum in any way they wish. They have been used in history, social studies, science, literature, geography, and to some extent mathematics. A limiting factor is computer time. Each student typically gets thirty minutes a day on a computer. This has generally meant that at any given time, only one unit or subject is being worked on via CSILE. In some cases a unit will follow a definite sequence of activities. For instance, it might begin with a videotape followed by whole-class discussion; then students will individually enter questions and study plans as CSILE notes; then they will do individual reading, entering what they learn as notes which others may comment on; whole class discussion or readings will intervene; finally selected text and graphic notes may be printed out and displayed on a bulletin board. In other cases, students will work in small groups and plan their own work, with only general guidance from the teacher (p. 208).

Learning Roles, Tasks, and Settings Used

The CSILE environment creates a semi-collaborative learning setting in which students are expected both to conduct independent work and to consult with colleagues about their work. At times a student may shift into a subordinate role, seeking advice and assistance from classmates. At other times, the same student may offer advice and pass on relevant information. For example, one comment that appeared in a CSILE database about inheritance was, "Mendel worked on Karen's question." As noted earlier, a unique feature is that this local network creates a communicative context in which students are not inhibited by overt dominance signals (e.g., tone of voice, others speaking more quickly or firmly, facial expressions, etc.) or by the need for immediate response. There is some evidence that students participate in CSILE discussions more equally than students in classroom discussions of the same topic (Bereiter & Scardamalia, 1993).

The teacher's role in CSILE has not been well specified. The teacher must initially teach students CSILE procedures and related word-processing, graphics, database search, and Internet skills. She must introduce topics to be reported/discussed through CSILE, and incorporate time for CSILE activity in the classroom program. (Note that this means that multiple settings must operate in the classroom, as children can't all work on CSILE at the same time. This implies an additional adult role—creating and participating in non-CSILE settings.) Beyond these responsibilities, the report on CSILE implies that the teacher should be reviewing the CSILE database as it evolves. The teacher might add comments to the database directly, contribute some teacher-authored notes, and/or discuss certain points with the class as a whole.

Effectiveness of the CSILE Program

Comparisons between CSILE students and comparable non-CSILE students in grades 3 to 6 have been reported for children in a Toronto school. Overall, CSILE students appear to gain .5 to .75 of a grade level on standardized language tests (reading comprehension, vocabulary, spelling), and show smaller but significant gains in standardized mathematics tests. (The language gains are not surprising—CSILE involves doing a lot of writing, reading and commenting.) On a number of other criteria, including "depth of explanation," "graphical knowledge representation," "portfolio ratings," and "constructive processes in reading," CSILE groups consistently showed significantly higher scores. CSILE and face-to-face cooperative discussion groups were compared in solving one of the

"Jasper" problems described in the previous section. Significantly more "high-level goals" were identified by the CSILE group, and students from the CSILE group became significantly more effective at solving math word problems. In short, participating in the CSILE environment for a year has benefits for students' language skills and comprehension, and for their problem-solving effectiveness.

Effectiveness of the CSILE Program for More vs. Less Advanced Children

Some evidence has been reported concerning the relative impact of the CSILE program on more versus less advanced students. Little difference is reported in the volume of notes and comments generated by the two groups. In contrast, others have reported that in "face-to-face" discussion groups, competitiveness and other social factors can disrupt the quality of discussion (Cohen, 1992; Salomon & Globerson, 1989). Unfortunately, no information on the *content* of more vs. less advanced students' notes and comments has been provided. We would be interested both in *process* data—what different students contribute in the form of notes and comments, and other possible impacts on classroom behavior—and in *summative* data, what educational gains are made by more and less advanced students in CSILE versus control classrooms. In principle, the CSILE environment appears to allow for relatively more "consulting" by all or most students. Whether this is actually being realized remains to be established.

We remain interested in the question of the dynamics of ability—in the impact of the CSILE experience on less-skilled writers (especially very poor and beginning writers), and on less-informed students. We suspect that CSILE *could* be especially valuable for such students. We would like to determine what the observed impact on such students has been to date, and what adaptations or teacher scaffolding may be helpful.

Reported Problems in Using the CSILE Program

As with the Jasper Project, successful CSILE activities are presently dependent on technological equipment (and teacher skills with this equipment), and on teacher and education system willingness to devote some scarce educational time to constructive tasks, rather than skills and formally taught strategies. In addition, CSILE presently requires the ongoing operation of the setting over a period of up to two hours, during which other worthwhile educational activities must be planned for non-CSILE students. This is not necessarily a liability—

such a situation could be viewed as an asset by any teacher who normally works with groups smaller than the whole class. Unfortunately, in our recent experience, we have found many teachers at the upper elementary (grades 4-6) and intermediate (grades 7-9) levels who have little experience with anything other than whole-class instruction, or who are working in rotary program structures that provide little opportunity for group work. If a rotary program is in place, CSILE would probably be best implemented in a lab or library setting that all students in a class could use simultaneously.

We have three other concerns. We understand from teachers using CSILE that unfortunate interpersonal dynamics can occur in CSILE communications, just as they can in face-to-face groups. This is far from being an insurmountable problem, but it points to the need to monitor CSILE activity and promote computer etiquette, just as students need to develop discussion and debating etiquette.

Reading and commenting on CSILE notes would be a time-consuming process for teachers, taking away time from planning, reviewing, or marking other work or classroom activities. It is interesting to note that some of the CSILE content discussed by Scardamalia et al. was not noted by the teacher until weeks after it had been generated. To help reduce this burden on teachers, programs for searching CSILE comments for "fruitful conversations" and students who "need a push" have been developed.[2]

As with the Jasper program, we suspect that wide-scale implementation will be difficult until the developers can become somewhat clearer about desirable teacher roles in relation to CSILE activities—both directly with students and in monitoring and feedback roles. Programs that explicitly set out to create consulting roles for students often leave teachers feeling uncertain about *their* roles or responsibilities. In time, this uncertainty must be reduced.

Why We Chose the CSILE Program

Like the Jasper Project, the CSILE project also illustrates *part* of a program—a learning setting without a specific task. The physical setting (networked computers) has been created, along with some student consulting roles (knowledge-constructing writing and commenting on peers' work). It is not surprising that CSILE researchers have incorporated Jasper tasks in their research. In general, the evolution of CSILE may depend in considerable part on the development of effective tasks to be used in the CSILE setting. However, it appears to us that the developers of CSILE have created a learning setting with real promise for involving a larger percentage of students in genuine consulting roles.[3]

The Fostering Communities of Learners Program

Areas of Growth Sought

Like Transactional Strategies Instruction and CSILE, the Fostering Communities of Learners (FCL) program began as an attempt to improve reading comprehension in elementary and middle schools. An important component of the FCL program is the Reciprocal Teaching learning setting developed by Brown and Palincsar (Brown & Campione, 1996).

Reciprocal Teaching (RT) was developed to teach at-risk readers from first through eighth grades, in groups of six or so participants. Each member of the group takes a turn leading a discussion about a text, a video, or other material that needs to be understood. Initially, an adult or an older student takes a turn as leader, with the younger or less competent group members following suit. Gradually, the group becomes capable of conducting its own reading activities in the absence of the adult or older peer leader. The group activities begin with a teacher-led question-and-answer session and conclude with a summary of the gist of the discussion. Along the way, the students are taught how to clarify any problems and to make predictions.

RT encourages the "externalization" of comprehension-monitoring activities and provides an avenue to nurture student discourse. The focus of RT is on the "core" skills of questioning, clarifying, summarizing, and predicting. Analysis of the social discourse of the RT groups indicates that approximately 75% consists of students asking and responding to questions (Rosenshine & Meister, 1994).

RT has proven effective in improving students' reading comprehension performance.[4] And as the RT program has evolved, the goals have broadened. As Brown and Campione (1996) explain, the goals now include the promotion of

> critical thinking and reflection skills underlying multiple forms of higher literacy: reading, writing, argumentation, technological sophistication, and so forth. Although billed as a thinking curriculum, the FCL program is embedded in deep disciplinary content. One cannot think critically, or otherwise, in a vacuum. Food for thought is needed to nourish critical thinking and reflection (p. 290).

In another part of the same article, Brown and Campione state their objectives:

> FCL encourages newcomers to adopt the discourse structure, goals, values, and belief systems of a community of research practice. The

> FCL community relies on the development of a discourse genre in
> which constructive discussion, questioning, querying, and criticism
> are the mode, rather than the exception (p. 305).

In short, they would like to see students become young university researchers.
A closely related objective is that students understand their interdependence
and learn how to work together, rather than separately, in coming to understand a topic. FCL emphasizes shared ownership, which promotes shared goals
and negotiated agreement on procedures and answers.

Teaching Methods

We should begin by noting that of all the programs outlined in this chapter, FCL
is the most complex, and we cannot do it justice in a few short pages. We refer
readers to Brown and Campione's (1996) chapter in Schauble and Glaser's *Innovations in Learning* for a more extended presentation.

The FCL program must be understood as a system involving a number of
components. Brown and Campione urge educators not to adopt pieces of the
system without understanding how the system as a whole functions. Conversely,
they stress that the components can undoubtedly be done differently—that their
"research seminars," "guided writing," etc., are not crucial in themselves, but
rather are crucial in the functions they serve as parts of a complete program.

With this caveat in mind, let us examine the FCL system. Brown and Campione
(1996) summarize the program as follows:

> At its simplest level, there are three key parts. Students engage in
> independent and group research on some aspect of a topic of in-
> quiry, mastery of which is ultimately the responsibility of all mem-
> bers of the class. This requires that they share their expertise with
> their classmates. This sharing is further motivated by some conse-
> quential task or activity that demands that all students have learned
> about all aspects of the joint topic. This consequential task can be as
> traditional as a test or quiz, or some nontraditional activity such as
> designing a "biopark" to protect an endangered species. These three
> key activities—(a) research, (b) in order to share information, (c) in
> order to perform a consequential task—are all overseen and coordi-
> nated by (d) self-conscious reflection on the part of all members of
> the community. In addition, the research-share-perform cycles of
> FCL cannot be carried out in a vacuum. All rely on the fact that the

participants are trying to understand deep disciplinary content (pp. 292-293).

The *research–share–consequential-task–group-reflection model* evolved from the "Jigsaw" method first developed by Aronson (1978). Essentially, this method involves teaching different groups of children different components of skills or knowledge that will be needed for a major task or project. The children are then regrouped so that the new groups include "experts" in each needed component. Thus, each has a consultative role to play. The FCL research team has elaborated on the learning methods used in the initial (or "research") stage of Jigsaw activity, as well as refining the final or "consequential" tasks to be used, and adding an intermediate stage ("cross-talk") in which all students come together to test how clearly each research group is able to present their area of expertise.

With their strong emphasis on reflection (which Brown and Campione define as student monitoring of their own and others' comprehension and progress), and on discourse about learning, the FCL developers clearly share our concern with bringing students to high or consultative levels of self-direction. The emphasis appears to be largely on the planning/application dimension of mastery, rather than on skill development. (This point will be addressed at greater length in the section on implications for less advanced students.) Again, there is an explicit assumption that dialoguing with others about knowledge will lead to internal monologue or thinking about similar tasks. In FCL implementations to date, FCL-based activity occupies approximately one third of a school day on a continuing basis.

Because the essence of the FCL program involves the deliberate orchestration of student roles and tasks in carefully sequenced learning settings, part of the discussion of methods involves an analysis of roles and settings in this program.

Learning Roles, Tasks, and Settings Used

Broadly speaking, the FCL program sequence involves two major groups of learning settings, with two basic tasks. In the "research" settings, the overall task is to learn or construct knowledge about a specified topic. (Note that students have probably been involved in specifying the topic.) In the "sharing" settings, the overall task is consequential, in the sense that results matter in some sense (presentation to others, grades, etc.). The overall task also requires bringing together the expertise of students from different research groups, while constructing some application of the knowledge gained in research groups. Several specific learning settings (or "participation structures," as Brown and Campione call them) have been developed for the basic program components of research and sharing. In each of these settings, the developers have deliberately structured student roles.

"Research" Component: Learning Settings, Roles, and Tasks. "Reciprocal Teaching" and "Research Seminars" are learning settings in which students increasingly assume the role of teacher as new information is studied and the group struggles to arrive at a joint understanding of the material. While a teacher or older student is usually present with the group, and initially provides much guidance in the form of questions, clarifications, and other prompts for students to apply strategies, the teacher gradually provides less and less direct guidance, as students take turns adopting a consulting role. The difference between Reciprocal Teaching and Research Seminars appears to lie largely in the strategies used for the comprehension task. In Reciprocal Teaching, the emphasis is on questioning, clarifying, predicting upcoming text and events, and summarizing sections of text. In Research Seminars, strategies include finding analogies to known phenomena, causal explanation, aspects of argumentation, and prediction of systems rather than events.

"Consultation with Experts," "Online Consultation," and "Cross-Age Teaching" are research settings in which students adopt acquisition or consolidation roles (except, of course, the older student experts who are providing consulting support). "Guided Writing" is a highly scaffolded setting in which research groups produce illustrated texts for teaching or helping others. An older student or teacher may do the actual typing of the text, and provides editorial assistance in the form of prompts (e.g., "Do you think the reader will be able to understand that?" or "Have you said how your animal gets food?"). Essentially, this involves consolidation roles for those being guided, and consultation roles for those guiding. Note that CSILE provides a setting in which guided writing can be pursued.

In general, the role of the teacher often involves guiding student activity as students attempt to understand (and later apply) areas of knowledge. Brown and Campione (1994) indicate that "guided discovery places a great deal of responsibility in the hands of the teachers, who must model, foster, and guide the 'discovery' process into forms of disciplined inquiry that may not be reached without such expert guidance" (p. 230).

"Sharing" Component: Learning Settings and Consequential Tasks. Two learning settings are described in the "sharing" aspect of FCL. One is "cross-talk," in

which research groups report their progress to the whole class. The rest of the students act as consultants by asking questions about material that is not clear. (As in any whole-class context, it would be interesting to know something about the levels of participation by high- and low-performing students in this activity.)

The other "sharing" setting is the Jigsaw group—which has a consequential task. Each student has a consulting role with respect to her area of expertise (acquired while in the "research groups"). Furthermore, all students in the group have a collaborative responsibility for the accomplishment of the consequential task. Such tasks provide an opportunity to assess the group's progress in mastering the areas studied in research groups, and in applying these areas of knowledge to at least one new problem. An example of a consequential task for second graders was inventing an imaginary creature, applying principles learned in the study of endangered species. Brown and Campione suggest that guided assessment of individual students can be carried out in the course of these consequential tasks (primarily through analysis of how much support is needed to accomplish tasks that are "one step beyond current performance").

In summary, the FCL program involves creating a number of learning settings with explicitly designed student roles ensuring consulting experiences for all students. Both intentional learning tasks and consequential ("results matter") tasks are used. The objective is to bring most students to high levels of consultation on tasks involving knowledge in the domain being studied, and to provide them with opportunities to reflect on their performance.

Effectiveness of the FCL Program

In studies of the FCL program, a variety of assessments have been provided, ranging from fairly traditional reading comprehension tests to analyses of changes in argumentation and explanation (Brown & Campione, 1994). In comparison to (presumably similar) non-FCL sixth-grade children, the FCL children (1) showed large gains in reading comprehension (65% versus 25% correct on a reading comprehension test that did not involve material covered in FCL); (2) applied more biological principles in constructing an imaginary animal (6 vs. 1); and (3) could answer many more short-answer questions concerning topics studied in the FCL classes, but only read about in the non-FCL classes. (It should be noted, however, that a Reciprocal Teaching control group showed similar, though somewhat smaller, gains in reading comprehension.) In addition, growth was reported for the FCL children over the year in argumentation and in clinical interviews which posed questions such as, "Could a cheetah change from a meat diet to a vegetable diet and survive?" Overall, in early trials, the program appears to be succeeding at improving students' abilities to comprehend texts. The authors stress that some of this improvement will necessarily be "local"—related to areas of new student expertise. It may be necessary in the future to evolve more appropriate tests for subject-specific learning.

Effectiveness of the FCL Program for More vs. Less Advanced Children

The FCL program was developed at an inner-city school in Oakland, California, primarily serving a black and Hispanic population. It should be noted, however, that this is a *magnet* school; enrollment involves active parental interest in their child's education. Brown and Campione note that there are a number of children in the school requiring special education services.

More than most writers, Brown, Campione, and their colleagues acknowledge the reality and magnitude of individual differences. We have previously quoted their rejection of the idea that there is a certain amount of work that "normal" students can do, or a certain amount of material that "normal" students can grasp, at particular ages. They are also clear about the problems of giving students highly standardized tests on which they simply can't succeed. However, we wish they would tell us more about what students who have trouble reading and writing *can* do as a result of participating in an FCL program, in comparison to similar students who have not participated in FCL. In the available report (Brown & Campione, 1994), some data apparently is taken "from only those students tackling grade-appropriate texts" (p. 250). Further research is needed to determine whether low-achieving students can benefit fully from the FCL experience.

Problems in Using the FCL Program

Several problems with implementing this program have been noted. As seen with Jasper, CSILE, and the others, programs that stress "understanding" topics in depth clash with typical education department demands that a wide range of topics be "covered." Furthermore, when in-depth coverage of a physical or social science topic is expected, teacher expertise in the topic may be necessary. This is not always available. (In our own experience, this problem can be partially addressed by selecting topics in which the teacher either *is* expert or wants to *become* more expert. However, this may not meet publicly mandated topic requirements.)

Teacher expertise at conducting an FCL program is also an issue (as with the other programs described here). Teachers need knowledge and skills in guiding learning, Reciprocal Teaching, organizing multi-group classrooms, etc., and in critical thinking about the topics being studied.

Finally, student misconceptions that arise in the course of a partially student-guided learning program can be problematic. The authors describe the example of a student conclusion that AIDS must be transmittable by mosquitoes. (To the best of public health knowledge, this is simply not true.) The point here is that teachers need to continually monitor the content of student-led teaching.

Why We Chose to Include the FCL Program

While the Jasper Project focuses on developing *tasks* suitable for fostering understanding, and the CSILE program focuses on developing a *learning setting* conducive to nurturing understanding, the Fostering Communities of Learners program focuses on developing student *roles* needed to nurture understanding. The FCL sequence of learning settings explicitly places students in consulting roles needed to bring them to high levels of self-direction and reflection. Furthermore, the FCL developers have created some sets of specific tasks that can be used for these purposes. It is not surprising that the further evolution of Jasper, CSILE, and FCL work is increasingly combining the methods developed within these three programs: Jasper and FCL tasks, CSILE learning settings, and FCL roles.

FCL is a complex, elaborate program. Compared to the other programs described, it requires a larger piece of the school day and a substantially more complex set of teacher roles. For it to become a "normal" part of most educational routines will involve a long period of teacher training and administrative support. Prior to that, clearer evidence on the effects of the program will be needed, especially with respect to the progress of low-achieving children. Some progress has been made, as the FCL format has been extended to areas of reading, math (Cobb, Wood, & Yackel, 1993), science (Brown et al., 1993), and social studies (Newman, Griffin, & Cole, 1989).

Overview of Programs Intended to Provide Higher Levels of Application and Self-Direction

The programs discussed in this chapter have a number of points in common.

1. They recognize that student competence and expertise are gained over long periods of time through concentrated, self-motivated learning.

2. They intentionally design a nurturing classroom environment that fosters individual and group problem solving, collaborative interpretive communication, negotiated agreements on procedures and products, and multiple student and teacher roles.

3. They are fundamentally concerned with building understanding and application of areas of knowledge, ranging from numbers to natural science, from writing to computer communication.

4. In each case, the approach is designed to enhance student understanding through dialogue, creating learning settings in which students' roles require them to initiate task-directive talk (or written language) with one another—sometimes from a position of authority or equality (as a teacher of recently-learned material, a player in a game, or a collaborator on a problem-solving or comprehension task). The tasks around which these interactions occur are primarily constructive—involving student planning responsibility, as well as performance responsibility. In each case, the authors emphasize that the kind of learning they are establishing should be an ongoing part of children's education and not a "one-shot" unit or experience.

5. The authors focus on presenting students with coherent content that is meaningful to them so they can apply their academic learning to important realistic problems, or as Brown (1997) comments, so "students learn to think deeply about serious matters."

6. Each program creates a metacognitive environment in which students learn to monitor their activities and in which they have to plan, orchestrate, oversee, and revise their learning efforts, and intentionally reflect on and self-direct their actions.

7. Students produce consequential products and activities that have meaning beyond the classroom, and are called upon to explain the procedures and processes they used to others.

8. The programs nurture inquiry, research, and transfer skills.

9. The authors of each program report measurable success in improving understanding, relative comparable children who received more conventional education. This is true for both conventional achievement measures and measures focused on understanding. In most cases, the authors state that conventional educational assessments provide only weak measures of the gains they seek, primarily because their approaches involve more in-depth study of a domain or discipline rather than the typical "survey" approach common in North American education.

10. All of the programs claim to be designed to benefit less-advanced stu-

dents. Two of them—Rightstart and Transactional Strategies Instruction—provide data on less advanced (or advantaged) students. These programs show explicit gains for such students. The FCL program has been developed and tested in an inner-city magnet school. We do not know to what extent this population can be described as educationally disadvantaged, and data on the accomplishments of less-advanced children within this population is not available.

It may also be helpful to note what these programs are *not*. When working in these programs, students are not simply repeating procedures demonstrated by others. They are not supplying fixed answers to fixed questions, or using algorithms in an unthinking rote fashion. For the most part, these programs provide relatively little instruction or introduction to new skills and concepts, compared to the time spent performing tasks which use acquired skills and concepts. To varying degrees, these programs assume that some skills and concepts have been acquired in other components of the school program (e.g., Jasper assumes that children can add, subtract, multiply, and divide fairly large numbers; CSILE assumes fairly strong word identification and spelling skills). On the other hand, in two of the programs—Rightstart and Transactional Strategies Instruction—basic skills and concepts are directly taught as needed, or otherwise addressed.

Overall, the programs examined in this chapter present encouraging evidence that emphasizing academic understanding and knowledge application by providing consultation roles on appropriate tasks can lead to enhanced comprehension and problem-solving skills. Nonetheless, we are left with some warnings and problems. Briefly, they include the following:

- Successful implementation of mastery- or understanding-focused education requires substantial teacher training or retraining. These are not programs that can be implemented as simply as a new textbook curriculum. They involve different teacher roles as well as different student roles. Inadequate teacher preparation or commitment can lead to what several writers referred to as "lethal mutations" of effective programs. A core issue is to what extent teachers have to "invent" each program, contrasted to the degree to which they can "learn" it—an issue not unlike that involved in the planning or application dimension of mastery presented in this book.
- Several authors noted that implementation of their programs was often in competition with educational objectives as specified by state or provincial departments of education. In an era of proliferating "standards"—

which involve both the content and the timing of learning—it is important to show that a stronger emphasis on mastery or understanding of academic skills and subjects has greater value for students than passing more factual questions on a standardized exam. In the long run, this will mean demonstrating improved achievement in colleges and universities and in the workplace. In the shorter run, it will mean demonstrating improved accomplishment (including staying in school) in subsequent years of school. (Such demonstrations will also require continued emphasis on comprehension and problem-solving in school programs.)

- Closely related is the issue of less advanced students. As long as our educational program is primarily concerned with producing "winners" and "losers," many will "lose." In the long run, we need a much higher percentage of students who can effectively use academic skills in a variety of contexts than now emerge from public education. It is not clear that tightening "standards" so that more will fail at specific ages is the way to achieve this.[5] Allowing more variation in rates of progress in mastering basic skills, while ensuring that most students gain consulting experience with relevant applications, is more likely to result in greater numbers of competent graduates.

- All dialogue-based programs depend to some degree on the collegiality and etiquette of the participants. Problems in this area were alluded to by several of the programs' developers. As noted in Chapter 9, students need to be taught how to be good helpers.

Endnotes

1. See Gregory et al. (1993), Pinnell et al. (1994), Rosenshine and Meister (1994), and Venezky (1996).

2. These are mentioned in Lamon et al. (1996, p. 272). The programs have not been published.

3. A number of computer-assisted programs have been developed that provide promising tasks for CSILE instruction. For example, Anderson and his colleagues (1995) have developed a computer-based "cognitive tutor" to teach students math skills such as algebra, geometry, problem solving, and programming. Schoenfeld and his colleagues (1987) have developed a computer-based high school instructional program to teach geometry. Not only do these programs result in increased student motivation, and reduced student discipline problems; in addition, the teachers' behavior also changed as they shifted from a "lecture" format toward the role of acting as facilitators, engaged in collaborative problem-solving with their students.

4. For detailed descriptions of Reciprocal Teaching, see Palincsar and Brown's (1984) article in *Cognition and Instruction*, and their chapter in Resnick's (1989) book, *Knowing, Learning, and Instruction*.

5. As we have noted earlier, if the primary function of the educational system is to perpetuate privilege, the current competitive educational model is appropriate. Moreover, if what we want to do is render 30–40% of the population ineligible for the limited number of jobs, the current curriculum-driven instructional approach will work. If, on the other hand, our goal is to increase the likelihood that all students will maximize their potential, then it is worthwhile to follow the principles behind these innovative programs and the teaching guidelines of this book.

Chapter Twelve

Lessons From Expert Teachers: Putting It All Together

Educating children is big business. Consider the figures for the U.S. Some 49 million students are being taught in kindergarten through grade 12, in 84,000 schools, by 2.5 million teachers, in 15,000 school districts. The average length of their instruction each year is 190 days. This costs taxpayers 300 billion dollars annually—approximately 275 billion dollars for public schools and 30 billion dollars for parochial schools (Mosteller et al., 1996).

With this potentially lucrative market, educators are inundated by innovators and promoters advocating for their particular version of educational reform. As Venezky (1996) notes:

> The current school reform theater is occupied by a group of brand name reform models that claim to be solutions for this country's schooling problems: Reading Recovery, Success for All, Accelerated Schools, Comer Schools, and others (p. 3).

We could add many additional educational reforms to this list, including Holistic Instruction, Instrumental Enrichment, Computer-Assisted Instruction, Multiple Intelligence Programs, Cultural Literacy Programs, Learning Style Instruction, Paideia Program, Roots and Wings, and others.[1]

Some of these instructional programs, like Reading Recovery, are focused on specific subject areas, while others represent full-scale reform models that seek systemic change in the culture, climate, and operation of the school. Often, the claims for the efficacy of these programs far exceed their documented results.

Our proposed educational approach does not fit either instructional approach. It is not focused on a specific subject area, and it does not propose to radically alter existing school procedures. Instead, our approach is designed to ensure that teachers are fully informed and responsive to the research literature on what practices constitute the best teaching. What do expert teachers do that results in their students' achieving? What can be done to bridge the gulf between what research tells us about effective instruction and what teachers actually do in their classrooms?

In order to answer these critical questions, we have carefully examined the literature on teacher expertise and on educational programs that have resulted in improved student performance, as described in Chapters 7 to 11. What do teachers who are judged to be expert—as determined by their students' overall performance, by objective measures of what their students have learned, or by years of experience—know and do to nurture their students' successes? A good deal of research, using classroom observations and laboratory studies, has been conducted to answer this important question (Brophy & Good, 1986; Leinhardt, 1988, 1990, 1992; Leinhardt & Greeno, 1986; Leinhardt & Smith, 1985; Rosenshine & Stevens, 1986; Shulman, 1980).

Like experts in other areas, expert teachers have been found to have more content knowledge and more pedagogical knowledge on how to teach than less expert teachers. Expert teachers know their subject matter well, whether it is teaching general skills like reading or a domain-specific area like math. They have an accumulated knowledge base about both the academic tasks they teach and about how students learn. Based on this knowledge, they select, represent, and explain concepts and procedures in an engaging, enthusiastic, and clear fashion.

The research literature also indicates that expert teachers are quicker to pick up cues that students are struggling, and that they more readily alter instruction accordingly. With experience comes an enhanced sensitivity to students' problems, many of which they can anticipate. Moreover, this information is stored in a more organized fashion, and its retrieval leads to the implementation of more effective teaching strategies. (This is reminiscent of the expert chess player, who evidenced superior pattern recognition and who had accompanying effective strategies or game plans.)

Expert teachers also have well-tuned, automated instructional tactics that allow them to perform teaching tasks without burdening their working memory, and without active metacognitive self-regulation. Yet such seemingly fluid performance disguises the lengthy preparation and planning that expert teachers engage in prior to teaching a lesson or unit (Sternberg & Horvath, 1995). The expert teachers' behaviors may look routine and scripted, as they model thinking, engage students in goal setting and deliberate practice, calibrate task difficulty, teach strategies directly, fade supports, and employ peer assistance. However, this appearance belies a mindfully vigilant educator in action.

Expert teachers also appear motivated to continually challenge their students to apply (extend, invent, and reinvest) their efforts, and to apply what they know to new tasks in new situations (Lepper et al., 1990). They are also cognizant that students learn and apply what interests them, so they more readily include authentic tasks that students find both challenging and meaningful (Newman & Wehlage, 1995). Expert teachers are as concerned with their students' self-confidence (self-efficacy and self-esteem), and with their causal explanations (to others and to themselves) about their failures and successes, as they are with the students' actual performance (Bereiter & Scardamalia, 1986; Dweck, 1986; Licht, 1993).

Expert teachers usually do not view themselves as merely conveying knowledge or teaching strategies to their students. Rather, they tend to view students as active participants, partners in learning, and "meaning makers," with whom they collaborate. They explicitly train and encourage their students to become their own, and each other's, teachers. Expert teachers work hard to convey ownership to their students; as one teacher noted, "I am in charge of getting out of their way. I am in charge of putting them in charge" (Pressley et al., 1995).

We propose that the present three-dimensional model of mastery captures what these expert teachers do. Expert teachers are skillful at moving students OVER along the X dimension of skills (and vocabulary), UP the Y dimension of self-direction (moving them from being initially "clueless," through being able to perform the task automatically, to being able to teach it to others), and finally, OUT along the Z dimension of planning and application, transferring what they have learned to new tasks and new situations.

Two additional things that expert teachers do are (1) evaluate, analyze, and critique their teaching efforts and (2) invite other teachers to be partners in the implementation and evaluation of their teaching efforts. Like experts in other areas, expert teachers are reflective, strategic, innovative, and self-evaluative, especially when their teaching objectives are not met. Such failures are often occasions for expert teachers to self-interrogate and analyze what they could do to improve their instruction. In the same way that teachers want their students to become self-directed learners, expert teachers can engage in a parallel self-reflective process, as described in Table 12.1 on the next page. How many of these questions do you, as a teacher, ask yourself?

An analogy that captures this dynamic and reflective teaching process is that of a web. The three dimensions of the model of mastery can be thought of as axes of the web. The web is woven from the threads of each of the three axes—

TABLE 12.1
Questions Teachers Can Ask Themselves
About Achieving Various Student Roles

Student Skill and Strategy Acquisition Roles

Have I determined that students

(a) can perform the taught skills and apply the taught strategies?

(b) can recite (demonstrate, write, diagram) the strategy from memory or para-phrase the strategy?

(c) can explain or define relevant language used with the skill or strategy?

(d) can understand the rationale for learning specific skills and strategies, and appreciate how learning these will help students achieve desired goals?

(e) feel confident that they will be able to use learned skills and strategies?

Have I created an inviting learning environment?

Have I calibrated the level of task difficulty, so it slightly exceeds the students' abilities?

Have I prepared the students for what is to be taught by accessing the students' prior knowledge, by providing an advance organizer and informed instruction, and by relating what is to be taught to the past (prior knowledge and experi-ence) and to future goals?

Have I anticipated possible misconceptions and procedural bugs that might interfere with students' skill performance or task accomplishment?

Have I adequately motivated (challenged) the students to accomplish assigned or self-selected tasks (bolstering their self-confidence)?

Have I paced the instruction, used reminders (provided predetermined gradu-ated prompts), and employed manipulatives?

Have I used direct instruction procedures (explanation, modeling, re-explana-tion, guided practice, and feedback)?

Have I enlisted the students as collaborators by giving them choices on task selection and employing discovery-learning procedures?

Have I taught students self-regulatory strategies such as self-monitoring behav-iors?

Student Skill and Strategy Consolidation Roles

Have I provided students with deliberate practice at a high level of mastery (e.g., an approximate 90% success rate on assigned tasks)?

Have I done this for all students in my class, even if this means that they are achieving 90% success rates on *different* skills and strategies?

Do the students need more assistance (temporarily) in using the skill or strat-egy?

Do I need to review, reteach, and provide more direct instruction?

Did I provide students with an opportunity to engage in goal setting that yields specific, proximal, and doable objectives?

Did I provide supports for students who are struggling or stuck?

Student Skill and Strategy Consultation Roles

Have I conveyed to students that I am as interested in learning about the processes they use to solve problems as I am in their answers?

Have I used student think-aloud procedures and the art of questioning to solicit the students' reflective processes?

Have I asked students to reflect in writing on the processes they used to perform the task or how they employ their strategies?

Have I engaged students in peer teaching (e.g., collaborative learning, cross-age peer tutoring, etc.)?

Have I provided learning settings in which all students in my class could successfully assume consulting roles in each major curriculum domain?

Student Application Roles

Have I assessed whether the students can employ learned skills and strategies when planning and performing other tasks and in other settings?

Have I used authentic learning tasks and activities that have value beyond the classroom (i.e., had students produce public products)?

Have I required students to describe how they performed a task or activity to others who are not part of the classroom?

Have I implemented the guidelines to help students achieve transfer of what they have learned? (For example, have I involved significant others? Have I trained explicitly for generalization? Have I followed the other transfer guidelines?)

Have I ensured that students take credit for successes and cope with and benefit from failures (i.e., attribute success to effort and strategy usage and view setbacks as learning opportunities)?

Have I built in authentic assessments that convey ownership to students?

Have I helped students help create and participate in a community of learners, so they develop a positive "possible self" vision of what they can achieve?

Have I ensured that all students in my class participate in consulting roles in applied settings?

Have I shared my teaching experiences with my colleagues and others?

Have I become a more expert teacher? In what specific ways?

skills and concepts (X), self-direction (Y), and strategies for real-world application (Z). Each teacher and their students can piece the web together somewhat differently. In fact, within a given classroom, the web may be woven somewhat differently at different times and for different students, depending upon the specific teaching objectives and the students' needs. At any one time, teachers may emphasize one dimension at the expense of the others. For students who are deficient in prerequisite skills, greater emphasis may need to be placed on skill acquisition and consolidation, while for those who have developed competence, the instruction may focus on developing consulting skills by means of collaborative learning and cross-age peer tutoring.

If students are to develop mastery, it is important that the instructional learning web include threads of all three dimensions *for all students.* Teachers need to guard against overlooking any of these dimensions. This is especially true for low-performing students, who often do not receive adequate opportunities to experience movement along each of the three dimensions. As Guthrie and Cox (1995) observe, "A genuine web cannot be woven with too few threads, and in an effective classroom, students must become weavers of their own web" (p. 12).

Expert teachers are expert at having their students weave their own webs, as they instill students with the lifelong desire to learn. These teachers have to be flexible, strategic, reflective thinkers.

We urge our readers to review their own classroom programs, using the questions in Table 12.1. Consider which settings in your program offer students acquisition, consolidation, and consultation roles. Consider which settings include application tasks. How many of your students currently have opportunities to master some of the skills and strategies you teach them? Can you find ways of extending such opportunities to other students in your program? If you can do so, your effort in reading this book (and ours in writing it) will not have been in vain.

Endnotes

1. Ross, Smith, and their colleagues have reviewed the strengths and weaknesses of nine educational programs. They note that the "characteristic features of all or most include cooperative learning, thematic units, student-centered instruction, integrated curricula, multi-age grouping, adoption of high-level performance standards, site-based school management, community and family connection to schools, and authentic assessment of student learning" (in press, p. 2). These programs have yet to demonstrate accountability in terms of achievement test scores.

References

Adams, M.J. (1990). *Beginning to read: Thinking and learning about print.* Cambridge, MA: MIT Press.

Alexander, K.L., & Entwistle, P.R. (1988). Achievement on the first two years of school: Patterns and processes. *Monographs of the Society for Research in Child Development* (2, Serial No. 218).

Ames, C. (1992). Classrooms: Goals, structures, and student motivation. *Journal of Educational Psychology, 84,* 261-271.

Anderson, J.R. (1982). Acquisitions of cognitive skill. *Psychological Review, 89,* 369-406.

Anderson, J.R. (1985). *Cognitive psychology and its implications.* New York: Freeman.

Anderson, J.R., (1987). Skill acquisition: Compilation of weak-method problem solutions. *Psychological Review, 94,* 192-210.

Anderson, J.R., Corbett, A.T., Koedinger, K.R., & Pelletier, R. (1995). Cognitive tutors: Lessons learned. *Journal of Learning Sciences, 4,* 167-207.

Anderson, J.R., Reder, L.M., & Simon, H.A. (1996). Situated learning and education. *Educational Researcher, 25,* 5-11.

Applebee, A., Langer, J., Mullis, I., Latham, A., & Gentile, C. (1994). *NAEP 1992 writing report card.* (Rep. No. 23-W01) Washington, DC: Office of Educational Research and Improvement, U.S. Department of Education.

Aronson, E. (1978). *The jigsaw classroom.* Beverly Hills, CA: Sage.

Bandura, A. (1993). Perceived self-efficacy in cognitive development and functioning. *Educational Psychologist, 28,* 117-148.

Barker, R.G., & Gump, P. (1964). *Big schools, small schools.* Stanford, CA: University Press.

Barone, M., & Taylor, L. (1996). Peer tutoring with mathematical manipulatives: A practical guide. *Teaching Children Mathematics,* Sept., 8-15.

Becker, W.C. (1977). Teaching reading and language to the disadvantaged: What we have learned from field research. *Harvard Educational Review, 47,* 518-543.

Benjamin Franklin Writings. (1987). New York: Literary Classics. (Original *Autobiography* published in 1868.)

Bereiter, C. (1995). A dispositional view of transfer. In A. McKeough, J. Lupart, & A. Marini (Eds.), *Teaching for transfer: Fostering generalization in learning.* Hillsdale, NJ: Erlbaum.

Bereiter, C., & Scardamalia, M. (1986). Educational relevance of the study of expertise. *Interchange, 17* 10-19.

Bereiter, C., & Scardamalia, M. (1993). *Surpassing ourselves. An inquiry into the nature and implications of expertise.* Chicago, IL: Open Court.

Bergeron, B., & Rudenga, E.A. (1996). Seeking authenticity: What is "real" about thematic literacy instruction? *The Reading Teacher, 49,* 544-557.

Bergeron, B., Wermuth, S., & Hammer, R.C. (1997). Initiating portfolios through shared learning: Three perspectives. *The Reading Teacher, 50,* 552-562.

Berliner, D.C., & Biddle, B.J. (1995). *The manufactured crisis: Myths, fraud, and the attack on America's public schools.* Reading, MA: Addison-Wesley.

Beyer, B.K. (1988). *Developing a thinking skills program.* Boston: Allyn & Bacon.

Biemiller, A. (1993). Lake Wobegon revisited: On diversity and education. *Educational Researcher, 22,* 7-12.

Biemiller, A., & Booth, D. (1994). *Towards higher levels of elementary school literacy.* Paper presented to the Royal Commission on Learning, Toronto, Ontario.

Biemiller, A., & Meichenbaum, D. (1992). The nature and nurture of student expertise. *Educational Leadership, 50(2),* 75-80.

Biemiller, A., & Morley, E. (1996, June). *Primary students' post-task reflections on task selection, maintenance and evaluation.* Paper presented at Jean Piaget Society, Philadelphia, PA.

Biemiller, A., & Richards, M. (1986). *Project Thrive. Vol. 2: Individualized intervention to foster social, emotional, and self-related functions in primary programs.* Toronto, ON: Ministry of Education (Ontario).

Biemiller, A., Shany, M., Inglis, A., & Meichenbaum, D. (in press). Factors influencing children's acquisition and demonstration of self-regulation on academic tasks. In D. Schunk and B.J. Zimmerman (Eds.), *Developing self-regulated learners: From teaching to self-reflective practice*. New York: Guilford.

Bivens, J.A., & Berk, L.E. (1990). A longitudinal study of the development of elementary school children's private speech. *Merrill-Palmer Quarterly, 36*, 443-463.

Bloom, B.S. (1964). *Stability and change in human characteristics*. New York: Wiley.

Bloom, B.S. (1976). *Human characteristics and school learning*. New York: McGraw-Hill.

Bloom, B.S. (Ed.). (1976a). *Taxonomy of educational objectives: The classification of educational goals. Handbook I. Cognitive domain*. New York: McKay.

Bloom, B.S. (Ed.). (1985). *Development of talent*. New York: Ballantine Books.

Blumenfield, P.C. (1992). Classroom learning and motivation: Clarifying and expanding goal theory. *Journal of Educational Psychology, 84*, 272-281.

Blumenfield, P.C., Soloway, E., Marx, R.W., Krajcik, J.S., Guzchal, M., & Palincsar, A. (1981). Motivating project-based learning: Sustaining the doing, supporting the learning. *Educational Psychologist, 26*, 369-398.

Borkowski, J.G., & Dukewich, T.L. (1996). Environmental covariations and intelligence: How attachment influences self-regulation. In D.K. Detterman (Ed.)., *Current topics in human intelligence, Vol. 5: The environment* (pp. 3-15). Norwood, NJ: Ablex.

Borkowski, J.G., & Muthakrishna, N. (1992). Moving metacognition into the classroom: "Working models" and effective strategy teaching. In M. Pressley, K.R. Harris, & J.T. Guthrie (Eds.), *Promoting academic competence and literacy in schools.* (pp. 477-501). Toronto: Academic Press.

Borkowski, J.G., & Thorpe, P.K. (1994). Self-regulation and motivation: A life-span perspective on underachievement. In D.H. Schunk & B.J. Zimmerman (Eds.), *Self-regulation of learning and performance*. Hillsdale, NJ: Erlbaum.

Bransford, J.D., Goldman, S.R., & Vye, N.J. (1990). Making a difference in people's ability to think: Reflections on a decade of work and some hopes for the future. In R.J. Sternberg & L. Okagaki (Eds.), *Influences on children* (pp. 147-180). Hillsdale, NJ: Erlbaum.

Brophy, J.E., & Good, T.L. (1986). Teacher behavior and student achievement. In M.C. Wittrock (Ed.), *Handbook of research on teaching* (3rd ed., pp. 328-376). New York: Macmillan.

Brown, A.L. (1995). The advancement of learning. *Educational Researcher, 23*, 4-12.

Brown, A.L. (1997). Transforming schools into communities of thinking and learning about serious matters. *American Psychologist, 52*, 399-413.

Brown, A.L., Ash, D., Rutherford, M., Nakagwa, K., Gordon, A., & Campione, J.C. (1993). Distributed expertise in the classroom. In G. Salomon (Ed.), *Distributed cognitions: Psychological and educational considerations* (pp. 188-218). New York: Cambridge University Press.

Brown, A.L., & Campione, J.C. (1994). Guided discovery in a community of learners. In K. McGilly (Ed.), *Classroom lessons: Integrating cognitive theory and classroom practice* (pp. 229-270). Cambridge, MA: MIT Press.

Brown, A.L., & Campione, J.C. (1996). Psychological theory and the design of innovative learning environments: On procedures, principles, and systems. In L. Schauble & R. Glaser (Eds.), *Innovations in learning: New environments for education* (pp. 289-325). Hillsdale, NJ: Erlbaum.

Brown, A.L., & Ferrara, R.A. (1985). Diagnosing zones of proximal development. In J.V. Wertsch (Ed.), *Culture, communication, and cognition: Vygotskian perspectives* (pp. 273-305). New York: Cambridge University Press.

Brown, A.L., & Kane, M.J. (1988). Preschool children can learn to transfer: Learning to learn and learning from example. *Cognitive Psychology, 15*, 1-38.

Brown, A.L., & Palincsar, A.S. (1989). Guided cooperative learning and individual knowledge acquisition. In L.B. Resnick (Ed.), *Knowing, learning, and instruction*. Hillsdale, NJ: Erlbaum.

Brown, R., Pressley, M., Van Meter, P., & Schuder, T. (1996). A quasi-experimental validation of transactional strategies instruction with low-achieving second-grade readers. *Journal of Educational Psychology, 88*, 18-37.

Bruer, J. (1993). *Schools for thought: A science of learning in the classroom*. Cambridge, MA: MIT Press.

Bryson, M., Bereiter, C., Scardamalia, M., & Joram, E. (1991). Going beyond the problem as given: Problem-solving in expert and novice writers. In R.J. Sternberg & R.A. Frensch (Eds.), *Complex problem solving* (pp. 61-84). Hillsdale, NJ: Erlbaum.

Cai, J., Magone, M.E., Wang, N., & Lane, S. (1996). A cognitive analysis of QUASAR mathematics performance tasks. *Research in Middle Level Education, 19*, 63-94.

Cai, J., & Silver, E. (1995). Solution process and interpretations of solutions in solving a division-with-remainder story problem: Do Chinese and U.S. students have similar difficulties? *Jour-*

nal for Research in Mathematics Education, 26, 491-497.

Cantalini, M. (1987). *The effects of age and gender on school readiness and school success*. Unpublished doctoral dissertation. Toronto, ON: University of Toronto.

Carnine, D.W., Granzin, A., & Becker, W. (1988). Direct instruction. In J.L. Graden, J.E. Zins, & M.J. Curtis (Eds.), *Alternative educational delivery systems* (pp. 327-349). Washington, DC: National Association of School Psychologists.

Carroll, J.B. (1963). A model of school learning. *Teacher's College Record, 64*, 723-733.

Carroll, J.B. (1985). The model of school learning: Progress of an idea. In C.W. Fisher & D.C. Berliner (Eds.), *Perspectives on instructional time* (pp. 59-72). New York: Longman.

Carroll, J.B. (1989). The Carroll model: A 25-year retrospective and prospective view. *Educational Researcher, 17*(1), 26-31.

Carver, S.M. (in press). The Discover Rochester Design Experiment: Collaborative change through five designs. In J. Hawkins & A. Collins (Eds.), *Design experiments: Integrating technology into schools*. Cambridge, UK: Cambridge University Press.

Case, R. (1985). *Intellectual development: Birth to adulthood*. San Diego, CA: Academic Press.

Case, R. (1992). *The mind's staircase: Exploring the conceptual underpinnings of children's thought and knowledge*. Hillsdale, NJ: Erlbaum.

Case, R. (1996). *Mathematics education for the information age*. Unpublished paper. Toronto, ON: University of Toronto.

Case, R., with Bruchkowsky, M., Capodilupo, A., et al. (1991). *The mind's staircase: exploring the conceptual underpinnings of children's thoughts and knowledge*. Hillsdale, NJ: Erlbaum.

Chall, J.S. (1983/1996). *Stages of reading development*. Fort Worth, TX: Harcourt Brace College Publishers.

Chase, W.G., & Simon, H.A. (1973a). Perception in chess. *Cognitive Psychology, 4*, 551.

Chase, W.G., & Simon, H.A. (1973b). The mind's eye in chess. In W. Chase (Ed.), *Visual information processing* (pp. 215-281). New York: Academic Press.

Chen, C., Lee, S.Y., & Stevenson, H.W. (1996). Long-term prediction of academic achievement of American, Chinese, and Japanese adolescents. *Journal of Educational Psychology, 88*, 750-789.

Chi, M.T., Bassok, M., Lewis, M., Reimann, P., & Glaser, R. (1989). Self-explanations: How students study and use examples to solve problems. *Cognitive Science, 13*, 145-182.

Chi, M.T., deLeeuw, N., Chiu, M.H., & La-

Vancher, C. (1994). Eliciting self-explanations improves understanding. *Cognitive Science, 18*, 439-478.

Chi, M.T., Feltovich, P.J., & Glaser, R. (1981). Categorization and representation of physics problems by high experienced subjects and low experienced subjects. *Cognitive Psychology, 5*, 215-281.

Chi, M.T., Glaser, R., & Farr, M. (Eds.). (1988). *The nature of expertise*. Hillsdale, NJ: Erlbaum.

Chi, M.T., & Van Leehn, K.A. (1991). The content of physics self-explanations. *Educational Psychologist, 1*, 69-105.

Cobb, P. (1994). Where is the mind? Constructivist and sociocultural perspectives on mathematical development. *Educational Researcher, 23*, 13-20.

Cobb, P., & Yackel, E. (1996). Constructivist, emergent, and sociocultural perspectives in the content of developmental research. *Educational Psychologist, 31*, 175-190.

Cobb, P., Wood, T., & Yackel, E. (1993). Discourse, mathematical thinking, and classroom practice. In E. Forman, N. Minick, & C.A. Stone (Eds.), *Contexts for learning: Sociocultural dynamics in children's development* (pp. 91-119). New York: Cambridge University Press.

Cochran-Smith, M. (1991). Elementary word processing and writing. *Review of Educational Research, 61*, 107-155.

Cognition and Technology Group at Vanderbilt. (1991a). Anchored instruction and its relationship to situated instruction. *Educational Researcher, 19*, 2-10.

Cognition and Technology Group at Vanderbilt. (1991b). Technology and the design of generative learning environments. *Educational Researcher, 31*, 34-40.

Cognition and Technology Group at Vanderbilt. (1994a). From visual word problems to learning communities: Changing conceptions of cognitive research. In K. McGilly (Ed.), *Classroom lessons: Integrating cognitive theory and classroom practice* (pp. 157-200). Cambridge, MA: MIT Press.

Cognition and Technology Group at Vanderbilt. (1994b). Multimedia environments for enhancing student learning in mathematics. In S. Vosnladon, E. Delorte, & H. Mandl (Eds.), *Technology-based learning environments: Psychological and educational foundations* (pp. 167-173). Berlin: Springer-Verlag.

Cognition and Technology Group at Vanderbilt. (in press). Learning Technology Center, Peabody College at Vanderbilt. In D.C. Berliner & R.C. Calfee (Eds.), *The handbook of educational psychology*. New York: Macmillan.

Cohen, E.G. (1994). Restructuring the classroom: Conditions for productive small groups. *Review of Educational Research, 64*, 1-35.

Corno, L. (1994). Student volition and education: Outcomes, influences and practices. In D.H. Schunk & B.J. Zimmerman (Eds.), *Self-regulation of learning and performance.* Hillsdale, NJ: Erlbaum.

Cronin, J.F. (1993). Four misconceptions about authentic learning. *Educational Leadership, 50,* 78-80.

Cunningham, A.E. (1990). Explicit versus implicit instruction in phonemic awareness. *Journal of Experimental Child Psychology, 50,* 429-444.

Cunningham, P.M., & Allington, R.L. (1994). *Classrooms that work: They can all read and write.* New York: HarperCollins.

Darling-Hammond, L., Ancess, J., & Falk, B. (1995). *Authentic assessment in action: Studies of school and students at work.* New York: Teachers College.

Davey, B., & McBride, S. (1986). Effects of question generation training on reading comprehension. *Journal of Educational Psychology, 78,* 256-262.

Day, J.D., Borkowski, J.G., Dietmeyer, D.L., Howsepian, B.A., & Saenz, D.S. (1992). Possible selves and academic achievement. In L.T. Winegar & J. Valsinar (Eds.), *Children's development within social context,* Vol. 2 (pp. 181-202). Hillsdale, NJ: Erlbaum.

de Groot, A.D. (1966). Perception and memory versus thought: Some old ideas and recent findings. In B. Kleinmuntz (Ed.), *Problem-solving* (pp 19-50). New York: Wiley.

Devin-Sheehan, L., Feldman, R.S., & Allen, V.L. (1976). Research on children tutoring children: A critical review. *Review of Educational Research, 46,* 355-385.

Dewey, J. (1933). *How we think.* Boston: D.C. Heath.

Duffy, G.D. (1993). Rethinking strategy instruction: Four teachers' development and their low achievers' understanding. *Elementary School Journal, 93,* 231-247.

Duffy, G.G., & Roehler, L.R. (1987a). *Improving classroom reading instruction: A decision making approach* (2nd ed.). New York: Random House.

Duffy, J.J., & Roehler, L.R. (1987b). Improving instruction through the use of elaboration. *Reading Teacher, 40,* 514-520.

Duncan, G.J., Brooks-Gunn, J., & Klebanov, P.K. (1994). Economic deprivation and early childhood development. *Child Development, 65,* 296-318.

Durkin, D. (1978). What classroom observations reveal about reading comprehension. *Reading Research Quarterly, 14,* 518-544.

Dweck, C.S. (1986). Motivational processes affecting learning. *American Psychologist, 41,* 1040-1048.

Eccles, J.S. (1993). School and family effects on the ontogeny of children's interests, self-perceptions, and activity choices. In J.E. Jacobs (Ed.), *Developmental perspectives on motivation: Vol. 40 of Nebraska Symposium.* Lincoln, NE: University of Nebraska Press.

Eccles, J.S., & Harold, R.D. (1993). Parent-school involvement during the early adolescent years. *Teachers College Record, 94,* 568-587.

Engleman, S., & Carnine, D. (1982). *Theory of instruction: Principles and applications.* New York: Irvington.

Englert, C.S., Torrant, K.L., & Mariage, T.V. (1992). Defining and redefining instructional practice in special education: Perspectives on good teaching. *Teacher Education and Special Education, 15,* 62-86.

Entrikin, V. (1992). Mind mapping. *The Mathematics Teacher, 85,* 444-445.

Epstein, J.L. (1992). School and family partnerships. In M. Aiken (Ed.), *Encyclopedia of educational research.* New York: Macmillan.

Ericsson, K.A., & Charness, N. (1994). Expert performance: Its structure and acquisition. *America's Psychologist, 49,* 725-747.

Ericsson, K.A., Krampe, R.T., & Tesch-Romer, C. (1993). The role of deliberate practice in the acquisition of expert performance. *Psychological Review, 100,* 363-406.

Ericsson, K.A., & Lehmann, A.C. (1996). Expert and exceptional performance: Evidence of maximal adaptation to task constraints. *Annual Review of Psychology, 47,* 273-305.

Ericsson, K.A., & Smith, J. (1989). *The study of expertise: Prospects and limits.* Hillsdale, NJ: Erlbaum.

Ericsson, K.A., & Smith, J. (Eds.). (1991). *Toward a general theory of expertise: Prospects and limits.* Cambridge, UK: Cambridge University Press.

Fantuzzo, J.W., King, J.A., & Heller, L.R. (1992). Effects of reciprocal peer tutoring on mathematics and school adjustment: A component analysis. *Journal of Educational Psychology, 84,* 331-339.

Ferretti, R.P., & Okolo, C.M. (1996). Authenticity in learning: Multimedia design projects in the social studies for students with disabilities. *Journal of Learning Disabilities, 29,* 450-460.

Fisher, C.N., & Berliner, D.C. (Eds.), (1995). *Perspectives on instructional time.* New York: Longman.

Fuchs, L.S., Fuchs, D., Bentz, J., Phillips, N.B., & Hamlett, C.L. (1994). The nature of student interactions during peer tutoring with and without prior training and experience. *American Educational Research Journal, 31,* 75-103.

Fuchs, L.S., Fuchs, D., & Hamlett, C.L. (1994). Strengthening the connection between assessment and instructional planning with expert systems. *Exceptional Children, 61,* 138-146.

Fuchs, L.S., Fuchs, D., Hamlett, C.L., Phillips, N.B., Karns, K., & Dutka, S. (1997). Enhancing students' helping behavior during peer-mediated instruction with conceptual mathematical explanations. *Elementary School Journal, 97,* 223-249.

Fuchs, L.S., Fuchs, D., Mathes, R.G., & Simmons, D.C. (1997). Peer-assisted learning strategies: Making classrooms more responsive to diversity. *American Educational Research Journal, 34,* 174-206.

Gagne, R., & Briggs, L. (1974). *Principles of instructional design.* New York: Holt, Rinehart & Winston.

Gamoran, A., Nystrand, M., Berends, M., & Le Pare, P.C. (1995). An organizational analysis of the effects of ability grouping. *American Educational Research Journal, 32,* 687-715.

Garcia-Coll, C., Lamberty, G., Jenkins, R., McAdoo, H.P., Crnic, K., Wasik, B.H., & Garcia, H.V. (in press). Toward an integrative-theoretical model for the study of developmental competencies in minority children. *Child Development.*

Gardner, H., Krechevsky, M., Sternberg, R.J., & Okagaki, L. (1994). Intelligence in context: Enhancing students' practical intelligence for school. In K. McGilly (Ed.), *Classroom lessons: Integrating cognitive theory and classroom practice* (pp. 105-128). Cambridge, MA: MIT Press.

Geary, D.C. (1994). *Children's mathematical development: Research and practical implications.* Washington, DC: American Psychological Association.

Gersten, R., & Brengelman, S.U. (1996). The quest to translate research into classroom practice: The emerging knowledge base. *Remedial and Special Education, 17,* 67-74.

Gill, A., & McPike, L. (1995). What can we learn from Japanese teachers' manuals? *American Educator,* Spring, 14-24.

Gisecke, D., Cartledge, G., & Gardner, R. (1993). Low achieving students as successful cross-age tutors. *Preventing School Failure, 37,* 34-43.

Good, T.L., & Brophy, J.E. (1994). *Looking in classrooms* (6th ed.). New York: HarperCollins.

Goodlad, J. (1984). *A place called school.* New York: McGraw-Hill.

Goodlad, S., & Hirst, B. (1989). *Peer tutoring: A guide to learning by teaching.* London: Kogan Page.

Goodlad, S., & Hirst, B. (1990). *Explorations in peer tutoring.* London: Blackwell Education.

Greenwood, C.R., Delquadri., J., & Carta, J. (1988). *Classwide peer tutoring.* Delray Beach, FL: Educational Achievement Systems.

Greenwood, C.R., Delquadri, J.C., & Hall, R.V. (1989). Longitudinal effects of classwide peer tutoring. *Journal of Educational Psychology, 81,* 371-383.

Greenwood, C.R., Dinwiddie, G., Bailey, V., & Schulte, D. (1987). Field replication of classwide peer tutoring. *Journal of Applied Behavior Analysis, 20,* 151-160.

Gregory, D., Earl, L., & O'Donoghue, B. (1993). *A study of reading recovery in Scarborough: 1990-1992.* Publication #92/93-15. Scarborough, ON: Scarborough Board of Education.

Griffin, S.A., Case, R., & Capodilupo, A. (1995). Teaching for understanding: The importance of the central conceptual structures in the elementary mathematics curriculum. In A. McKeough, J. Lupart, & A. Marini (Eds.), *Teaching for transfer: Fostering generalization in learning.* Hillsdale, NJ: Erlbaum.

Griffin, S.A., Case, R., & Siegler, R.S. (1994). Rightstart: Providing the central conceptual prerequisites for first formal learning of arithmetic to students at risk for school failure. In K. McGilly (Ed.), *Classroom lessons: Integrating cognitive theory and classroom practice.* Cambridge, MA: MIT Press.

Griffith, J. (1996). Relation of parental involvement, empowerment, and school traits to student academic performance. *Journal of Educational Research, 90,* 33-41.

Guskey, I.R. (1985). *Implementing mastery learning.* Belmont, CA: Wadsworth.

Gutentag, R.E. (1984). The mental effort requirement of cumulative rehearsal: A developmental study. *Journal of Experimental Child Psychology, 37,* 92-106.

Gutentag, R.E., Ornstein, P.A., & Siemens, I. (1987). Children's spontaneous rehearsal: Transitions in strategy acquisition. *Cognitive Development, 2,* 307-326.

Guthrie, J.T., & Alao, S. (1997). Designing contexts to increase motivations for reading. *Educational Psychologist, 32,* 95-105.

Guthrie, J.T., & Cox, K.E. (1998). Portrait of an engaging classroom: Principles of concept-oriented reading instruction for diverse students. In K. Harris, S. Graham, & D. Deshler (Eds.), *Teaching every child every day: Learning in diverse schools and classrooms.* Cambridge, MA: Brookline Books.

Guthrie, J.T., & McCann, A.D. (1996). Idea circles: Peer collaborations for conceptual learning. In L. Gambrele & J. Almasi (Eds.), *Lively discussions* (pp. 87-105). Newark, DE: International Reading Association.

Gutierrez, R., & Slavin, R.E. (1992). Achievement effects of the nongraded elementary school: A best evidence synthesis. *Review of Educational Research, 62*, 333-376.

Harris, K.R., & Graham, S. (1996). *Making the writing process work: Strategies for composition and self-regulation.* Cambridge, MA: Brookline Books.

Hart, B., & Risley, T.R. (1997). *Meaningful differences in the everyday experiences of young American children.* Baltimore, MD: Paul H. Brookes.

Hegarty, M., Mayer, R.E., & Monk, C.A. (1995). Comprehension of arithmetic word problems: A comparison of successful and unsuccessful problem solvers. *Journal of Educational Psychology, 87*, 18-32.

Hess, R.S., & D'Amato, R.C. (1996). High school completion among Mexican-American children: Individual and family background variable. *School Psychology Quarterly, 11*, 353-368.

Hirano-Nakanishi, M. (1986). The extent and prevalence of pre-high school attrition and delayed education for Hispanics. *Hispanic Journal of Behavioral Sciences, 8*, 61-76.

Hodgkinson, H.L. (1992). *A demographic look at tomorrow.* Washington, DC: Center for Demographic Policy, Institute for Educational Leadership.

Hoover-Dempsey, K.V., & Sandler, H.M. (1995). Parental involvement in children's education: Why does it make a difference? *Teachers College Record, 97*, 310-331.

Huston, A.C. (1995). Children in poverty and public policy. *Developmental Psychology Newsletter, Fall*, 1-8.

Hutchinson, N. (1987). *Instruction of representation and solution in algebraic problem solving in learning disabled adolescents.* Doctoral dissertation, Simon Fraser University.

Hutchinson, N. (1993). Effects of cognitive strategy instruction on algebraic problems solving of adolescents with learning disabilities. *Learning Disabilities Quarterly, 16*, 34-63.

Inglis, A., & Biemiller, A. (submitted for publication). *Fostering self-direction in grade four tutors: A cross-age tutoring program.* Submitted to the *Journal of Educational Psychology.*

James, W. (1890). *The principles of psychology.* Cambridge, MA: Harvard University Press.

Jerman, M.E., & Mirman, S. (1974). Predicting the relative difficulty of verbal arithmetic problems. *Educational Studies in Mathematics, 4*, 306-323.

Johnson, D.W., & Johnson, R.T. (1982). *Joining together: Group theory and group skills* (2nd ed.). Englewood Cliffs, NJ: Prentice Hall.

Johnson, D.W., & Johnson, R.T. (1986). *Learning together and alone* (2nd ed.). Englewood Cliffs, NJ: Prentice Hall.

Johnson, D.W., & Johnson, R.T. (1994). *Learning together and alone: Cooperative, competitive, and individualistic learning* (4th ed.) Boston: Allyn & Bacon.

Kammen, M. (1996). A teacher's implementation of authentic assessment in an elementary science classroom. *Journal of Research in Science and Teaching, 33*, 859-877.

Katz, L.G., & Chard, S.C. (1989). *Engaging children's minds: The project approach.* Norwood, NJ: Ablex.

Kellogg, R.T. (1994). *The psychology of writing.* Oxford, UK: Oxford University Press.

King, A. (1990). Enhancing peer interaction and learning in the classroom through reciprocal questioning. *American Educational Research Journal, 27*, 664-687.

King, A. (1991). Effects of training in strategic questioning in children's problem-solving performance. *Journal of Educational Psychology, 83*, 307-317.

King, A. (1994). Guiding knowledge construction in the classroom: Effects of teaching children how to question and how to explain. *American Educational Research Journal, 31*, 338-368.

King, A., & Rosenshine, B. (1993). Effects of guided cooperative questioning on children's knowledge construction. *Journal of Experimental Education, 61*, 127-148.

Knapp, M.S., & Associates (1995). *Teaching for meaning in high poverty classrooms.* New York: Teachers College Press.

Knapp, M.S., & Shields, P.M. (1991). *Better schooling for the children of poverty: Alternatives to conventional wisdom.* San Francisco: McCutchan.

Knapp, M.S., Shields, P.M., & Turnbull, B.J. (1997). *Academic challenges for the children of poverty: Summary report.* Washington, DC: Office of Policy and Planning, U.S. Department of Education.

Kohlberg, L., Ricks, D., & Snarey, J. (1984). Childhood development as a predictor of adaptation in adulthood. *Genetic Psychology Monographs, 110*, 91-172.

Kozol, J. (1991). *Savage inequalities: Children in America's schools.* New York: Crown.

Lamon, M., Secules, T., Petrosino, A.J., Hackett, R., Bransford, J.D., & Goldman, S.R. (1996). Schools for thought: Overview of the project and lessons learned from one of the sites. In L. Schauble & R. Glaser (Eds.), *Innovations in learn-*

ing: New environments for education (pp. 243-288). Hillsdale, NJ: Erlbaum.

Lane, S. (1993). The conceptual framework for the development of a mathematics performance assessment instrument. *Educational Measurement: Issues and Practice*, Summer, 16-23.

Lane, S., Liu, M., Ankenmann, R.D., & Stone, C.A. (1996). Generalizability and validity of mathematics performance assessment. *Journal of Educational Measurement*, 33, 71-92.

Langer, E.J. (1993). A mindful education. *Educational Psychologist*, 28, 43-50.

Langer, P., Kalk, J., & Searls, D. (1984). Age of admission and trends in achievement: A comparison of Blacks and Caucasians. *American Educational Research Journal*, 21, 61-78.

Lehrer, R., Erickson, J., & Connell, T. (in press). *Learning by designing hypermedia documents: Computers in schools.*

Leinhardt, G. (1988). Situated knowledge and expertise in teaching. In J. Calderhead (Ed.), *Teacher's Professional Learning*. London: Falmer Press.

Leinhardt, G. (1990). On teaching. In R. Glaser (Ed.), *Advances in instructional psychology: Vol. 4*. Hillsdale, NJ: Erlbaum.

Leinhardt, G. (1992). What research on learning tells us about teaching. *Educational Leadership*, 49, 20-25.

Leinhardt, G., & Greeno, J.G. (1986). The cognitive skills of teaching. *Journal of Educational Psychology*, 78, 75-95.

Leinhardt, G., & Smith, D.A. (1985). Expertise in mathematics instruction. *Journal of Educational Psychology*, 77, 247-271.

Lepper, M.R., Aspinwall, L., Mumme, D., & Chabay, R. (1990). Self-perception and social perception in tutoring: Subtle social control strategies in expert tutors. In J.M. Olson & M.P. Zanna (Eds.), *Self-inference process: The Ontario Symposium*, Vol. 6, Hillsdale, NJ: Erlbaum.

Licht, B. (1993). Achievement-related belief in children with learning disabilities: Impact on motivation and strategy learning. In L.J. Meltzer (Ed.), *Strategy assessment and instruction for students with learning disabilities* (pp. 247-270). Austin, TX: Pro-Ed.

Linn, R.L. (1993). Educational assessment: Expanded expectations and challenges. *Educational Evaluation and Policy Analysis*, 15, 1-16.

Linn, R.L., Baker, E.L., & Dunbare, E.S. (1991). Complex, performance-based assessment: Expectations and validation criteria. *Educational Researcher*, 20, 15-21.

Lloyd, D.N. (1978). Prediction of school failure from third-grade data. *Educational and Psychological Measurement*, 38, 1193-1200.

Locke, E.A. (1990). *A theory of goal setting and task performance*. Englewood Cliffs, NJ: Prentice-Hall.

Loera, P.P., & Meichenbaum, D. (1994). The "potential" contributions of cognitive behavior modification to literacy training for deaf students. *American Annals for the Deaf*, 138, 87-95.

Markus, H., & Nurius, P. (1986). Possible selves. *American Psychologist*, 41, 954-969.

Maurogenes, N.A., & Galen, N.D. (1978). Cross-age tutoring: Why and how? *Journal of Reading*, 22, 344-353.

McGill-Franzen, A., & Allington, R.L. (1991) The gridlock of low reading achievement: Perspectives on practice and policy. *Remedial and Special Education*, 12(3), 20-20.

McGilly, K. (Ed.) (1994). *Classroom lessons: Integrating cognitive theory and classroom practice*. Cambridge, MA: MIT Press.

McIntosh, P., Vaugh, S., Schumm, J.I., Haeger, D., & Lee, O. (1993). Observations of students with learning disabilities in general education classrooms. *Exceptional Children*, 60, 249-261.

McKeough, A. (1992). A neo-structural analysis of children's narrative and its development. In R. Case (Ed.), *The mind's staircase: Exploring the conceptual underpinnings of children's thought and knowledge* (pp. 171-188). Hillsdale, NJ: Erlbaum.

McTighe, J., & Lyman, F.T. (1988). Cueing thinking in the classroom: The promise of theory and embedded tools. *Educational Leadership*, 45, 18-24.

Meichenbaum, D. (1977). *Cognitive behavior modification: An integrative approach*. New York: Plenum Press.

Meichenbaum, D., & Biemiller, A. (1992). In search of student expertise in the classroom: A metacognitive analysis. In M. Pressley, K. Harris, & J. Guthrie (Eds.), *Promoting academic competence and literacy: Cognitive research and instructional innovation* (pp. 3-56). New York: Academic Press.

Mercier, C.D., Jordan L., & Miller, S.P. (1994). Implications of constructivism for teaching math to students with moderate to mild disabilities. *Journal of Special Education*, 28, 290-306.

Mertens, R. (1996). The IMPACT project: Parental involvement in the curriculum. *School Effectiveness and School Improvement*, 1, 411-426.

Mertens, R., & Voss, J. (1993). *Partnership in mathematics: Parents and school*. London: Falmer Press.

Minstrell, J. (1989). Teaching science for understanding. In L.B. Resnick & L.E. Klopfer (Eds.), *Towards the thinking curriculum*. New York: Association Curriculum Development.

Mosle, S. (1996). The answer is national standards. *New York Times Magazine*, (Oct.), 44-48.

Mosteller, F., Light, R.J., & Sachs, J.A. (1996).

Sustained inquiry in education: Lessons from skill grouping and class size. *Harvard Educational Review, 66*(4), 797-828.

Myrick, R.D., & Bowman, R.P. (1991). *Children helping children: Teaching students to become friendly helpers.* Minneapolis, MN: Educational Media Corp.

Nagy, W.E., & Anderson, R.C. (1984). How many words are there in printed school English? *Reading Research Quarterly, 19,* 304-330.

National Assessment of Educational Progress (1992). *NAEP 1992 mathematics report card for the nation and the states.* Washington, DC: National Center for Educational Statistics, Report No. 23-ST02.

National Commission on Excellence in Education. (1993). *A nation at risk: The imperative for educational reform.* Washington, DC: Author.

Neumann, R.A. (1996). Reducing Hispanic dropout: A case of success. *Educational Policy, 10,* 22-45.

Newman, D., Griffin, P., & Cole, M. (1989). *The construction zone: Working for cognitive change in school.* New York: Cambridge University Press.

Newman, F.M. (1990). Higher order thinking in teaching social studies: A rationale for the assessment of classroom thoughtfulness. *Journal of Curriculum Studies, 22,* 41-56.

Newman, F.M., & Associates. (1996a). *Authentic achievement: Restructuring schools for intellectual quality.* San Francisco, CA: Jossey-Bass.

Newman, F.M., Marks, H.M., & Gamoran, A. (1996b). Authentic pedagogy and student performance. *American Journal of Education, 104,* 280-312.

Newman, F.M., & Wehlage, G.G. (1995). *Successful school restructuring. A report to the public and educators.* University of Madison, WI: Wisconsin Education Center.

Nickerson, R.S., Perkins, D.N., & Smith, E.E. (1985). *The teaching of thinking.* Hillsdale, NJ: Erlbaum.

Nuthall, G. (1995). Understanding student thinking and learning in the classroom. In B.J. Biddle, T.L. Good, & I.F. Goodson (Eds.), *The international handbook of teachers and teaching.* London: Kluwer Academic Publishers.

Oakes, J. (1985). *Keeping track: How schools structure inequality.* New Haven, CT: Yale University Press.

Oakes, J. (1990). *Multiplying inequalities: The effects of race, social class, and tracking on opportunities to learn mathematics and science.* Santa Monica: RAND.

Oakes, J. (1992). Can tracking research inform practice? Technical, normative, and practical considerations. *Educational Researcher, 21,* 12-21.

Oakes, J., Gamoran, A., & Page, R.N. (1992). Curriculum differentiation: Opportunities, outcomes, and meanings. In P.W. Jackson (Ed.), *Handbook of research on curriculum* (pp. 570-608). Washington, DC: American Educational Research Association.

Oakes, J., & Guiton, G. (1995). Matchmaking: The dynamics of high school tracking decisions. *American Education Research Journal, 32,* 3-33.

Osguthorpe, R.T., & Scruggs, T.E. (1986). Special education students as tutors: A review and analysis. *Remedial and Special Education, 7,* 15 - 26.

Paas, F.G.W.C., & Van Merrienboer, J.J.G. (1994). Variability of worked examples and transfer of geometrical problem-solving skills: A cognitive load approach. *Journal of Educational Psychology, 86,* 122-133.

Page, R.N. (1991). *Lower track classrooms: A curriculum and cultural perspective.* New York: Teachers College Press.

Palincsar, A.S. (1986). The role of dialogue in providing scaffolded instruction. *Educational Psychologist, 21,* 73-98.

Palincsar, A.S., & Brown, A.L. (1984). Reciprocal teaching of comprehension-fostering and comprehension: Monitoring activities. *Cognition and Instruction, 2,* 117-175.

Palincsar, A.S., & Brown, A.L. (1986). Interactive teaching to promote independent learning from text. *Reading Teacher, 39,* 771-775.

Palincsar, A.S., & Klenk, D. (1993). Broader visions encompassing literacy, learners, and contexts. *Remedial and Special Education, 14,* 19-25.

Pallas, A.M., Natriello, & McDill, E.L. (1989). The changing nature of disadvantaged population: Current dimensions and future trends. *Educational Researcher, 18,* 16-22.

Perkins, D. (1991). Educating for insight. *Educational Leadership, 49,* 4-8.

Perkins, D. (1992). *Smart schools: From training memories to educating minds.* New York: Macmillan.

Perkins, D.N., & Salomon, G. (1988). Teaching for transfer. *Educational Leadership, 46,* 22-32.

Perkins, D.N., & Salomon, G. (1989). Are cognitive skills context-bound? *Educational Researcher, 46,* 16-25

Piaget, J. (1964). Development and learning. In T.R. Ripple & V. Rockcastle (Eds.), *Piaget rediscovered.* Ithaca, NY: Cornell University Press.

Pianta, R.C., Steinberg, M.S., & Rollins, K.B. (1995). The first two years of school: Teacher-child relationships and reflections in children's classroom adjustment. *Developmental and Psychopathology, 7,* 295-312.

Pinnell, G.S., Lyons, C.A., Deford, D.E., Bryk,

A.S., & Seltzer, M. (1994). Comparing instructional models for the literacy education of high-risk first graders. *Reading Research Quarterly, 29,* 9-38.

Pressley, M., Borkowski, J.G., & Schneider, W. (1987). Good information processing: What it is and what education can do to promote it. *International Journal of Educational Research, 13,* 857-867.

Pressley, M., Burkell, J., Coriglia-Bull, T., Lysynchuk, L., McGoldrick, J.A., Schneider, B., Snyder, B.L., Symons, S., & Woloshyn, V.E. (1990). *Cognitive strategy instruction that really improves children's academic performance* (1st ed.). Cambridge, MA: Brookline Books.

Pressley, M. El-Dinary, P.B., Brown, R., Schuder, T., Bergman, J.L., York, M., & Gaskins, I.W. (1995). A transactional strategies instruction Christmas Carol. In A. McKeough, J. Lupart, & A. Marini (Eds.), *Reaching for transfer: Fostering generalization in learning.* Hillsdale, NJ: Erlbaum.

Pressley, M., El-Dinary, P.B., Marks, M.B., Brown, R., & Stein, S. (1992). Good strategy instruction is motivating and interesting. In K.A. Renninger, & A. Krapp (Eds.), *The role of interest in learning and development* (pp. 333-358). Hillsdale, NJ: Erlbaum.

Pressley, M., Snyder, B.L., & Cariglia-Bull, T. (1987). How can good strategy use be taught to children? Evaluation of six alternative approaches. In S.M. Cormier & J.D. Hagman (Eds.), *Transfer of learning* (pp. 81-120). New York: Academic Press.

Pressley, M., & Woloshyn, V. (1995). *Cognitive strategy instruction that really improves children's academic performance* (2nd ed.). Cambridge, MA: Brookline Books.

Pressley, M., Woloshyn, V., Lysynchuk, L.M., Martin, V., Wood, E., & Willoughby, T. (1990). A primer of research in cognitive strategy instruction: The important issues and how to address them. *Educational Psychology Review, 2,* 2-58.

Raphael, T.E., & Pearson, P.D. (1985). Increasing student awareness of sources of information for answering questions. *American Education Research Journal, 22,* 217-237.

Reed, S.K., Dempster, A., & Ettinger, M. (1985). Usefulness of analogous solutions for solving algebraic word problems. *Journal of Experimental Psychology: Learning, Memory and Cognition, 111,* 106-125.

Rekrut, M.D. (1994). Peer and cross-age tutoring: The lessons of research. *Journal of Reading, 37,* 356-363.

Resnick, L.B. (Ed.) (1989). *Knowing, learning, and instruction: Essays in honor of Robert Glaser* (pp. 393-451). Hillsdale, NJ: Erlbaum.

Riley, J.P. (1986). The effects of teachers' wait-time and knowledge comprehension questioning on science achievement. *Journal of Research in Science Teaching, 17,* 469-475.

Rogoff, B. (1990). *Apprenticeship in thinking: Cognitive development in social context.* New York: Oxford University Press.

Rogoff, B. (1994). Developing understanding of the idea of communities of learners. *Mind, Culture, and Activity, 1,* 209-229.

Rogoff, B., & Wertsch, J.V. (1984). *Children's learning in the "zone of proximal development."* San Francisco: Jossey-Bass.

Rosenbaum, J.E. (1976). *Making inequality: The hidden curriculum of high school tracking.* New York: Wiley.

Rosenbaum, J.E. (1980). Social implication of educational grouping. *Review of Research in Education, 8,* 361-401.

Rosenshine, B. (1995). Advances in research on instruction. *Journal of Educational Research, 88,* 262-268.

Rosenshine, B., & Meister, C. (1994). Reciprocal teaching: A review of the research. *Review of Educational Research, 64,* 479-530.

Rosenshine, B., & Meister, C. (1996). Cognitive strategy instruction in reading. In J. Shimron (Ed.), *Literacy and education: Essays in memory of Dina Feitelson* (pp. 119-145). Cresshill, NJ: Hampton Press.

Rosenshine, B., Meister, C., & Chapman, S. (1996). Teaching students to generate questions: A review of intervention studies. *Review of Educational Research, 66,* 181-221.

Rosenshine, B., & Stevens, R. (1986). Teaching functions. In M.C. Wittrock (Ed.), *AERA Handbook of Research and Teaching* (3rd ed., pp. 371-391). New York: Macmillan.

Ross, S.M., Smith, L.J., & Associates (in press). Scaling up the NAS designs in Memphis: A synthesis of first year results. *School Effectiveness and School Improvement.*

Roth, W.M. (1996). Where is the context in contextual word problems? Mathematical practices and products in grade 8 students' answers to story problems. *Cognition and Instruction, 14,* 487-527.

Rowe, M. (1974). Wait-time and rewards as instructional variables, their influence on language, logic, and "fate control," Part 1: Wait time. *Journal of Research in Science Teaching, 23,* 335-342.

Rowe, M.B. (1986). Wait time: Slow down may be speeding up. *Journal of Teacher Education, 37,* 43-50.

Salomon, G. (1989). Rocky roads to transfer: Re-thinking mechanisms of a neglected phenom-enon. *Educational Psychologist, 24*(2), 113-142.

Salomon, G., & Globerson, T. (1987). Skill may not be enough: The role of mindfulness and transfer. *International Journal of Educational Re-search, 11,* 823-627.

Salomon, G., & Globerson, T. (1989). When teams do not function the way they ought to. *Interna-tional Journal of Educational Research, 13,* 89-93.

Salomon, G., & Perkins, P.N. (1987). Transfer of cognitive skills from programming: When and how? *Journal of Educational Computing Research, 3,* 149-169.

Salomon, G., & Perkins, P.N. (1988). Rocky roads to transfer: Rethinking mechanisms of a ne-glected phenomenon. *Educational Psychologist, 18,* 42-50.

Sameroff, A.J., Seifer, R., Baldwin, A., & Baldwin, C. (1993). Stability of intelligence from preschool to adolescence: The influence of social and fam-ily risk factors. *Child Development, 64,* 80-97.

Sameroff, A.J., Seifer, R., Barocas, B., Zax, M., & Greenspan, S. (1987). IQ scores of 5-year-old children: Socio-environmental risk factors. *Pe-diatrics, 79,* 343-350.

Samuels, S.G. (1980). The age-old controversy between holistic and subskill approaches to beginning reading revisited. In C.M. McCollough (Ed.), *Inchword: Persistent problems in reading education.* Newark, DE: International Reading Association.

Saxe, G.B. (1988). Candy selling and math learn-ing. *Educational Researcher, 17,* 14-21.

Scanlon, D.M., & Vellutino, F.R. (1997). A com-parison of the instructional backgrounds and cognitive profiles of poor, average, and good readers who were initially identified as at risk for reading failure. *Scientific Studies of Reading, 1,* 191-216.

Scardamalia, M., Bereiter, C., & Lamon, M. (1994). The CSILE project: Trying to bring the class-room into World 3. In K. McGilly (Ed.), *Class-room lessons: Integrating cognitive theory and class-room practice* (pp. 201-228). Cambridge, MA: MIT Press.

Schoenfeld, A.H. (1985). *Mathematical problem-solv-ing.* San Diego, CA: Academic Press.

Schoenfeld, A.H. (1987). *Cognitive science and math-ematics education.* Hillsdale, NJ: Erlbaum.

Schuder, T. (1993). The genesis of transactional strategies instruction in a reading program for at risk students. *Elementary School Journal, 94,* 183-198.

Schunk, D.H., & Zimmerman, B.J. (1994). *Self-regulation of learning and performance: Issues and education applications.* Hillsdale, NJ: Erlbaum.

Scruggs, T.E., & Richter, L. (1985). Tutoring learn-ing disabled students: A critical review. *Learn-ing Disability Quarterly, 8,* 274-286.

Shany, M., & Biemiller, A. (1995). Assisted read-ing practice: Effects on performance for poor readers in grades 3 and 4. *Reading Research Quar-terly, 30,* 382-395.

Sharp, C. (1995). What's age got to do with it? A study of patterns of school entry and the im-pact of season of birth on school attainment. *Educational Research, 37,* 251-261.

Shephard, L.A., & Smith, L.A. (1990). Synthesis of research on grade retention. *Educational Lead-ership, 47,* 84-88.

Sherman, A. (1994). *Wasting America's future: The Children's Defense Fund report on the costs of child poverty.* Boston: Beacon Press.

Sherwood, R., Kinzer, C., Hasselbring, T., & Bransford, J. (1987). Macrocontents for learn-ing: Initial findings and issues. *Journal of Ap-plied Cognition, 1,* 93-108.

Shulman, L.S. (1987). Knowledge and teaching: Foundations of the new reform. *Harvard Educa-tional Review, 19,* 4-14.

Silber, E.A. (1986). Using conceptual and proce-dural knowledge: A focus on relationships. In J. Hiebert (Ed.), *Conceptual and procedural knowl-edge: The case of mathematics* (pp. 181-198). Hillsdale, NJ: Erlbaum.

Silver, E.A., & Cai, J. (1996). Analysis of arith-metic problem posing by middle school stu-dents. *Journal of Research in Mathematics Educa-tion, 27,* 521-539.

Simon, H.A., & Gilmartin, K. (1973). Simulation of memory for the chess positions. *Cognitive Psychology, 5,* 29-46.

Slavin, R.E. (1978). Student teams and achieve-ment divisions. *Journal of Research and Develop-ment In Education, 22,* 39-49.

Slavin, R.E. (1987a). Ability grouping and student achievement in elementary school: A best-evi-dence synthesis. *Review of Educational Research, 57,* 293-336.

Slavin, R.E. (1987b). Mastery learning reconsid-ered. *Review of Educational Research, 57,* 175-215.

Slavin, R.E. (1993). Ability grouping in the middle grades: Achievement effects and alternatives. *Elementary School Journal, 93,* 535-552.

Slavin, R.E. (1995). *Cooperative learning: Theory, research and practice.* (2nd ed.). Boston: Allyn & Bacon.

Slavin, R.E. (1996). Neverstreaming: Preventing learning disabilities. *Educational Leadership,* Feb., 4-7.

Slavin, R.E. (1996). Research on cooperative learn-ing and achievement: What we know, what we need to know. *Contemporary Educative Psychology, 21*, 43-69.

Solomon, D., Battistich, V., Ham, A. (1996). Teacher beliefs and practices in school communities that differ in socioeconomic level. *Journal of Experimental Education, 64*, 327-347.

Stanovich, K.E. (1986). Matthew effects in reading: Some consequences of individual differences in the acquisition of literacy. *Reading Research Quarterly, 21*, 360-406.

Stanovich, K.E. (1994). Constructivism in reading education. *Journal of Special Education, 28*, 259-274.

Sternberg, R.J., & Horvath, J.A. (1995). A prototype view of expert teaching. *Educational Researcher*, August-September, 9-17.

Sternberg, R.J., Wagner, R.K., Williams, W.M., & Horvath, J.A. (1995). Testing common sense. *American Psychologist, 50*, 912-927.

Stevens, R.J., & Slavin, L.E. (1995). The cooperative elementary school: Effects on students' achievement, attitudes, and social relations. *American Educational Research Journal, 32*, 321-351.

Stevenson, H.W., & Lee, S. (1990). Contexts of achievement: A study of American, Chinese and Japanese children. *Monograph of the Society for Research in Child Development, 55*, Nos. 1-2.

Stevenson, H.W., & Lee, S. (1995). The east Asian version of whole-class teaching. *Educational Policy, 9*, 152-168.

Stevenson, H.W., Lee, S., Chen, C., Stigler, J.W., Hsu, C., & Kitamura, S. (1990). Contexts of achievement: A study of American, Chinese, and Japanese children. *Monographs of the Society for Research in Child Development* (Serial No. 221).

Stevenson, H.W., Lee, S.Y., & Stigler, J. (1986). Mathematics achievement of Chinese, Japanese, and American children. *Science, 231*, 693-699.

Stevenson, H.W., & Lee, S.Y. (1990). Contexts of achievement: A study of American, Chinese, and Japanese children. *Monograph of the Society for Research in Child Development, 55*, No. 1-2.

Stevenson, H.W., & Stigler, J.W. (1992). *The learning gap: Why our schools are failing and what we can learn from Japanese and Chinese education*. New York: Summit Books.

Stigler, J.W., Lee, S.Y., & Stevenson, H.W. (1987). Mathematics classrooms in Japan, Taiwan, and the United States. *Child Development, 58*, 1272-1285.

Stigler, J.W., Lee, S.Y., & Stevenson, H.W. (1990). *Mathematical knowledge of Japanese, Chinese and American elementary school children*. Reston, VA: National Council of Teachers of Mathematics.

Stokes, T.F., & Baer, D.M. (1979). An implicit technology of generalization. *Journal of Applied Behavior Analysis, 10*, 349-367.

Swanson, J.M. (1992). *School-based assessments and interventions for ADD students*. Irvine, CA: K.C.

Swing, S.R., & Peterson, P.L. (1982). The relationship of student ability and small-group interaction to student achievement. *American Educational Research Journal, 19*, 259-274.

Tharp, R.G., & Gallimore, R.G. (1991). *Rousing minds to life: Teaching, learning and schooling in a social context*. New York: Cambridge University Press.

Tirozzi, G., & Uro, G. (1997). Education reform in the United States. *American Psychologist, 52*, 241-249.

Tobin, K.G. (1983). The effects of wait time on classroom learning. *European Journal of Science Education, 5*, 35-48.

Tsurunda, G. (1994). *Putting it together: Middle school math in transition*. Portsmouth, NH: Heinemann.

U.S. Department of Education (1993). *Reinventing Chapter 1*. Washington, DC: Author.

Valdes, G. (1992). Bilingual minorities and language issues in writing: Toward profession-wide responses to a new challenge. *Written Communication, 9*, 48-136.

Vellutino, F.R., & Scanton, D.M. (1987). Phonological coding: Phonological awareness, and reading ability. *Merrill Palmer Quarterly, 33*, 321-363.

Venezky, R. (1996). *An alternative perspective on Success for All*. Unpublished manuscript, University of Delaware.

Von Glasersfeld, E. (1995). Sensory experience, abstraction, and teaching. In L.P. Steffle & J. Gale (Eds.), *Constructivism in education* (pp. 369-383). Hillsdale, NJ: Erlbaum.

Vygotsky, L.S. (1962). *Thought and language* (E. Hanfmann & G. Vaker, Trans.). Cambridge, MA: MIT Press.

Vygotsky, L.S. (1978). *Mind in society: The development of higher psychological processes* (M. Cole, V. John-Steiner, & E. Souberman, Eds. and Trans.). Cambridge, MA: Harvard University Press.

Ward, E., Johnson, J., Bain, H.C., Fulton, B.D., Zaharis, J.B., Achilles, C.M., Lintz, M.N., Folger, J., & Breda, C. (1994). *The state of Tennessee's Student/Teacher Achievement Ratio (STAR) project: Technical report 1985-1990*. Nashville: Tennessee State Department of Education.

Webb, N.M. (1989). Peer interaction and learning in small groups. *International Journal of Educational Research, 13*, 21-40.

Webb, N.M. (1991). Task-related verbal interaction and mathematics learning in small groups.

Journal of Research in Mathematics Education, 22, 366-389.

White, K.R., Taylor, M.J., & Moss, V.D. (1992). Does research support claims about the benefits of involving parents in early intervention programs? *Review of Educational Research, 62,* 91-125.

Whitehead, A.N. (1929). *The aims of education.* New York: Macmillan.

Wood, D. (1988). *How children think and learn.* Oxford, UK: Basil Blackwell.

Wood, D.J., Bruner, J., & Ross, G. (1976). The role of tutoring in problem solving. *Journal of Child Psychology and Psychiatry, 17,* 89-100.

Wood, D.J., & Middleton, D. (1975). A study of assisted problem solving. *British Journal of Psychology, 66,* 181-191.

Yasutake, D., Bryan, T., & Dohrn, E. (1996). The effects of combining peer tutoring and attribution training in students' perceived self-competence. *Remedial and Special Education, 17,* 83-91.

Zimmerman, B.J. (1986). Development of self-regulated learning: Which are the key subprocesses? *Contemporary Educational Psychology, 16,* 307-313.

Zimmerman, B.J., & Schunk, D.H. (Eds.) (1989). *Self-regulated learning and academic achievement: Theory, practice and research.* New York: Springer-Verlag.

Zimmerman, B.J., & Schunk, D.H. (Eds.) (1994). *Self-regulation of learning and performance.* Hillsdale, NJ: Erlbaum.

Index

About the Authors

Donald Meichenbaum, Ph.D. (e-mail dmeich@watarts.uwaterloo.ca), is Professor Emeritus, University of Waterloo, Ontario, Canada. He was educated at the City College of New York and at the University of Illinois. For the last 30 years he has conducted research on the development of self-regulation and metacognitive development. He has pioneered work on cognitive behavioral interventions with children and their teachers and families. This work has led him to focus on issues of generalization and academic performance. He has published extensively, and in a survey reported in *The American Psychologist*, fellow clinicians have voted him "one of the ten most influential psychotherapists of the century."

Andrew Biemiller, Ph.D. (e-mail a.biemiller@utoronto.ca), is a professor at the Institute of Child Study, a part of the Ontario Institute for Studies in Education at the University of Toronto. Educated at Harvard and Cornell Universities, Dr. Biemiller was a part of Project Literacy at Cornell in the 1960's—a research program which combined classroom and laboratory research on reading. Through both research and teaching, he has remained involved in the practice of education. Biemiller has taught preservice teachers and graduate students for thirty years. His published research includes classroom studies of beginning reading and laboratory studies of reading processes, as well as studies of self-direction related to the work reported in this book.